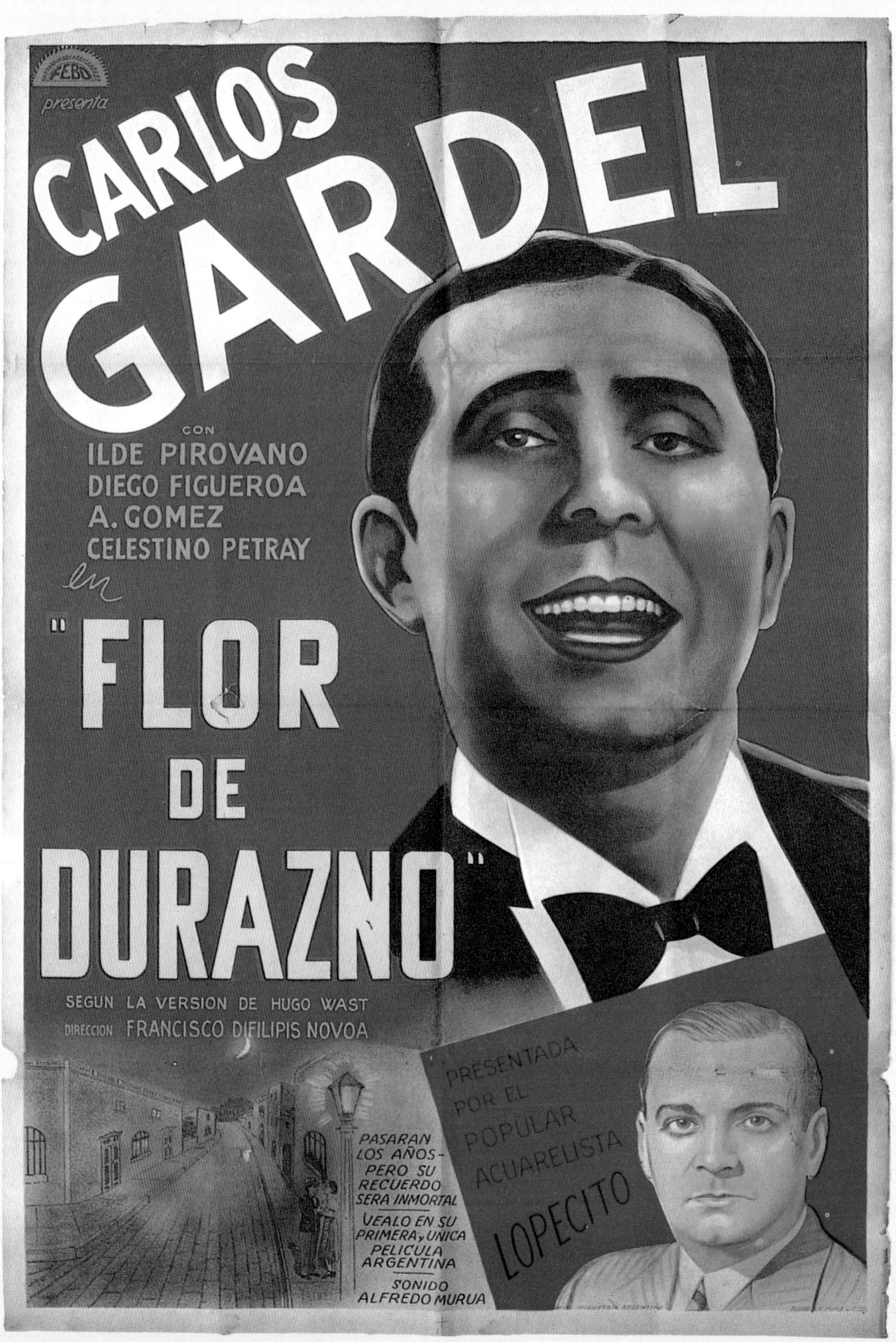
FEBO
presenta
CARLOS
GARDEL
CON
ILDE PIROVANO
DIEGO FIGUEROA
A. GOMEZ
CELESTINO PETRAY
en
"FLOR
DE
DURAZNO"
SEGUN LA VERSION DE HUGO WAST
DIRECCION FRANCISCO DEFILIPIS NOVOA
PASARAN
LOS AÑOS-
PERO SU
RECUERDO
SERA INMORTAL
VEALO EN SU
PRIMERA y UNICA
PELICULA
ARGENTINA
SONIDO
ALFREDO MURUA
PRESENTADA
POR EL
POPULAR
ACUARELISTA
LOPECITO

Created and Directed by Hans Höfer

Edited and Produced by Deirdre Ball

APA PUBLICATIONS

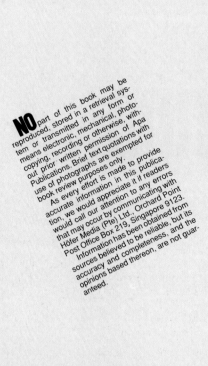
ARGENTINA

ABOUT THIS BOOK

Insight Guide: Argentina was the first in a series on South American countries by Apa Publications of Singapore. This large country at the southeast base of the continent was chosen to launch this series because so little had been published about it and because there was so much to tell.

Apa Founder **Hans Höfer** published his first travel guide, a prize-winning book about Bali, in 1970. Using his training in the Bauhaus tradition of his native West Germany, Höfer developed a formula for a new kind of travel literature that combined outstanding photography, fine writing and clear, objective journalism. Höfer's conception was drawn on his education in book design, printing and photography.

The Insight Guides are designed for the serious traveler who wants to know the history, culture and society of the country he is visiting, going beyond the usual visitor's introduction. To accomplish that goal, Höfer appoints a single project editor for each book and gives that editor responsibility for gathering the best available writers and photographers in the region. For *Insight Guide: Argentina*, the project editor was **Deirdre Ball** who had spent 18 months in Buenos Aires as a free-lance writer and teacher of English.

Raised in Beirut and educated at Yale University, Ball has lived and worked as an editor and free-lance journalist in Montana and Cairo. Commuting from the U.S. and her new home in Brazil, Ball assembled a team of outstanding Argentine writers and photographers.

Ball reserved for herself the chapters on Geography (From Jungles to Glaciers), People (In Search of a National Identity), the West (Cuyo) and Gauchos (Wild Orphans of the Pampa).

The Prehistory chapter was written by Argentine archaeologist **Elena Decima**. Decima has worked on digs throughout South and Central America, including the Tunel site on Tierra del Fuego. Decima also wrote the chapter on the Córdoba's Colonial Past.

The job of writing about Argentina's long and complicated history after the arrival of the Spanish fell to **Philip Benson**. After receiving his degree in history from Harverford College, Benson taught high school history in East Jerusalem, Cairo and Buenos Aires. Since completing a Masters at Brown University, he has been teaching in São Paulo. Benson wrote a second piece for the book on travelers' accounts (Descriptions of Argentina: 1800-1920).

Tony Perrottet brought his deft journalistic touch to the "Argentina Today" piece. Raised and educated in Australia, Perrottet has worked as a stringer for various Australian, British and U.S. newspapers.

The daunting task of explaining the sprawling complex of Buenos Aires was undertaken by free-lance writer **Patricia Pittman** who has been involved in Latin American affairs since her student days at Yale University. She first went to Argentina in 1982 on a one-year grant to work with a human rights organization and now works as a consultant for both Americas Watch and the Ford Foundation.

The pieces on the tango (The Sultry Tango) and the economy (Economics, Politics and Labor) were written by journalist **Judith Evans**. Evans received a Masters in history from the University of California at Berkeley, and has lived in Buenos Aires off and on since 1972. She is currently a correspondent for the *Wall Street Journal*, and contributes pieces to *The Independent* (U.K.) and the *New York Times*.

Buenos Aires-based food and wine critic **Dereck Foster** wrote the pieces on food (Dining out in Buenos Aires) and wine (The Wines of Argentina). Foster has been a columnist for the *Buenos Aires Herald* and now publishes his own magazine, *Aromas y Sabores*. His published books include *The Argentines, how they live and work*, and *The Wines of Argentina*.

Journalist, explorer and publisher **Federico Kirbus** wrote the chapters on the Vacation Coast (Gamblers and Gambolers: the Vacation Coast) and the Northwest (Color and History: The Mag-

Ball

Benson

Pittman

Foster

Kirbus

nificent Northwest). He operates the *Adventurismo* tour company and writes travel articles for various publications.

Another contributor whose articles are based on long years in the field is **Maurice Rumboll**, who wrote the pieces on Wildlife (Wild Argentina) and the Northeast (River Journey to the Northeast). Educated in Argentina, England and Scotland, he worked for many years in the Argentine national park service, including a stint as chief naturalist at Iguazú.

The chapter on Patagonia (The Windy Expanse) was written by the three Bariloche-based authors, **Hans Schulz, Carol Jones** and **Edith Jones.** Schulz is an anthropologist who manages Polvani Tours. Carol Jones is the granddaughter of a Texas cowboy who moved to Patagonia in the 19th century. She runs a dude-ranch near Bariloche. Her mother, Edith, worked for years as an English teacher and headmistress at the local Woodville School.

The piece on the Welsh (The Welsh in Patagonia) was written by **Parry Jones**, a Welshman who lives in Bucks County, Pennsylvania. A retired high school history teacher, Jones in 1986 traveled to Patagonia to investigate the small but flourishing Welsh communities there.

The articles on Tierra del Fuego (The Uttermost South) was written by **Rae Natalie Prosser Goodall** who moved to Argentina in 1963, after receiving degrees from Kent State University (Ohio) in education and biology. She is a researcher at the *Centro Austral de Investigaciones Científicas*, in Ushuaia, specializing in marine mammals. She has also completed several studies of the flora and fauna of the islands, and a guide, *Tierra del Fuego*.

The sports editor of the *Buenos Aires Herald*, **Eric Weil**, was the co-author of the Sports feature (From the Kings of Sport to the Sport of Kings). Weil has also contributed stories on a number of topics to the *British Broadcasting Corporation* and the *Daily Mail* (U.K.). Co-author **Doug Cress**, a journalist based in Los Angeles, worked for many years at *The Washington Post*.

The grueling task of compiling the Travel Tips was accomplished with grace and thoroughness by **Hazel McCleary**. Familiar with all nitty-gritty of the tourist trade, McCleary has worked for several years at Cosmopolitan Tours in Buenos Aires.

The original maps were put together for the guide by **Isabel Juárez de Rosa**, a native of Quilmes, outside Buenos Aires. Juárez works for the *Servicio de Hydrografia Naval*, and has had several maps published before.

Nearly a quarter of the photos were contributed by **The Photoworks**, which is directed by photographer **Alex Ocampo**. The co-founder of The Photoworks, the late **Roberto Bunge** is represented and remembered with many fine, and often rare, photos.

Nearly all of the archival material and many of the Buenos Aires photos were shot by **Fiora Bemporad**, a respected professional working in Buenos Aires.

Many more photos, including most of the delightful wildlife shots, were taken by **Roberto Cinti** and **Carlos Passera**, who head up the **Photohunters** agency.

Focus, an agency founded by **Marcelo Brodsky**, was the source for many shots by a group of up-and-coming professionals.

Jorge Schulte contributed a number of his exquisite photos of the northwest. Other Argentine photographers included are **Eduardo Gil** (Bs. As.), **Pablov Cottescu, Arlette Neyens, Gabriel Bendersky** and **Ricardo Trabucco** (all based in Bariloche) and **Natalie** and **Thomas Goodall** (Ushuaia). The works of New York photographers **Don Boroughs** and **Joe Hooper** are also represented.

The editor would like to thank the following institutions for their support: the Argentine Secretariat of Tourism (and its former director, Francisco Manrique), Aerolineas Argentinas, the Philately Division of the Argentine Central Post Office, the Cervecería Cuyo y Norte (Mendoza) and the Graded School of São Paulo.

– APA PUBLICATIONS

Rumboll

C. Jones

P. Jones

Goodall

Weil

CONTENTS

History & Geography

13 Welcome to Argentina
—by Deirdre Ball

17 From Jungles to Glaciers
—by Deirdre Ball

24 Before the Spanish
—by Elena Decima

31 Caudillos, Tyrants and Demagogues
—by Philip Benson

38 *The Case of the Afro-Argentines*
—by Philip Benson

44 *Evita*
—by Philip Benson

50 Argentina Today
—by Tony Perrottet

54 Economics, Politics and Labor
—by Judith Evans

59 In Search of a National Identity
—by Deirdre Ball

73 Descriptions of Argentina: 1800-1920
—by Philip Benson

Places & Features

**87 Putting Together the Pieces:
An Argentine Itinerary**
—by Deirdre Ball

91 Mi Buenos Aires Querido
—by Deirdre Ball

92   City of Contradictions
  —by Patricia Pittman

102   _Politics in the Streets_
  —by Patricia Pittman

106   _Dining out in Buenos Aires_
  —by Dereck Foster

118   _The Sultry Tango_
  —by Judith Evans

**135   Gamblers and Gambolers:
  The Vacation Coast**
  —by Deirdre Ball

136   Mar Y Sierras
  —by Federico B. Kirbus

145   The Tranquil Central Sierras
  —by Deirdre Ball

146   Córdoba's Colonial Charm
  —by Elena Decima

159   Mesopotamian Meanderings
  —by Deirdre Ball

161   River Journey to the Northeast
  —by Maurice Rumboll

**173   Color and History:
  the Magnificent Northwest**
  —by Deirdre Ball

175   Ancient Settlements
  —by Federico B. Kirbus

193   The Wing Country
  —by Deirdre Ball

194   The Cuyo
  —by Deirdre Ball

196 The Wines of Argentina
—by Dereck Foster

209 Romantic Patagonia
—by Deirdre Ball

210 The Windy Expanse
—by Hans Ablert Schulz,
   Edith Jones and Carol Jones

223 *The Welsh in Patagonia*
—by Parry Jones

241 Distant Land of Fire
—by Deirdre Ball

243 Uttermost South
—by Rae Natalie P. Goodall

261 Wild Argentina
—by Maurice Rumboll

**275 From the Kings of Sport
to the Sport of Kings**
—by Eric Weil and Doug Cress

285 Wild Orphans of the Pampa
—by Deirdre Ball

Maps

86 Argentina
91 Buenos Aires and Surroundings
96 Buenos Aires: Capital Federal
101 Buenos Aires: City Center
172 Northwest
195 Cuyo
208 Patagonia
230 Lake District
246 Land of Fire and Malvinas
300 Buenos Aires Subway

TRAVEL TIPS

294 *Getting There*

294 *Travel Essentials*

295 *Getting Acquainted*

296 *Communications*

297 *Emergencies*

298 *Getting Around*

301 *Where to Stay*

303 *Food Digest*

304 *Culture Plus*

306 *Nightlife*

307 *Shopping*

308 *Sports*

310 *Further Reading*

311 *Useful Addresses*

*For detailed Information
See Page 293*

WELCOME TO ARGENTINA

Some of Argentina's characteristics are world-famous, while its other charms have gone unheralded. Everyone knows it is the home of the tango, but almost no one is aware that the highest peak in the Americas, Aconcagua, lies on its western border; Argentine beef is world-renowned, but few have heard about the rare glacial formations of the Lake District; and while the name Tierra del Fuego is familiar to most, not many know that Ushuaia, on its lower shore, is the southernmost town in the world.

Beyond the sophisticated metropolis of Buenos Aires, rough-riding gauchos, and the wide-open spaces of Patagonia and the pampas, Argentina will astonish the visitor with fine wines, jungle waterfalls, colonial cities and penguin colonies. One can create a vacation here with activities as diverse as horseback trekking in the Andes and gambling in a seaside casino. There are polo matches, ski tournaments, German Oktoberfests and Welsh Eisteddfods.

While certain attractions in Argentina have long been appreciated by select groups, such as climbers in search of a challenge and ornithologists pursuing filled-out life lists, the country has gone virtually undiscovered by the traveling world at large. Argentina is enough off the beaten track that one can romp on the resort beaches surrounded by only Argentines, and it is possible, on a lucky day, to have a national park all to oneself.

As the visitor goes about enjoying the refinements of Buenos Aires or the natural beauties of the interior, he or she should make a point of meeting Argentines along the way. An afternoon spent chatting with a bunch of spirited *porteños* in a café, or talking horses with a seasoned gaucho in Patagonia will help one to appreciate the Argentines' unique culture, of which they are justifiably proud.

Preceding pages: movie poster with Tango's most famous star, Carlos Gardel; valley of the Río Pinturas; Iguazú Falls; late afternoon on the Pampa; Mount Fitz Roy in Santa Cruz. Left, couple dancing the tango.

Argentina is a land of many riches, but silver is not one of them. This is something that the early Spanish explorers did not know when they gave the country its name (*argentum* is the Latin name for silver).The precious ore was discovered in great quantities to the north, in Bolivia and Peru, but no matter, the name stuck here.

Present day Argentina is an enormous country, eighth largest in the world and second largest, in population and area, in South America, after Brazil. It comprises 22 provinces and one national territory, which includes part of Tierra del Fuego, several South Atlantic islands and a 49 degree wedge of Antartica which ends at the South Pole. However, the antarctic sector overlaps with claims by Chile and Britain, and the South Atlantic islands in question are currently under British control.

The disputed territories aside, Argentina covers an area of nearly 1.1 million square miles (2.8 million square km). The islands and antarctic land together cover an additional 480,000 square miles (1.2 million square km). The country is 2,170 miles (3,500 km) long and 868 miles (1,400 km) across at its widest point.

As one might expect, a country covering this much terrain has a great diversity of topography and climate. While most of Argentina lies within the temperate zone of the Southern Hemisphere, climates range from tropical in the north to subantarctic in the south. In general, the climate of the country is moderated by the proximity of the oceans on either side of the cone and this influence is heightened the further south one goes, as the continent narrows and the two oceans meet. The towering barrier of the Andes to the west also plays an important part. This diversity of environments has endowed Argentina with a broad spectrum of plant and animal life.

The country can be roughly divided into six geographical zones: the fertile central

pampas, marshy Mesopotamia in the northeast, the forested Chaco region of the central north, the high plateau of the northwest, the mountainous desert of the west, and the windy plateaus of Patagonia. Within these areas one can find everything from steamy subtropical jungles to the lofty continental ice cap, and just about any kind of environmental feature in between.

Grassy heartland: The pampas are, perhaps, the terrain that Argentina is most

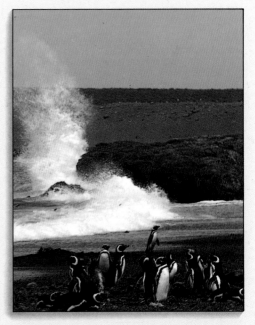

known for. These fertile alluvial plains were the home of the legendary gaucho, and today they are the base for a large percentage of the nation's economic wealth. These grasslands cover much of the central region of Argentina, stretching south, west and north in a radius of 600 miles (970 km) from the city of Buenos Aires. Argentines boast of the richness of the pampean earth, some saying the topsoil reaches a depth of six feet (two meters), others say the soil reaches 16 feet (five meters). Whatever the figure, there is no doubt that the region is a primary asset to the nation. Early European explorers invariably remarked on the extreme and vast flatness of

Preceding pages: iceberg on Lago Argentino. Left, husband and wife in the Northwest. Above, Magellanic penguins.

these prairies. And they are flat; miles and miles level as a tabletop.

There is little vegetation that is native to the pampas. In some areas there is a fine low grass, while in others there are tall, coarse grasses, or low scrub. The only tree that grew here originally, the ombú, is not even really a tree; it's a weed. Although it grows to a substantial size, its moist fibers are useless as fuel. Historically, its most useful function was to provide shade for tired gauchos as they rested beneath its branches to sip their afternoon *mate*. Over the years, many non-indigenous plants have been brought in. Tall rows of trees serving as windbreaks can be seen everywhere and break the monotony of

Virtually all of the *pampa humeda* has been carved up and cultivated. Many of Argentina's wealthy landowners have their *estancias* here, properties which sometimes run to hundreds of thousands of hectares.

The dry pampa lies further to the west, where the Andes help bring about a drier environment.

The smoothness of the pampa is broken up at several points by low-lying sierras. The major ranges are the Sierra de Tandil and the Sierra de la Ventana in the east, and several parallel ranges in the central provinces of Córdoba and San Luis.

The Río de la Plata River Basin has as its tributaries more than six major rivers,

the landscape.

The pampa has two subdivisions: the humid pampa (*pampa humeda*) and the dry pampa (*pampa seca*). The first is the more easterly portion, which lies mostly in the province of Buenos Aires. This wetter area supports much of the nation's agriculture; grains, primarily wheat, are grown here. This is also the heart of the nation's cattle industry. The grass-feeding of the cattle is what gives Argentine beef its celebrated flavor. The development of the pampa took a large leap with the building, by the British, of an extensive railway system and the importation of British breeds of cattle.

among them the Paraná, the Uruguay, and the Paraguay. It drains a huge area of South America, including eastern Bolivia, most of Paraguay and Uruguay, and a large part of southern Brazil. It finds its outlet in the Río de la Plata estuary, its mouth just northwest of Buenos Aires. The delta area of the river is laced with countless small waterways which have created a unique marshy ecosystem. The major port of Buenos Aires was developed along the marshy banks of the estuary, but constant dredging is needed to keep the channels free from silt deposits.

Subtropical forests: The isolated northeast reaches of Argentina is referred to as

Mesopotamia, as most of it lies between the Paraná and Uruguay Rivers. The whole area is crosscut by rivers and streams, and a great deal of the land here is marshy and low. The region receives a lot of rainfall.

The southern sector, with its swamps and low, rolling hills, is supported by an economy of sheep, horse and cattle raising. This is one of the major wool-producing areas of the country.

Towards the north, the climate becomes subtropical and very humid. The economy here is based on agriculture, with the principal crops being yerba *mate* (a form of tea) and various types of fruit. Enormous tracts of the virgin forest have been lost to an

The hunting ground: The north-central part of Argentina is called the Chaco. It is the southern sector of the Gran Chaco, which extends into Bolivia, Paraguay and Brazil, and that borders on the north with Brazil's Mato Grosso region. In the local dialect, *chaco* means "hunting ground," and across this wide and largely undeveloped region there are many forms of wildlife that would justify the name.

The area is covered by flat jungle plains and the drier chaqueña savanna, and the climate ranges from the tropical to the subtropical. The Chaco lies within the Río de la Plata river basin, and although it is dry much of the year, the summer rains always cause

increasingly important lumbering business. Towards the northern tip of Misiones, a plateau of sandstone and basalt rises from the lowlands. The landscape is characterized by a rough relief and fast-running rivers. Along the northern border with Brazil sits the magnificent Iguazú Falls, which has over 275 separate cascades dropping over 200 feet (60 meters) through the lush subtropical forest.

Left, rainbow over the Pampa. Above, going upriver in Mesopotamia.

extensive flooding.

The forests of the area contain high quality hard woods, and lumbering has become a major industry. In the cleared areas of the forest, cotton is grown and there is some ranching. One of the region's most important economic activities is the harvesting of the quebracho tree. This tree produces a resin used in the tanning of leather, and fine leathers are a major by-product of the cattle industry in Argentina.

High desert: Going west from the Chaco, one reaches the plateau region of the northwest, where the bordering Andes create an arid or semi-arid environment over much of the terrain. Here the elevation rises steadily until reaching the altiplano (high plateau) on the northern border with Bolivia. Along this stretch, the Andes are divided into two parallel *cordilleras* (ranges), the Salta-Jujeña to the west and the Sierra Subandinas to the east.

The Puna is a dry cold desert that stretches over the Andes, north from the province of Catamarca towards Bolivia and covers part of northern Chile as well. Here the population, largely of mestizo stock, raises goats, sheep and llamas.

Further to the east, much of the provinces of Tucumán, Salta and Jujuy have a mountain tropical climate, with mild winters.

Along with cattle ranching, there are vineyards, olive and citrus groves, and tobacco and sugar cane plantations. Vegetable farms lie in the valleys and piedmonts.

Grapes and oil: The central western section of Argentina, comprising the provinces of San Juan, Mendoza and San Luis is known as the Cuyo. The Andes here become a single towering range, with many peaks over 21, 780 feet (6,600 meters). West of the city of Mendoza lies Aconcagua, at 23, 034 feet (6,980 meters) the highest peak in the Western Hemisphere. Just south of Aconagua is the Upsallata Pass, the *Camino de los Andes*, which at its highest point of 12, 540 feet

(3,800 meters) crosses over into Chile.

Fingers of desert extend eastward from the glacial mountains into the plains. Much of the area is dry and wind-eroded, with scrub vegetation. Rivers nourished by the melting snows of the Andes cut through the desert.

It is these rivers which, through extensive irrigation, allow for large scale agriculture in the region. The Cuyo is the heart of Argentina's wine country; the arid climate, sandy soil, and year-round sunshine makes this ideal for viticulture. Citrus fruits are also grown.

The Cuyo area is blessed with mineral wealth. Copper, lead and uranium are mined, and oil discovered here and in Patagonia has made Argentina nearly self-sufficient in that vital resource.

Open steppe: South of the Rio Colorado, covering more than a quarter of Argentina, is Patagonia, where a series of dry plateaus drop from the Andes towards the rugged cliffs of the Atlantic coast. The Patagonian Andes are lower than those to the north, and are dotted with lakes, meadows, and glaciers. Many of the slopes are forested.

The central steppes are battered by sharp winds, and towards the south the winds become nearly constant. The terrain has been eroded by these winds, and by rivers and glaciers. In the low, wide river valleys of northern Patagonia, fruit and vegetable farming is made possible with irrigation. Towards the south, the rivers run through deep, flat-bottomed canyons. Although there is rainfall throughout most of the year, the climate is cold and doesn't allow for much vegetation. The plains are covered by grasses, shrubs and a few hardy trees. Sheep raising is the major economic activity.

To the south, between the Strait of Magellan and the Beagle Channel, lies Tierra del Fuego. The climate here is subantarctic, and although that sounds rather intimidating, it could be worse, given the latitude. The nearness of the Atlantic and the Pacific waters helps to moderate the temperatures somewhat, and some parts of the island are quite green.

Left, giant Cardones Cactus of the Northwest. Right, Cerro Torre, in Glacier National Park.

Argentina and Chile were the last areas into which early humans moved in their quest for new lands and new food resources. Looking beyond and north from Argentina, the story began many years before and many miles away, when the first group of Asians entered the North American continent. It is a theory accepted by most archaeologists that the early Americans came via the Bering Strait in one of the many Ice Ages, at a time when seas were a great deal lower than at

present. The Bering Strait became a perfect bridge between America and Asia.

If we accept the early archaeological dates of the Yukon Valley in Alaska, placing the first waves of immigrants at about 24,000 to 29,000 B.C., it is possible that the early Americans reached the southern tip of South America by 9,000 B.C.. The Fells cave site, a few miles from the Straits of Magellan, seems to corroborate this theory.

What were the factors that influenced the movement of people and the settlement of groups throughout America? The Ice Age, with its many advances and retreats, was a serious obstacle in the early years. The

movement through North America was extremely difficult when two huge ice sheets covered most of the continent.

Though the effects of the Ice Age in South America are not yet completely understood, it is thought that, as in North America, advances and retreats of the ice characterized the Pleistocene in the Southern Hemisphere.

Different climate: The last ice advance in South America occurred between 9,000 and 8,000 B.C., provoking different effects than in North America. No ice sheets covered the pampas of Argentina or the jungles of Brazil. The principal manifestation was that the great chain of mountains that is the spine of South America, the Andes, had more ice than it does today. The environment was also different since many more lakes existed and sea level was lower, rendering many areas, now under water, very tempting campsites. The Atlantic side, which today has a large and not very deep submarine platform, was very likely much wider, creating with the pampas and Patagonia a still larger plain. The rainfall pattern was also different during the Pleistocene and areas like the now arid Patagonia were then covered with grass.

What did the first Spaniards find when they finally entered Argentina during the 16th century? Certainly not the great cities and pyramids of Meso-America or a great empire like the one the Peruvian Incas had built in only 100 years. Rather they found a country sparsely populated from the Northwestern Puna to the tip of Tierra del Fuego. This population was not homogeneous in its cultural development.

Forts and farming: The Northwest zone was definitely the most culturally developed. This area received throughout the centuries the influences that diffused from Bolivia (during the peak of the Tiahuanaco empire) and Peru (especially during the expansion of the Inca empire, which incorporated northwestern Argentina within its great realm).

The early-16th century found the natives of the northwest living in architecturally simple stone houses, in towns with populations that might have reached 3,000 people in some cases, making this area the most densely populated. Many of the towns were walled, located on hilltops for defense purposes, and had ceremonial buildings. Intensive agriculture and irrigation was practiced everywhere and domestic animals, mostly camelids like the llama and alpaca, were used by the people.

Most of the arts reached a high level of development; good ceramics, wood carvings, excellent metalworking (mostly cop-

Ceramics were made but were rather crude, and little to no metal was worked in the area. Many of the metal pieces were imported from the Northwest.

Fish and nomads: Life in the Northeastern region of Argentina had many of the characteristics of that in the Central Mountains except that the presence of two big rivers, the Paraná and the Uruguay, added a new dimension in that economy: fishing. Though pottery was known, metallurgy seems to

per and bronze pieces) and stone sculptures have been found from the different groups. Tribes and confederations of tribes politically organized the people.

The Central Mountains and around Santiago del Estero was a less developed area. Small villages existed in this region, in some cases with semisubterranean houses. Though agriculture was practiced, hunting and collecting still played an important role.

Preceding pages: the Cueva de las Manos, in Santa Cruz. Left, ruins of a Quilmes Indian settlement, Tucumán. Above, ancient stone tools.

have been absent. Unfortunately this is one of the less archaeologically studied areas.

The last region, which encompasses the southern half of the country from southern Santa Fe and Córdoba to the southernmost islands, had very little to no architecture. Many of the groups here were nomadic and erected temporary settlements with simple houses of branches or hides. Almost no agriculture was practiced, with hunting (both on land and at sea) and collecting playing important roles. Pottery was either not known or, when practiced, very crude. Metalworking was unknown until the Chilean Araucanian migrations. Most of the tools were of stone or bone and in both mediums they reached a highly developed technology. In Patagonia it is estimated that some of these roaming bands had, at times, up to 150 members.

Dating difficulties: Archaeologists have been able to confirm and expand backwards most of the information collected by the first visitors. What is the story of each region and how did they develop to the stages that the Spaniards encountered?

Though there are many archaeological sites throughout the country, the dating of many of them is still not satisfactory and only a few can be ascribed to the end of the Pleistocene and beginning of the Holocene, around 10,000 to 9,000 B.C.. Many archaeologists call the earliest cultural tradition the Hunting Tradition or the Hunting and Collecting Tradition. As the words suggest, these early groups that roamed the country lived from the hunting of big game and the collection of plants, seeds and fruits. Many of the animals hunted and eaten are now extinct. Many of the early sites are either rockshelters or caves.

Colorful caves: The Fells and Pailli Aike caves, located on the southern tip of the continent, contain horse, guanaco and ground sloth bones, together with those of humans. In southern Chile the Eberhardt cave has remains of Mylodon and Onohippidon. The Los Toldos site, in Santa Cruz, is a group of caves with horse bones. All of these sites have stone tools which include points, scrappers, and knives; some of them have bone tools and Eberhardt has worked hides. The sites represent seasonal occupations within a pattern of nomadism that followed the food resources.

The Los Toldos caves have walls and ceilings covered with paintings, mostly of hands, done in what is called negative technique (the hand is placed on the wall and the paint applied around it). Because some of the stone artifacts from the early levels have paint remains, it is thought that the cave paintings also correspond to the early levels, i.e. circa 9,000 B.C..

Stone points: The hunting tradition survived for several thousand years, throughout the country, and until the European contact in some areas. These manifestations appear in the different regions in the form of archaeological sites which have certain common characteristics: absence of ceramics and metal, no clear sign of the practice of agriculture (though by 2,500 B.C., some milling stones are present in some of the places), and the presence of stone and bone tools and objects for personal decoration. Both the stone and bone tools exhibit change through time. One of the most useful tools for gauging change is the stone point, as its development reflects technological advances, functional changes, specialization in hunting, and discovery of new and better raw materials.

Sea hunters: As mentioned earlier, development was uneven throughout the country and certain areas, within the Patagonia and

Tierra del Fuego zones, never moved beyond the Hunting Tradition Stage. The Tunel site, on the Beagle Channel, on the southern coast of Tierra del Fuego, testifies to that. After a first occupation, oriented toward guanaco hunting, the inhabitants (either the same or different groups) converted to a sea-oriented economy. For 6,000 years, that is until their full contact with the Europeans (by the late 1800s), their economy and way of life remained within a mostly sea hunting, sea collecting pattern, complemented by guanaco hunting and seed and fruit collection. The lack of revolutionary changes does not reflect primitiveness or cultural backwardness but a successful and, with time, comfortable adaptation to the local environment by people who knew the resources and exploited them.

Agriculture arrives: In other areas of the country the Hunting Tradition gave way eventually to agriculture. The transformation was from a pattern of collecting fruits, seeds and leaves when and where they could be found (nomadism being of course a consequence of this regime) to an organized pattern of planting, tending and collecting the fruits within a more restricted area, usually under sedentary patterns of settlement.

Within the New World, Mexico and the Andean area were the centers of domestica-

tion. The vegetables and fruits that with time became the main staples of all the pre-Colombian societies and later of the European settlements—maize, potatoes, squash, beans, peppers—appear in either Meso-America or the Andean area by approximately 5,000 B.C..

Standing stones: The advent of agriculture is often closely followed by the development of ceramic skills. It is possible that

Left and above, decorated menhirs found in the Province of Tucumán.

the harvesting of crops and the new phenomenon of surplus food was an incentive for the making of containers which could hold and store seeds and fruits. Although pottery appeared in the New World during the 4th millenium B.C., it is not seen in Argentina's archaeological record until circa 500 B.C..

This period of transition between hunting and collecting patterns and sedentary agriculture is called either Incipient Agriculture or Early Ceramic (when ceramic is present). The Ceramic Period is usually subdivided into Early, Intermediate and Late, according to the different styles that succeeded each other in the different areas. One should remember once again that most of the ceramic cultures occurred in the northern half of Argentina.

To the Early Ceramic Period, which extended from around 500 B.C. to 600 A.D., belong several cultures which occupied an arch extending from the center of Jujuy to the eastern part of San Juan. One of the early complexes is the Tafi culture of Tucumán, which is noted for its stone sculptures. Some of these beautiful carved monoliths (some of which reach 10 feet/three meters in height) have very stylized human faces.

The area's people lived in settlements formed by groups of houses arranged around a patio. Their diet included *quinoa* (an Andean cereal), potato and possibly maize, and they practiced llama herding. Mounds have been found, which were used either for burials or as platforms for special structures.

Another extraordinary example of excellent stone sculpture is found at the site of the Alamito culture, on the Tucumán-Catamarca border. The statues here (both of women and men) reached an unusual level of development, with an almost abstract style both powerful and expressive.

In contrast to these stone-oriented cultures there is Condorhuasi, a culture in which ceramic art reached levels of expression not known in any other groups. Strange figures, often with both animal and human characteristics, sit and crawl with globular bodies and legs, painted in white and red, cream and red or black and red combinations.

Corn and tweezers: The Middle Ceramic Period, from 650 A.D. to 850 A.D., witnessed the development and continuation of the preceding cultures, the existence of full agricultural communities and llama and alpaca herding.

Architecture was still not impressive, at times just clay walls, probably with straw or wood roofs. Ceramic art continued to be very developed, but stone work declined. Metalworking was by then highly developed, with the making of bronze and copper axes, needles, tweezers, bracelets and disks with complicated designs. The distinct differences in the quantity of artifacts found in the graves is a clear indication that by now social stratification existed. The lack of monumental works or clear examples of organized labor points to a still simple political organization.

The Aguada complex (mostly from Catamarca and La Rioja) is a good representative of this period.

Inca invasion: The Late Ceramic Period, from 850 A.D. to 1480 A.D. witnessed some changes. The settlements became larger, some in defensible locations, and thick walls made of round stones are found in many of these sites. Llama and alpaca herding was practiced on a large scale. Roads, cemeteries, irrigation works and what were probably ceremonial centers appeared.

The ceramic urn (used for the burial of children) is one of the markers of the period. These vessels (between 16 and 24 inches/40 and 60 cm in height) often have painted human faces showing what could be tear marks. Other markers for this period are beautiful metal disks or breastplates with human head and snake motifs on them.

Finally, in 1480 A.D., the Inca armies arrived and conquered the Northwestern region of Argentina. Remains of Inca roads, tambos (places of rest, supply and storage), and forts or *pucarás* can be found in the region. The Incas introduced their styles and artistic values and many of the pieces of this period are just local reproductions of original Inca pieces.

Hands and feet: A last word should be dedicated to the cave and rock paintings and decorations. Examples of this form of art are now being found throughout the country, but it is in Patagonia where it has been most thoroughly studied. Within this area several styles have been recognized. One of them is the style of the painted hands, which is present in many caves, some of them with hundreds of hand representations. The painting is done with the negative technique, and the depictions are mostly of left adult hands. An excellent example of this type of painting is found at the Cave of the Painted Hands in Santa Cruz.

Another style is the naturalist style or scenes style. It often depicts whole scenes related to dancing ceremonies and the hunting and corralling of guanacos. Along the Upper Pinturas River, in Santa Cruz, several such paintings can be found on the walls of the gullies.

Footprint paintings constitute another style, and the geometric design style completes the range of motifs.

As can be seen, the Spaniards found, upon their arrival, a mosaic of cultural developments ranging from groups which were still practicing a hunting and collecting mode of subsistence to others that were moving to the threshold of civilization. The story of the area's uneven cultural development goes back to approximately 10,000 B.C. and it is still not completely revealed. The continuing work of archaeologists is slowly but surely filling the gaps in our understanding of the prehistory of Argentina.

Left, well-worn grinding stone. Right, petroglyph, thought to depict the devil, at Talampaya.

The history of Argentina has been written in blood, from her earliest days under the colonial administration of the Spaniards until very recently. There have been periodic outbursts of democratic rule but the tradition of representative government does not run deep in the people of this remote nation.

Paradoxically, Argentina has assisted in the liberation of minds and souls throughout Latin America, exerting intellectual power and military force on behalf of other Latin peoples during the course of her history.

Admirable achievements and depressing lowpoints have marked the development of the Argentine nation as she has struggled to liberate herself first from a distant master and then from the cruel and selfish local potentates, the *caudillos*. Heroic actions such as San Martín's crossing of the Andes, and the liberation of workers from a status similar to serfdom have, unfortunately, been overshadowed by an ultra-nationalistic conceit that borders on hubris and has proved time and again to be self-defeating.

The conflict between Buenos Aires and the interior, a problem that persists today, has also been a major obstacle in the development of the nation.

The first explorers: The first half of the 16th century was a period of intense exploration on behalf of the Portuguese and Spanish Crowns. Not quite 10 years after Columbus' first voyage to the new world, Amerigo Vespucci was probing the eastern shores of South America. Today, many credit him with the discovery of the Río de la Plata, although standard Argentine accounts cite Juan de Solís as the first European to sail these waters.

Solís reached the Río de la Plata estuary in 1516 and named the river Mar Dulce or Sweet Sea. Not long after, while Solís was leading a small party ashore, he was killed along with all but one of his sailors, by Charrua tribesmen. After killing the Spaniards, the natives then ate them in full view of the remaining crew onboard.

In 1520, Ferdinand Magellan, on his voyage to the Pacific, was the next explorer to reach what is now Argentina. Sebastian Cabot, sailing under the Spanish flag, and drawn by rumors of a mountain of silver, was the next to explore the Río de la Plata region in 1526. His three-year search proved fruitless, but he is credited with having established the first settlement, later abandoned.

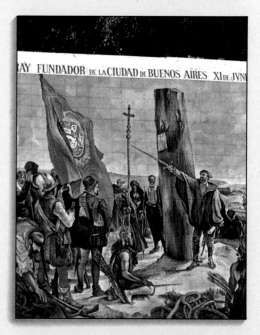

The Spanish nobleman Pedro de Mendoza led a very large expedition to the area, also drawn by reports of great wealth. On February 3, 1536, he founded Santa Maria de los Buenos Aires. The natives were at first helpful and fed the Spaniards, but then they turned furiously against them. As one of Mendoza's soldiers wrote, "The Indians attacked our city of Buenos Aires with great force....There were around 23,000 of them....While some of them were attacking us, others were shooting burning arrows at our houses, so that we wouldn't have time to see to both problems and save our houses....In this attack they burned four

Left: top, Paraná river culture, and bottom, the early difficult years of the settlement at Buenos Aires. Right, mural depicting the resettlement of Buenos Aires.

large ships." The natives finally retreated under the fire of Spanish artillery.

Mendoza and his men never did locate any great mineral wealth and eventually left Buenos Aires for the more hospitable Asunción, in Paraguay.

A second group of Spaniards, this time approaching overland from Chile, Peru and Upper Peru (today's Bolivia), was more successful in founding lasting settlements. The northwest towns of Santiago del Estero, Catamarca, Mendoza, Tucumán, Córdoba, Salta, La Rioja and Jujuy were all founded in the second half of the 16th century, with Santiago del Estero being the oldest continuously settled outpost (1551).

For all of the following century and most of the 18th, the northwest was the center of most activity in Argentina. This was mostly due to the King of Spain's 1554 prohibition of traffic on the Río de la Plata. Manufactured goods from Spain and human chattel from Africa were shipped to South America via Panama and then Peru. The king's order was to benefit greatly the Spanish colonial cities of Lima and Mexico City but it kept the Río de la Plata estuary isolated and commercially backward.

Northwest/Central supremacy: While Argentina was part of the Peruvian viceroyalty until 1776, two areas of the colony became important centers. Tucumán developed into a successful agricultural region, supplying wheat, corn, cotton, tobacco and livestock to neighboring Upper Peru. Somewhat later, Córdoba attained status as a center of learning, with the establishment of the Jesuit university in 1613. Córdoba also prospered, owing to its central location and fertile lands. By contrast, Buenos Aires, which had been refounded in 1580, was a small town that relied on smuggling for its income. Because all manufactured goods had to come the long route from Spain, their prices were very high, and this led to the cheaper contraband traffic.

West to East shift: The decline of the Andean mining industries, coupled with growing calls for direct transatlantic trade, finally persuaded the Spanish Crown to establish the new viceroyalty of Río de la Plata, which had its administrative center at Buenos Aires.

With a new viceroyalty, which included Uruguay, Paraguay and parts of Upper Peru

and the Argentine, Spain hoped to exert greater control on a region that was growing more important. Buenos Aires experienced an explosion in population, as the city increased in numbers from 2,200 in 1726 to well over 33,000 by 1778.

Upwards of one-quarter of the population was Afro-Argentine and held in bondage. Many others were of mixed Indian and Spanish parentage, a natural consequence of the paucity of Spanish women in the viceroyalty. Another important appearance in the demographic picture was the rise of the gaucho which came with the large ranches in the latter half of the 18th century. The gaucho represented a culture very different from that of the perfumed and groomed inhabitants of Buenos Aires.

The growing importance of the viceroyalty of the Río de la Plata did not go unnoticed in Europe. The Franco-Hispanic alliance during the Napoleonic Wars (1804-15) resulted in a loosening of Argentina's ties with the motherland, when Spain's fleet was destroyed by the English navy. The Spanish colonies in Latin America were open for English attention.

The British invade: In 1806 and again the following year, the British invaded Buenos Aires. During the first invasion, the inept Spanish viceroy fled to Montevideo, across the Río de la Plata, taking with him many of his troops. The retaking of the city was left to Santiago de Liniers, who organized the remaining Spanish troops and the local inhabitants, including one battalion of Blacks. The British were quickly routed but were to return soon.

After seizing Montevideo, the British attempted the recapture of Buenos Aires with an army of 10,000. They were met by Liniers and his men, and women pelting rooftiles and throwing boiling oil on them from above. The city's streets were turned into what the British called, "pathways of death." The English commander of the expedition promptly evacuated his troops.

Beyond the immediate consequences of repelling the invaders, a number of very important effects stemmed from the confrontations with the British. Pride in the colony was a natural outcome of having defeated a large and well-trained army with a mostly local militia. Tensions arose between the criollos (Argentine-born colonists) and the Spanish troops, who realised they could not be of any assistance to the Crown in the troubled Iberian Peninsula. The creation of a rudimentary provisional government also helped to foster an independent-minded local elite. Thoughts of a booming economy without the strictures and regulations of a Crown that could not even protect the colony began to enter the minds of the criollos.

Independence steps: Napoleon Bonaparte's invasion of Spain in 1808 provided the final push for a rupture in relations; a *cabildo abierto* (open town council) in Buenos Aires deposed the Spanish viceroy and created a revolutionary junta to rule in

much more of a tortured process than the criollo intellectuals could have imagined. Indeed, a civil war was in the making after what Argentines call the May Revolution. On May 25, 1810, an autonomous government was set up in Buenos Aires. This date is celebrated in Argentina as the nation's day of independence, although a formal declaration was not made until 1816.

These early years were not easy; the people of the viceroyalty were split along regional, class and political lines. The Unitarios, or Unitarians, were intent upon having a strong central government which would be based in offices in Buenos Aires while the Federales, or Federalists, hoped to

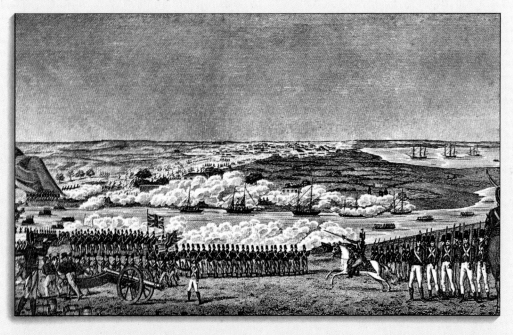

his stead. Bernardino Rivadavia, Manuel Belgrano and Mariano Moreno were three criollo intellectuals, who, inspired by European liberal thought, focused their energies on creating a new nation based on a reordering of colonial society. The old order—the rich merchants, the *estancieros* (large landowners), members of the clergy and, indeed, the whole colonial administrative structure—was violently opposed to any tampering with its status.

A house divided: This lack of unity made the realization of an independent nation

Above, the first British invasion, 1806.

establish a loose confederation of autonomous provinces.

A confusing series of juntas, triumvirates and assemblies rose and fell, as one group would have the upper hand for a brief period only to lose the advantage to another. Whatever unity the viceroyalty had was soon shattered, as Uruguay, Paraguay and Bolivia went their separate ways. The eight original jurisdictions of the viceroyalty dwindled to three; these three then fragmented into seven provinces.

Before this loose group of provinces further disintegrated, a congress was called to maintain whatever unity was left. On July 9,

1816 the congress at Tucumán formally declared independence under the blue and white banner of the United Provinces of South America.

Enter San Martín: The task of ridding the continent of Spanish armies remained. José San Martín was to execute one of the boldest moves of the South American wars of liberation. Gathering a large army, San Martín crossed the icy Andes at Mendoza in 21 days and met and defeated a Spanish army at Chacabuco (1817) in Chile. He again engaged the Spaniards, this time at Maipú (1818), where he ended the Spanish menace to Chile once and for all.

San Martín's next move was no less auda-

Hall, a contemporary of San Martín's, had this to say: "There was little, at first sight, in his appearance to engage attention; but when he rose up and began to speak, his great superiority over every other person I had seen in South America was sufficiently apparent....General San Martín is a tall, erect, well-proportioned, handsome man, with a large aquiline nose, thick black hair, and immense bushy whiskers extending from ear to ear under the chin; his complexion is deep olive, and his eye, which is large, prominent and piercing, jet black; his whole appearance being highly military... I have never seen any person, the enchantment of whose address was more irresistible...The

cious than his crossing of the Andes. He amassed a fleet of mostly English and American ships to convoy his army the 1500 miles to Lima. The Spanish army evacuated the city without fighting, wishing to keep their forces intact. It was at this time, in 1822, that San Martín met the other great liberator of South America, Simón Bolívar, at Guayaquil. What actually was discussed at this meeting is not known and has kept historians guessing. The upshot, though, was San Martín's retirement from battle, leaving the remaining honors to be garnered by Bolívar.

Of San Martín and his motivations, Basil

contest in Peru, he said, was not of an ordinary description—not a war of conquest and glory, but entirely of opinion; it was a war of new and liberal principles against prejudice, bigotry and tyranny."

San Martín was elevated to a position of sainthood by Argentines but this only happened posthumously. Every town in Argentina has a street named after him and every classroom a portrait of the general crossing the Andes on a white horse. When he re-

Left, the Latin American liberator, San Martín. Above, the formal declaration of independence, July 9, 1816, in Tucumán.

turned to Buenos Aires in 1823 from his campaigns on behalf of Argentina, he received no acknowledgement for the services he rendered his country. Soon afterwards San Martín left for France, where he was to die in obscurity.

Continued disorder: The period from independence to the commencement of Juan Manuel de Rosas' dictatorship in 1829 were difficult years for the United Provinces of the Río de la Plata (the earlier and grander name had to be dropped with the fragmentation of the original grouping of provinces). Bernardino Rivadavia, a man of great vision, valiantly but vainly attempted to shape the country's future.

He was interested in establishing a constitution for the nation, forming a strong central government, dividing up the land in more equitable shares, and drawing immigrants to the United Provinces. His plans were quickly sidetracked, however, by *caudillos* in the interior, none too anxious to surrender any of their power, and the draining Cisplatine War (1825-1828) with Brazil over the status of Uruguay. When Rivadavia resigned from the presidency of the United Provinces in 1827 and went into exile, there was little to show for his efforts. The region remained as anarchic as ever.

Caudillo and tyrant: One of Latin American history's most intriguing, if bloodthirsty, figures must be Juan Manuel de Rosas, who ruled much of Argentina as his personal domain for over 20 years. Rosas forged a coalition of rough gauchos, wealthy landowners and others who represented the Federalist cause, in his quest for power, and this combination proved a formidable one for many years. Above all else, Rosas is remembered for the terror to which he and his followers subjected the new nation.

Although born in Buenos Aires in 1793, Rosas was a product of the open pampa. It was here on his family's *estancia* that he learned to ride and fight and toss the boleadoras as well as any of the gauchos he kept company with, gaining their respect and later their support.

Rosas became wealthy in his own right at an early age. By his mid-twenties, he owned thousands of acres and was a successful businessman, having helped to establish one of the first meat-salting plants in his province. Rosas chose well in marrying Maria de la Encarnacion Escurra, daughter of another rich family. She would later prove invaluable to Rosas' ascent to power, plotting and organizing subtly and effectively on her husband's behalf.

In order to stem the rising tide of anarchy that followed the exile of Rivadavia, Rosas was asked to become the governor of the province of Buenos Aires in 1829. Rosas, a powerful *caudillo* and experienced military man, seemed the perfect individual to restore order and stability. The major problem with the Federalists was that there was little unity among the various factions. Federalists in the provinces demanded autonomy and an equal footing with Buenos Aires, while those espousing the Federalist cause in Argentina's major city were not willing to surrender their premier position.

As governor with extraordinary powers, Rosas signed the Federal Pact in 1831 which tied together the provinces of Buenos Aires, Entre Ríos, Santa Fe and Corrientes. His opposition, the Unitarian League, was dealt a severe blow when its leader, José Maria Paz, was unhorsed by a Federalist soldier wielding boleadoras. Paz was taken prisoner and jailed by Rosas. By 1832 the Unitarians had suffered a number of reverses on the battlefield and, for the moment, did not pose a deep threat to the Federalists.

When Rosas' first term as governor ended in 1832, he refused to accept another stint in office because the council of provincial representatives was unwilling to allow Rosas to maintain his virtually unlimited authority.

Darwin and Rosas: In the midst of this struggle, Rosas did not absent himself from combat. He took command of the campaign against the native Argentine tribes in the south, and earned himself even more dubious glory by wiping out thousands.

It was during this Desert Campaign of 1833-34 that the British naturalist Charles Darwin was entertained by Rosas. Of his meeting with Rosas, Darwin wrote: "General Rosas is a man of extraordinary character; he has at present a most predominant influence in this country and may probably end up by being its ruler...He is moreover a perfect gaucho: his feats of horsemanship are very notorious. He will fall from a doorway upon an unbroken colt, as it rushes out of the Corral, and will defy the worst efforts of the animal. He wears the Gaucho dress and is said to have called upon Lord Ponsonby in it, saying at the time he thought the costume of the country the proper and therefore the most respectful dress. By these means he obtained an unbounded popularity in the Camp, and in consequence despotic power. A man a short time since murdered another; being arrested and questioned he answered, "the man spoke disrespectfully of General Rosas and I killed him," in one week's time the murderer was at liberty. In conversation he is enthusiastic, sensible and very grave. His gravity is carried to a high pitch."

Though Rosas was campaigning in the south, he was not out of contact with events

in Buenos Aires. His wife waged a "dirty war" to have her husband reinstated as governor, forming the Sociedad Popular Restauradora and its terror-wing, the *mazorca*. Through the Sociedad Popular Restauradora, Doña Encarnación hampered the efforts of the three governors who followed Rosas to rule effectively.

The junta finally acquiesced to Rosas' demands in 1835; he was to have all the power necessary to defend the national cause of the Federalists without restrictions. Rosas assumed his post as Restorer of the Laws and governor in a regal ceremony on April 13, 1835.

Rosas now had the means to institute the most personal of regimes. The red color of the Federalists became the distinguishing factor in dress. Women wore scarlet dresses and men red badges that proclaimed "Federation or Death." Decorating in blue, the hated color of the "savage Unitarians," could be cause enough for imprisonment or execution, so deep ran the paranoid streak of the Rosistas (followers of Rosas).

The horror: While Rosas did not create the brutal methods of repression that so characterized his regime, he did give a certain order and system to them in making himself supreme dictator. Generally speaking, Rosas' victims were not massacred wholesale but rather executed on an individual basis. Long lists of suspected Unitarians and what property they possessed were drawn up by Rosas' effective spy network, the police, the military and justices of the peace.

The methods of silencing opponents ranged from exile to imprisonment to execution. The favored manner of despatching them was throat-cutting, reflecting the traditions of the gauchos. W. H. Hudson, naturalist and chronicler of the pampas, wrote that the Argentines "loved to kill a man not with a bullet but in a manner to make them know and feel that they were really and truly killing." Another method of killing was lancing; two executioners, standing on either side of the prisoner, would plunge lances into the body simultaneously.

Throat-cutting, lancing, castration and the carving out of tongues were acceptable means at the disposal of the violent caudillos but it was only under Rosas that these methods were institutionalized. The actual number of those who perished remains unclear, but estimates range in the thousands. Whatever the correct number, Rosas created and maintained a climate of fear for over 20 years.

With Rosas at the helm, the Argentine state did not prosper. Rosas meddled in the affairs of neighboring Uruguay often, expending scarce resources in the process, but he was never able to conquer its capital, Montevideo. Extreme xenophobia on Rosas' part also kept the country from attracting needed immigrants and foreign capital. Indeed, during two periods, the first from 1838-40 when French troops occupied a customs house on the River Plate, and then during the 1845-47 Anglo-French blockade of the river, the finances of Buenos Aires suffered severely. Rosas' treatment of European nationals and his extreme paranoia, and the resulting consequences from these did not help the growth of the nation.

In response to the atmosphere of terror and lack of freedom, Argentines in secret and in exile organized to overthrow Rosas. These intellectuals, whose ranks included such luminaries as Bartolomé Mitre, Juan Bautista Alberdi and Domingo Faustino Sarmiento, provided the words necessary to galvanize the opposition.

A quick end: Justo José de Urquiza, a *caudillo* who had long supported Rosas, turned against the Restorer and organized an army that soon included thousands of volunteers, and even many Uruguayans and Brazilians. On February 3, 1852 Urquiza's army engaged Rosas' demoralized and rebellion-weary troops at Caseros, near Buenos Aires. "The battle," as Mitre later wrote, "was won before it was fought." A new age in Argentina's history had begun, with Urquiza intent on consolidating the nation as one unit and not a collection of semi-independent provinces; progress in all areas came quickly.

State foundations: The period from Rosas' downfall to 1880 was a time of organizing the nation-state and establishing the institutions required to run it. The major conflict of this period was an old one: the status of Buenos Aires in relation to the interior. This issue was finally settled in 1880 by federalizing the city and making it something like the District of Columbia in the United States.

Urquiza's first task was to draw up a constitution for Argentina. A constitutional convention was held in the city of Santa Fe and this meeting produced a document modeled on the U.S. Constitution. Among its provisos were the establishment of a bicameral legislature, an executive chosen by an electoral college, and an independent judiciary. The Argentine constitution was accepted by the convention on May 1, 1853. Not surprisingly, Urquiza was chosen as the first president. During his tenure, he established a national bank, built schools and improved transportation in the republic.

Left, the tyrant Juan Manuel de Rosas. Right, a Rosas soldier in Federalist colors.

What plagued Urquiza and the development of the nation was the uncertain role of Buenos Aires. Until 1862 there were, in fact, two Argentinas, one based in the wealthy port city of Buenos Aires and the other in the interior with its capital at Paraná. A congress met in Buenos Aires in 1862 and it was decided that Buenos Aires would become the capital city of both the republic and the province.

Bartolomé Mitre, an historian and former governor of the province of Buenos Aires became the next president. While the task of creating a national infrastructure was of great importance to Mitre, he found himself distracted by the Paraguayan War (1865-

Soldado de Rosas - Buenos Aires
Monvoisin - Oleo - 1842

1870) in which the triple alliance of Brazil, Uruguay and Argentina subdued the Paraguayan dictator Francisco Solano López only after five bloody years of fighting. The conflict placed hard financial burdens on the young republic and its citizens but Argentina did receive a large chunk of territory (the provinces of Formosa, Chaco and Misiones) for her efforts.

Mitre was succeeded by Domingo Faustino Sarmiento whose role in promoting education in Argentina has taken on mythic proportions. It was during Sarmiento's administration (1868-1874) that Argentina made enormous strides in development.

THE CASE OF THE AFRO-ARGENTINES

Sherlock Holmes would have been hard-pressed to solve one of Argentina's most fascinating puzzles, that of the vanished Afro-Argentines. Historians throughout the years have offered diverse explanations. Ordinary citizens are ready with stories that range from the plausible to the ludicrous.

What is certainly true is that Argentines of African heritage did exist in large numbers and even comprised 30 percent of Buenos Aires' population for almost 40 years (1778 - 1815). Slaves were first brought to Argentina in the 16th century by their Spanish owners. Due to the pe-

culiar trading arrangements with the Spanish Crown, most slaves were imported to Buenos Aires via Panama and Peru and then overland from Chile, thereby driving their price greatly upwards. Tens of thousands of Africans were shipped via the conventional routes but some were brought in illegally, directly into the port of Buenos Aires and down from Brazil.

Argentine slaves were generally domestic servants but also filled the growing need for artisans in the labor-short colony. While the degree of their labor differed greatly from that of plantation workers in Brazil and the United States, they suffered similarly. Families were torn apart, gruesome punishments awaited runaways and blacks' status in society was kept low, through law and custom, even after emanciption.

In the post-independence era, the move to free slaves was fitful at best; the road to freedom was a long one, Argentine history textbook accounts notwithstanding. While the majority of slaves had gained their liberty by 1827 (through military service, the largess of friendly masters or by purchasing their own freedom), some remained in bondage until 1861. One early 1800s law stipulated that the children of slaves would be free upon birth, though their mothers would remain slaves. However, it was not unusual for slaveowners to spirit their pregnant slaves to Uruguay, where slavery was still legal, and then bring both mother and child back to Argentina as slaves.

The North American professor George Reid Andrews has done much research to uncover the fate of the blacks in his important work, *The Afro-Argentines of Buenos Aires, 1800-900,* but he offers no definitive conclusions. Rather he has explored, in depth, some of the more likely theories regarding their disappearance.

Reid Andrews researches four strong possibilites. A great percentage of Afro-Argentine males served in the army, organized into their own battalions. Many of them might have perished in the incessant warfare during and after independence. Miscegenation, or the mixing of races, is an explanation that many ascribe to. This might also seem sensible given the degree to which the black community was swamped by the hundreds of thousands of European immigrants who reached Argentina after the mid-1800s. The great yellow fever epidemic of 1871 and the general ill health and horrendous living conditions of the blacks is also cited as a possible factor. Finally, Reid Andrews explores the decline of the slave trade (outlawed in 1813) and its impact on a community that would not have its numbers refreshed with new shipments of human chattel.

Census figures for the city of Buenos Aires from 1836 to 1887 point to a steep decline in the numbers and percentages of blacks, from a figure of 14,906 or 26 percent of the total population to 8,005 or 1.8 percent.

The contributions blacks made to Argentine society have, for the most part, been written out of the records. After the early-19th century, Afro-Argentines, for all intents and purposes disappeared or were intentionally made to vanish. One must sift through prints and photographs of the late 1800s to discover that this group, although on a decline, remained a part of the greater community. In these representations we might see blacks working as gauchos or as street vendors or artisans in Buenos Aires.

Hundreds of thousands of immigrants poured into the city of Buenos Aires, railroads were built, and the use of barbed-wire fencing spread, thereby controlling the open range. Sarmiento continually stressed the need to push for a removal of the "barbaric" elements within Argentine society, namely the *caudillos* and the gauchos. Groups such as these had kept Argentina from advancing at a faster rate, thought Sarmiento.

Following Sarmiento came President Nicolás Avellaneda whose inauguration in October, 1874 almost never occurred. Mitre, fearing a decline in Buenos Aires' prestige at the hands of such non-*porteños* as Sarm-

Golden age:
In 1880, Argentina entered its golden age which lasted until the outbreak of the First World War. An enormous number of European immigrants arrived while exports to Europe soared; this was made possible, in part, because of technological advances which permitted ships to carry refrigerated beef to the Old World. There was a corresponding growth in the intellectual fields, as well. Newspapers were founded, political parties were begun, writers were published and a world-class opera house, the Teatro Colón, opened in Buenos Aires.

This is not to say that all was well in Argentina. Politics remained closed to most

iento, Avellaneda and Julio Roca led a revolt against the government. It took three months to crush this rebellion.

Avellaneda's minister of war, Roca headed a series of expeditions against the natives of Patagonia in the infamous Conquest of the Desert which was concluded by 1879. Thousands upon thousands of square miles were opened up for settlement and exploration after this war of genocidal proportions.

Left, Afro-Argentine street vendor, 1844. Above, Indians captured during the Desert Campaign.

Argentines; a few had taken it upon themselves to run the country. The middle-class, supporting the new political party, the Radical Civic Union, pressed for entry into what had been a government run by a small group of conservative families. Workers also became politicized and were attracted to the Socialist Party and the anarchists. Strikes hit turn-of-the-century Argentina and labor unrest grew. The workers found themselves expendable as the country struggled to pay back international loans and as imports began to exceed exports.

One of the worst periods of governmental repressions occurred in 1919. In what was

INMORTALIDAD

DO

EL DIA

JOTE

EL JUICIO

Lit. J. Ribas y H^no Rino

called the *Semana Tragica* (Tragic Week), troops opened fire on strikers and many lives were lost.

The Radical Civic Union governed Argentina from 1916 until 1930. Hipólito Yrigoyen served as president for all but six of those years.

With the coming of the Great Depression, the military swept Yrigoyen from office. With this move, a new element entered modern Argentina's political body. The pattern was to be followed all too frequently over the next half-century.

The Radicals staged a comeback with the ascension of Roberto Ortiz in the fraudulent elections of 1937. Ironically, Ortiz then set

been long. Even today, 15 years after his death, the man and his ideology are strongly influential in Argentina. He elicits the most powerful of responses from the citizenry: complete adoration or utter revulsion. In his name, governments have fallen, terrorist acts committed and workers organized.

His greatest achievement was to harness the energy of the Argentine laborer. Through the workers Perón established a new force in the politics of his country, one that today must always be reckoned with.

Perón's background indicated no pro-labor tendencies. He attended a military college and rose through the ranks as a career officer. While stationed in Italy in 1939 as a

about to restore voter confidence by annulling corrupt elections that followed. Ortiz died in office and was succeeded by Vice-President Ramón Castillo, who reversed his predecessor's campaign to cleanse the political system of corruption. It was this man's blatant dishonesty and fickle policies that triggered the military's coup d'etat in 1943. The significance of the intervention this time around cannot be underestimated for it was during this regime that Juan Perón emerged to lead his nation.

A demagogue's demagogue: Although Juan Domingo Perón served as president for only 11 of the past 40 years, his shadow has

military observer, Perón became impressed by the nationalism of the fascists. The state's intervention in Italy's economy also seemed logical to Perón. On his return to Argentina, Perón involved himself deeply in the secret military organization, the GOU (*Grupo Obra de Unificacion* or Unification Task Force), which was composed of Young Turks bent on remodeling Argentina's political system along the lines of those in Germany and Italy.

The GOU overthrew Castillo on June 4, 1943. Perón was given the post of Secretary of the Labor and Social Welfare Ministry from which he was to build his power base.

He promulgated a series of labor reforms—job security, child labor laws, pensions among them—that were immensely popular with the working class. Furthermore, Perón tied union and nonunion members together through the national welfare system, a move that assured him control over and allegiance from most workers.

The military became uneasy with Perón's growing power and arrested him. This led to a series of demonstrations, capped by a gigantic display in the Plaza de Mayo by the *descamisados* (shirtless ones or poor workers). Perón's consort, Eva Duarte, and labor leaders were behind these actions, rallying support for the imprisoned Perón. Within

ambassador to Buenos Aires ironically contributed to electing the man described by Washington as a fascist.

In the years immediately following World War II, Argentina was wealthy and seemed to be a nation on the move. The country possessed a healthy surplus in its treasury, workers' salaries increased greatly, and industrialization proceeded apace. Although storm clouds were gathering on the economic horizon, nobody seemed to notice: this was a golden age when every family could eat fine steak twice a day, and it is little wonder that Argentina re-elected Perón to a second term in 1951 with a massive 67 percent majority.

weeks he was free. He would soon marry Eva to legitimize their relationship in the eyes of the voters and the Church. Perón sensed correctly that his moment on the national stage had arrived. In the presidential elections of 1946, Perón won with a majority of 54 percent. The clumsy U.S. intervention in these elections through its

Preceding pages: a caricature of Argentine political life, 1893, from the magazine *Don Quijote*. Left, the masses turn out for Loyalty Day, 1946. Above, Perón and Evita appear on the balcony of the Casa Rosada.

Severe droughts and a decrease in the international prices of grains led to a fifty percent increase in Argentina's trade deficit. Eva Perón's death shortly after her husband's second inauguration left him without one of his most successful organizers and contributed to the malaise the nation was experiencing. Without Eva, Perón seemed to lose his willpower and left many decisions to be made by his increasingly radical acolytes. The president's affair with a 13-year-old did not sit well with the more traditionally minded.

Middle-class revolt: A triumvirate of middle-class forces gathered to push Perón

EVITA

Although Maria Eva Duarte de Perón, known throughout the world as Evita, lived in the limelight ever so briefly, her impact on Argentine politics was enormous and even continues today, more than 35 years after her death.

Evita was venerated by the Argentine working class, mocked by the *grandes dames* of Buenos Aires society, and misunderstood by the military establishment. Through all of this she came to symbolize a wealthy Argentina, full of pride and with great expectations immediately following the Second World War.

Her meteoric rise from her beginnings as a poor

villager in the backwaters of the interior to a status as one of the most intriguing, engaging, and powerful figures in a male-dominated culture is a tale worth retelling because of its uniqueness.

Evita was born in the squalid village of Los Toldos in 1919, one of five illegitimate children her mother bore to Juan Duarte. After her father's death, the family moved to the northwestern provincial town of Junín, under the patronage of another of her mother's benefactors. It was in Junín, at the age of 14, that she became determined to become an actress, and when given the opportunity to flee the dusty town, she grabbed it. Evita ran off to Buenos Aires, the cultural mecca of Latin America, in the company of a young tango singer.

As an aspiring 15-year-old actress, Evita

faced almost insurmountable odds in landing jobs in the theater. She led a miserable existence, often falling ill and never having much to eat. Her opportunities took a dramatic leap forward when a rich manufacturer fell for Evita and provided her with her own radio show. Shortly thereafter, Evita's voice became a regular feature on the airwaves of Radio Argentina and Radio El Mundo.

Evita's energy was boundless; her work pace became frenetic and she made powerful friends. Her lack of acting talent and sophistication did not seem to hinder her ability to attract some very important people to her cause. Among her admirers were the president of Argentina and, more importantly, the Minister of Communications, Colonel Imbert, who controlled all radio stations in the country.

Evita met Colonel Juan Domingo Perón, the reputed power behind the new military government, at a fund-raiser for victims of the devastating 1944 San Juan earthquake, in which thousands died. She did not tarry in catching the widower; Evita left the fund-raiser on the arm of the strongman.

Though exactly half Perón's 48 years, Evita, at numerous turns, assisted her husband's rise to power in ways that were beyond the imagination of even the most astute politicians. When Perón became Minister of Labor and Welfare, Evita convinced him that his real power base should be the ignored masses of laborers living in the horrible *villas miserias* (slums) that still ring the capital city. A slew of pronouncements issued forth from the ministry instituting minimum wages, better living conditions, salary increases and protection from employers. The working class, for the first time in Argentina's history, began to see some of the profits of its labor. Additionally, and most brilliantly, Perón empowered and shepherded the giant Confederacion del Trabajo (CGT or General Confederation of Labor), which embraced many unions. In the process, recalcitrant labor leaders were picked up by the police and sent to prisons in Patagonia.

It was not long before Evita called Perón's constituency—the *descamisados*, the shirtless ones—to his aid. An army coup was on the point of success when Evita called all her chips in. Upwards of 200,000 *descamisados* entered the capital city and demanded that Perón be their president. Perón accepted the mandate of the Argentine people.

Evita, now married to Perón, cemented her ties with the workers by establishing the Social Aid Foundation. Through this charity, scores of hospitals and hundreds of schools were built, nurses trained, and money dispensed to the poor. Evita also furthered the cause of women's rights and suffrage and formed the first women's political party, the Peronista Feminist Party. Although a cult was developing around her personality, she would always tell the people in her countless speeches that all credit should go to her husband and that she would gladly sacrifice her life for him, as they should sacrifice theirs.

Perhaps Evita's finest personal and political moment came with her long tour of Europe, during which she met Franco, dictator of Spain,

Family and friends were placed in high positions well above their levels of competence.

The people's heroine was dying by 1952, a victim of uterine cancer, but she kept up her intense work schedule. At her last speech, on May Day, her husband had to hold her up as she spoke to the *descamisados* .

Evita's death on July 26, 1952 brought the country to a standstill. Her body was embalmed, and at her wake thousands paid their respects.

In 1955, Evita's corpse disappeared, stolen by the military after they had deposed Juan Perón. It was carried to Germany and then Italy, where it

Pope Pius XII, and the Italian and French foreign ministers.

She absolutely dazzled post-war Europe with her jewels and elegant gowns. Her rags-to-riches story was told and retold in the press, and she was even on the cover of *Time* magazine.

On the negative side, Evita would brook no criticism of her husband. Newspapers were closed, careers destroyed, and opponents jailed on trumped-up charges. She could be extremely vindictive, never forgetting an insult, even if it were years old.

Left, the glamorous First Lady. Above, the Peróns with their pet poodles.

was interred for 16 years under another name. After negotiations, it was finally returned to her husband in Spain. Evita's long odyssey came to an end when Juan Perón died in Argentina in 1974. Her coffin was brought from Spain and lay in state next to that of the one she said she would die for.

Even though efforts to have her canonized in Rome met with polite refusal, Evita still holds near-saint status in Argentina. Graffitti proclaiming *Evita Vive!* (Evita lives!) can be seen everywhere. At the Duarte family crypt in the Recoleta Cemetery, devotees still leave flowers and a continual guard is kept to prevent vandalism. Her epitaph, which reads, "Don't cry for me Argentina, I remain quite near to you," still rings true, decades after her early death.

from office in 1955. Students resented the total Peronist control over their institutions, while the church hierarchy felt threatened by Perón's secular views regarding education, divorce and prostitution. The armed forces, having been removed from the center of attention, were convinced that they would see their power diminished. A church-sponsored demonstration drew 100,000 to the center of Buenos Aires, and was soon followed by the rebellious airforce's bombing of the Casa Rosada and the Plaza de Mayo. The army struck back against the dissident airforce while Peronist mobs burned churches.

Events were rolling out of control for Perón as the navy then rebelled, joined by some army units in the interior. Perón spared his country enormous bloodshed by not making good his promise to arm the workers and instead fleeing to Paraguay.

The interregnum that was to follow, before Perón's triumphant return, lasted 18 years. During this period, Argentina would suffer nine leaders, none of whom succeeded in taming the economic demons that tormented the country's health.

It would be difficult to describe these years in a positive light. The military constantly meddled in politics, overthrowing elected presidents and installing generals when it was felt that the professional politicians were not guiding the country correctly. Perón's followers were alternately persecuted or allowed to organize and run for office.

Perón's influence continued to be felt although he was in exile. No group, not the military nor the other political parties such as the UCRP (People's Radical Civic Union) and the UCRI (Intransigent Radical Civic Union), could totally ignore the strongman or his workers' party.

Arturo Frondizi was the first president to be freely elected after Perón in February 1958 and his tenure was marked by a state of seige, an economic downturn and many (35) coup attempts. What brought Frondizi down was his decision to allow Peronists to participate in the congressional elections of 1962. Frondizi's attempts to accommodate the Peronists disturbed the Argentine military; they ordered him to annul the election results and when he refused to declare all Peronist wins illegal, the army stepped in.

Arturo Illia did not fare much better when he won the presidential elections in 1963. While the economy was stronger than under Frondizi's administration, inflation remained oppressively high. Illia's minority government stood little chance of survival; the military was apprehensive over the president's inability to hold back the increasingly popular Peronist party, then called the Popular Union.

The next in line to try his hand at governing Argentina was General Juan Carlos Onganía, leader of the 1966 coup against Illia. Onganía ushered in an extremely repressive era; political parties were banned, Congress dissolved and demonstrations outlawed. The economic situation reached new lows. Foreign ownership of companies hit 59 percent in 1969, as workers' real income slumped sharply.

The famed Cordobazo (Córdoba coup) of 1969 precipitated Onganía's departure from government. Argentina's second largest city was the focus of anti-government activity among a new alliance of students, workers and businessmen, all of whom had been badly hurt by Onganía's policies. For two days Córdoba became a war zone, as soldiers battled demonstrators. Over 100 were killed or wounded in the street-fighting.

Onganía was ousted by General Lanusse and representatives of the other branches of the military. An obscure general assumed the presidency, lasting only nine months in office. Lanusse himself then took charge and prepared the nation for a return to civilian elections which were to be held in 1973.

Continued interferences and repression by the military spawned the growth of a number of guerrilla groups in Argentina, chief among them the Montoneros and the People's Revolutionary Army (ERP). The use of torture and murder by Lanusse led to a new cycle of violence in which both sides were engaged. Over 2,000 political prisoners languished in jail, reflective of the very broad subversion laws Lanusse decreed.

In this climate, the presidential election of 1973 took place. Perón chose Héctor Cámpora to run as his proxy as the head of the Peronist Justicialist Party. On a familiar platform of national reconstruction, Cámpora won just under half of the vote. The Peronists had come back strongly and the time to end their leader's exile had arrived.

Round two: Perón's return to Argentina did not have auspicious beginnings. Two million were on hand at the international airport to greet the aging man they thought could restore order to the economy and dignity to the working class. Riots among different groups of demonstrators and security police at the airport turned into pitched battles that left hundreds dead.

Héctor Cámpora resigned from office and in the new presidential elections Perón easily emerged as victor. Following past form, Perón's wife was given political power, in this case as vice president. The president's initial efforts at national reconciliation appeared to work but again the economy began

vice on one of Argentina's most bizarre and sinister figures, José López Rega. This Rasputin-like character wielded great power and founded the infamous rightist terror group, the *Alianza Argentina Anticomunista.* Reportedly, under Lopéz Rega's influence, Isabel even took to employing astrological divination as a means to determine national policy.

Isabel Perón's inability to come to grips with Argentina's chronic economic problems, as well as her failure to curb rising terrorism, led the military to intervene yet again. In a move that was widely expected and hoped for, they removed the last Perón from the Casa Rosada on March 24, 1976.

to unravel and with it the fragile unity Perón had achieved.

The sudden death of Juan Domingo Perón on July 1, 1974 brought Isabel to the supreme position in the land, but her administration was an unmitigated disaster. She was no Evita and had little to offer Argentina besides her husband's name. Her government was marked by ultraconservatism, corruption and repression.

Additionally, Isabel came to rely for ad-

Above: left, President Onganía confers with General Lanusse, 1967, and right, Perón's third wife, Isabel.

The Proceso: Although the military had never proved itself any abler in solving the nation's problems, there seemed to be a different attitude with this band of uniformed men steering the nation. Each of the four successive juntas made a point of coordinating efforts among their various branches of the armed forces. The first junta tried to lend legitimacy to its leadership by amending the constitution. This amendment, the Statute for the National Reorganization Process, called for the ruling junta to shoulder responsibility of both executive and legislative functions of the state. From this amendment the period of military rule from 1977-1983 has come to be known as the *Proceso.*

General Videla was chosen as the first president and he attacked the problem of leftist guerrilla action through a campaign dubbed the "dirty war." It was during Videla's time in office that the majority of *desaparecidos* (disappeared) vanished. Anyone suspected of anti-government activity, and this was loosely interpreted by the military, could be made to disappear.

Nuns, priests, schoolchildren and whole families were kidnapped, raped, tortured and then murdered by a nefarious coalition of the military, police and right-wing deathsquads acting in the name of Christian-

was in this dirty war that the military lost all claims to representing the civilized and often touted European standard of conduct which Argentines believe they uphold.

Attempts by university professors and students to gain greater control over their institutions were regarded as subversive, and so the universities were gutted. The heavy hand of censorship in the media also fell across the country.

International condemnation, the pleas of human rights groups and the efforts of the mothers of the disappeared—the Mothers of the Plaza de Mayo who have marched every Thursday since the late 1970s, demanding to know what had become of their children—

ity and Democracy. The estimates of the numbers of *desaparecidos* (also known as the NNs or no names) range from 10,000 to 40,000 people, of whom only a tiny fraction were actual terrorists who had been involved in kidnappings or bombings. The military had, in fact, decided to "cleanse" Argentine society of any left-wing influence, real or imagined, by eliminating union leaders, intellectuals and student radicals—even, in one famous case, executing a group of high school students who had staged a protest against rising bus fares.

The whole campaign was conducted secretly, abductions often occurring at night. It

did not alleviate the problem of state-sponsored terrorism.

Videla was succeeded by General Viola who was then forced from office and replaced by General Galtieri. In economic matters, the military fared no better than it had in politics. The foreign debt soared to $45 billion while the inflation rate went from bad to worse, unemployment increased and the peso was constantly devalued. It was in this climate that General Galtieri and his junta chose to try something new.

The Malvinas conflict: It was ironic that the Argentine military, having won its dirty war against its own people, was forced from power attempting to achieve what it had been trained to do, namely fight a conventional conflict. General Galtieri hoped to divert his people's attention from the worsening domestic situation through the traditional method of turning their eyes to foreign matters, in this case the British-occupied Malvinas (Falkland) Islands.

The ensuing South Atlantic War was a brief but bloody engagement begun on April 2, 1982 with the Argentine invasion of the islands and ending with their surrender at Port Stanley on June 14.

The disputed Malvinas or Falkland archipelago appeared the perfect target for Galtieri: the islands lay more than 8,000

miles (13,000 km) from Great Britain and their tiny population was heavily outnumbered by sheep. However, Galtieri and the other military commanders did not consider the possibility that Britain would actually fight to retain her claims to the islands. This major miscalculation was one of many the Argentine junta was to make in the following weeks. Technically, tactically and politically Argentina's rulers blundered badly.

Left, demonstration by the Mothers of the Plaza de Mayo. Above, democracy returns with Alfonsín's inauguration, December 10, 1983.

The conscripted army was ill-prepared for battle against trained professionals and did not put up much of a fight, while the navy stayed in port after a British submarine sank the General Belgrano heavy cruiser on May 2. Perhaps the country's honor was kept a bit less tarnished by the brilliant and courageous performance of its air force, which delayed the inevitable.

Although, initially, most Argentines were wildly enthusiastic in their support of the military's adventurism, their euphoria quickly collapsed. The people were soon to realize that their government had consistently fabricated stories of success in the field and that rather than having achieved a glorious repossession of what all Argentines feel is theirs, the country was made to suffer a humiliating blow.

General Galtieri resigned three days after the Argentine surrender and was replaced a week later by the retired general, Reynaldo Bignone. Bignone's attempts to curb inflation failed as the rate rocketed to 433 percent in 1983. Additionally, the junta was under increased pressure to lift its state of seige and hold elections for a civilian government; massive demonstrations at the Plaza de Mayo helped to force the government to honor its promises.

The military, knowing its days in power were numbered, sought to protect itself from anticipated criminal prosecution for human rights abuses by issuing its own study, *The Final Document of the Military Junta on the War Against Subversion and Terrorism*. This white paper praised the efforts of the armed forces in combating and defeating terrorism and denied any administration involvement in the barbaric actions which were undertaken during the dirty war. As an extra protective measure, the government proclaimed a general amnesty for all those involved in the "extralegal" efforts to crush the opposition.

The election campaign of 1983 was one full of surprises. Many analysts expected a Peronist return to power or possibly a coalition government. A majority of voters, however, selected Raúl Alfonsín and his Radical Party to lead the nation out of the years of repression and economic distress. Alfonsín was sworn in as president on December 10, one day after the military junta had dissolved itself.

Dancing in the streets of Buenos Aires greeted the inauguration of Raúl Alfonsín as President of the Nation at the end of 1983, ending nearly eight years of military rule. The last of the juntas slunk from the Casa Rosada through the side exit, to the boos and hisses of an awaiting crowd. Argentines continued celebrating for days, convinced that a new democratic era would bring social justice and economic prosperity.

These high hopes have faded in the face of

corner of Florída and Lavalle, while every new organization bandies the word "democratic" about with gleeful abandon.

The vibrant new atmosphere of Argentina today is still partly a reaction against the conservative moral values of the military and the Church. The strict censorship of the dictatorship was lifted early in 1984, and once prohibited ideas such as contraception and abortion could be discussed openly on radio and television. Over the indignant pro-

Argentina's formidable contemporary economic and political problems. Nearly a decade of civilian rule has brought new freedoms and moments of euphoria, but also bitter disappointments.

Breaking out: The return to democracy brought with it an immediate sense of release after the suffocating restriction of the dictatorship. Participation in public life has returned to normal after the military repression, with street traffic in Buenos Aires regularly blocked by demonstrating unionists and students with their booming drums and protest songs. Groups of gesticulating men are constantly seen discussing politics on the

tests of the Church, Argentine audiences were finally exposed to cinema classics such as Bertolucci's *Last Tango In Paris,* which was previously banned by the military as "unhealthy."

The lifting of censorshop provided a new creative freedom, luring exiled Argentine artists back from abroad. Dozens of banned books have been re-released and new literary works are still appearing in small-circulation magazines; a new wave of Argentine cinema has gained momentum after years of stagnation and the theater scene has likewise been injected with a new burst of energy.

In the world's eye: The international press closely followed the return of democracy in Argentina, initially regarding it as a brave but doomed attempt. Tired of being regarded as a pariah nation, Argentines themselves became keen for acceptance and clutched at any sign of national accomplishment.

The genial grin of President Alfonsín became a familiar sight in newspapers and television reports across the world, as foreign governments showered him with hu-

prizes at international festivals. Director Luis Puenzo won the 1985 Academy Award for Best Foreign Film with *La Historia Oficial,* a story about a woman who discovers that her adopted daughter is the child of one of the "disappeared," and Argentina still produces the most polished films in Latin America.

Tackling the economy: The farewell gift from the military government to the new democracy in 1983 was a desperately sick

man rights awards and messages of support. Alfonsín set out to change Argentina's image as a country of rabid and irrational nationalists. A negotiated settlement with Chile on the Beagle Channel dispute was overwhelmingly approved by plebiscite, while Argentina has shown that its claims to the Falkland/Malvinas Islands will only be pursued peacefully.

Although Argentine writer Jorge Luis Borges died without receiving the Nobel Prize, Argentine cinema began sweeping up

Left, newsstand in Buenos Aires. Above, local chapter of the Radical Party.

economy. Inflation was running riot, the foreign debt had soared, unemployment was rising and anybody who had money was sending it overseas rather than investing in Argentina.

The Radical Party initially hoped that Alfonsín's benign and fatherly reassurance in television messages would restore confidence. It didn't, and inflation rose to over 1000 percent annually. Argentines became accustomed to daily fare increases on the bus ride to work and spending their pay packets before they lost value. Joking tales are still told of being chased around supermarkets by attendants trying to mark up goods.

Alfonsín finally accepted the measures suggested by the International Monetary Fund (IMF) and he announced a surprising new plan: three zeros were to be lopped from the value of the peso, creating a new currency called the austral. All prices and wages were frozen, while government spending was cut.

Instead of a storm of protest, most Argentines initially accepted the plan. The government was surprised at its own audacity in virtually ending inflation by decree.

Sadly, the Radicals were uncertain about what to do next. They reinstated the plan with various modifications, but failed to stimulate the economy, while Argentines' wages slid behind. The massive bureaucracy kept devouring national funds, while industry stagnated.

Dealing with the military: At the same time as dealing with Argentina's economic woes, Alfonsín took on the country's other great plague: the armed forces.

When the last of the junta leaders handed over power after the Falklands/Malvinas war, the military were discredited in the eyes of the Argentine public as never before. Alfonsín's first action as president was to revoke the sweeping amnesty the officers had bravely given themselves before scrambling from the Casa Rosada.

Within a week, a commission was established to investigate the fate of the "disappeared" after the coup of 1976, headed by respected author Ernesto Sabato. Non-stop media coverage, followed by publication of the commission's findings (in a still-available book called *Nunca Mas*, or "Never Again") forced many skeptical Argentines to accept the accuracy of the horrifying reports they had previously brushed off as exaggerations.

Soon after, the chiefs of the Army, Navy and Air Force who had led the first three military juntas were put on trial. This was an historic event, marking the first time in Latin American history that a military government was being held accountable for its deeds in office, but many Argentines expected a more severe result. As massive crowds demonstrated outside the Palace of Justice, the verdict came down: life sentences for ex-President Videla and Admiral Massero, lesser sentences for three others, while four were acquitted.

Alfonsín had hoped that the trial of the generals would be a symbolic end to this bloody period of Argentine history. Instead, human rights lawyers filed for hundreds more trials against the middle and lower ranking military officers who had carried out the grisly campaign of kidnap, torture and murder.

Unfortunately, the trials proved to be a rallying point within the military: during the Easter weekend of 1987, soldiers fortified their barracks and went into rebellion against the prosecutions. Alfonsín had to stage a theatrical helicopter dash to a rebel base, demanding their surrender, while civilian rallies were held around the country in support of democracy. But few people protested when, weeks later, trials were cut to a handful.

Even this was too much for the military, and two more rebellions followed until the government ended further trials of officers altogether.

The Peronist revival: The deepening economic crisis in the late 1980s allowed the Peronist party to bounce back from the shock of losing the 1983 election—the first defeat in the party's history. In mid-1989, amongst massive street celebrations by Peronists waving banners of Juan and Evita Peron, the party's flamboyant candidate Carlos Menem won the presidential elections by a landslide.

Recognized around Argentina for his giant grey-streaked sideburns, Menem is a "man of the people" who had worked as a truck driver and laborer before entering the union movement and becoming Governor of rural La Rioja province. Before beginning his push for the presidency, he could be found yelling his support for soccer teams in Buenos Aires, driving a rally car in the provinces or at nightclubs with local TV stars. He was a popular man.

The situation Menem inherited was disastrous. With inflation completely out of control at 200 percent a month, the austral crumbling and food riots rocking the country, Alfonsín had decided to resign and hand over the presidential sash to Menem several months before his term was over. Menem's policies quickly proved to be a surprise for his critics and supporters alike: announcing that "the fiesta is over," he abandoned one Peronist sacred vow after another to begin the severest period of austerity that Argentina has seen.

Bloated state-owned companies like the national airline, Aerolineas Argentinas, and the telephone company ENTEL were privatized and massive layoffs ordered. Government subsidies and controls over the economy were sacrificed on the altar of the free market. Despite months of protests by Menem's former Peronist supporters, the unheard-of reforms went through, cementing a new friendly relationship with the United States—with Menem going so far as to offer Argentine troops to serve in the Gulf War of 1991.

In relations with the military, Menem

of crisis, Menem's policies brought inflation to a virtual halt, although at the price of widespread unemployment. In January 1992, the austral was replaced by yet another new currency called the peso, pegged to the US dollar—and middle-class Argentines began reappearing in the hotels of Miami and shops of New York, buying big once again, as in the days of old.

There are still many doubts about Argentina's future. Economists believe that there is a long way to go before its economy will be out of trouble. Menem's administration has been marked by constant corruption scandals. Women in Argentina are still largely excluded from public life, and the

shocked human rights activists by pardoning the former junta leaders who had been convicted for their "dirty war" crimes, undoing what many had seen was the greatest achievement of the Alfonsín years. Choosing a date between Christmas and New Year to minimize international attention, Menem ignored nearly a million-strong demonstration of protesters in Buenos Aires to sign the generals' release.

Looking to the future: After a long period

Above, President Carlos Menem, elected in 1989.

imbalances remain not only between Buenos Aires and "the interior" but also between the glittering and international wealth of the capital's northern suburbs and the misery of the urban slums which are located only a bus ride away.

Yet, despite the chaos of the last decade, civilian rule has become firmly established in Argentina, the army forgotten. While the Argentines continue to criticize the government and one another with astonishing vigour, they remain for the present united on one point: democracy, for all its shortcomings, is preferable to the strait jacket of military rule.

In 1937, at the close of what was, up to then, Argentina's most difficult decade, the country's per capita GDP was $510, a figure equal to that of Austria and only slightly behind that of France, placing Argentina among the world's wealthiest nations. By 1973 Argentina had joined the less developed nations, with the per capita GDP figure falling behind as Austria's doubled and that of France tripled. This stark fact draws attention to the drama of Argentina, perhaps the only country in the world which, in the 20th century, has experienced such a rapid slide from riches to rags.

The fabled wealth of Argentina, which led *fin de siecle* Parisians to coin the phrase "rich as an Argentine," was built on livestock. From the earliest days of colonization until the Great Depression, exports of animals and animal products dominated economic life. From roughly 1600 to 1750, the backward and unimportant outposts along the Rio de La Plata delta survived by exporting the hides from the wild cattle and horses that flourished on the vast open pampa plain. It was a culture based on leather, which was used for everything from shelter to clothing, with the surplus traded mainly to Upper Peru for use as containers in the Spanish mines. Over the 18th century, semi-tamed herds gradually replaced the wild animals and the rural economy began taking shape.

The rural economy's most important characteristic is the extensive landholding pattern. These properties, with the development of the livestock business, became the forerunners of today's *estancias*.

The most profound changes to occur, and the ones that would lay the foundation for Argentina's golden age, were the development of methods for chilling and then freezing meat, innovations in shipping that allowed on-the-hoof cattle exports and the construction of railway networks that made more intensive ranching and farming possible. The results were both rapid and impressive: land under cultivation increased 15 times between 1872 and 1895, while cereal exports expanded greatly from 1870 to 1900. Behind this accelerated economic growth lay the increased demand for foodstuffs created by the British factory system—Great Britain would remain Argentina's main trading partner until World War II.

The new processed meat and cereals economy required a work force, and by the 1890s Argentina was receiving thousands of mostly Italian and Spanish immigrants. The population grew from 1.8 million in 1869 to over four million by 1895, with an additional 50,000 migrant workers per year arriving to do seasonal harvest work. With land already in the hands of the great *estancieros*, immigrants settled in a small number of growing towns (Rosario, Santa Fe, Bahia Blanca), but the majority established themselves in Buenos Aires.

The enormous influx of Europeans—three out of every four persons living in Buenos Aires in 1910 was European-born—combined with the continental tastes of the wealthy elite made the capital city one of the great cosmopolitan centers in the charmed days before the First World War.

The war in Europe was a great stimulus to the Argentine economy in two ways. First, the belligerents' need for agricultural products skyrocketed, and second, the paralysis of European trade flows of manufactured goods encouraged local production. The weak artesanal urban economy began to fill domestic demand as imports fell by 50 percent. This unplanned industrial boomlet revealed weaknesses in the Argentine economy—such as dependence on imported raw materials, lack of energy resource development, lack of a capital goods sector—that would only become more obvious during the Great Depression, when the nation had to rely once more on local production.

The incipient growth of an industrial sector also emphasized the social strains in a society that had barely begun to absorb a huge immigrant population. Outbreaks of labor unrest and mass protests against poor living conditions were sharp reminders that the immigrants had brought with them the anarchist, socialist and syndicalist ideas of Europe's working classes. The disturbances also led to nativist backlashes, as in 1919 when fear of the Russian Revolution and prejudice against the new arrivals led a minority of middle and upper class groups to form vigilante committees that terrorized workers and Jews during what has come to be called the *Semana Tragica* (Tragic Week).

The rise of Hipolito Yrigoyen, Argentina's first modern populist leader, was the consequence of the economic and social changes experienced from the late 1880s through World War I. President from 1916 to 1922 and elected again in 1922, he was also the first president to be overthrown by a military coup in 1930.

With that coup Argentina entered what has been a long agony of political and economic instability. The Depression and World War II deepened the trend toward local industrial development, increasing the number of large factories and with them, the number of workers. By the early 1940s, the inequities in income distribution and lack of political fair play had created a sense of frustration among lower middle class and working class people while the war-engendered economic boom developed a new sense of national destiny. Into that atmosphere stepped Argentina's most controversial and influential political figure—Juan Domingo Perón.

Under Perón, who was elected President in 1946 and again in 1951, Argentina underwent a period of intense industrialization based on the wealth generated by agricultural exports. Lending the power of the state to organizing the underprivileged workers, especially in the largest industries, Perón built a solid base of followers that would remain faithful through years of political censorship and despite his 17 years in exile.

The social base of Peronism was constructed on the trade unions. In the three years before he became president Perón took charge of the newly created Labor Ministry, a post which he used to encourage the organization of workers, who up to that time had a low level of trade union membership. By the time Perón was ousted, Argentina had come to have a very high percentage of unionization estimated at over 50 percent of its actively employed population. The country's modern union movement thus began, and has remained, a very politicized one, always tied to Peronism. Given their size and commitment to this political movement, the unions have naturally played an important role in contemporary politics.

Economically, Peronism left a contradictory heritage that continues to weigh on efforts to modernize, rationalize and streamline the productive apparatus to this day. Under strong protection from imports, local manufacturing grew but remained inefficient, costly, uncompetitive and unable to provide sustained growth. At the same time, continued dependence on imported raw materials and capital goods, vulnerability to agricultural price cycles and the burden of a state sector designed to provide high levels of employment and social welfare, led to a series of balance of payments crises, beginning in the late 1950s.

Perón's return to power and the subsequent efforts to revive the 1940s economic model deepened the crisis, which, coupled with a militant labor offensive and an urban guerilla campaign, threatened Argentina with chaos.

Since 1983 Argentina has once again enjoyed civilian democratic government. The new government, elected in May 1989, operates under the Constitution of 1853, a document modeled on the U.S. constitution. The structures of government are therefore very similar to those of the U.S., with three separate spheres of power.

There are two major political parties in Argentina; the Radical Civic Union and the Justicialist Party (Peronists), which between them have accounted for approximately 80 percent of the vote in the last three elections. A group of center right parties, including the Union of the Democratic Center and several provincial parties, represent a much smaller force which reached seven percent in the 1991 mid-term elections.

There are in addition a number of tiny, floundering leftist parties, the largest of which is the Intransigent Party.

Walking the streets of Buenos Aires, a visitor with an untrained ear might think he's hearing an awful lot of Italian being spoken. From the look of some of the city's streets he might momentarily forget he is in South America, and think he is in Europe. Such are the illusions generated by Argentina's mixed social heritage.

Who are the Argentines? Trying to define the national character can be a difficult task. Asking an Argentine about this, and one is likely to get an agonized response. Many in this country are very quick to confess to a national identity crisis; "We don't know if we're Europeans or Latin Americans," they'll tell you.

Jokes abound about the confused nature of the Argentine psyche. One line has it that an Argentine is an Italian who speaks Spanish, lives in a French house and thinks he is British. Another holds that the Mexicans descended from the Aztecs, the Peruvians descended from the Incas, and the Argentines descended from boats.

All of this uncertainty has been created by the fact that Argentina is a nation of immigrants. Many other countries also have this cultural mix, but the dynamics of the influx were different here. The melting pot phenomenon that took place in the United States, over a long period of time, did not really happen here. Too many people arrived in Argentina in too short a time, and the country is still trying to work things out, to develop an identifiable cohesion.

In the beginning, things were much simpler. The original native inhabitants of Argentina were divided into many distinct tribes across the land, but their numbers were few. The first European settlers, in the 16th century, were almost all Spanish, and those coming in over the next 300 years were predominantly Spanish as well. A minority population of mestizos (mixed Indian and Hispanic stock) developed early on. A large number of Africans were brought in as

Preceding pages: *porteño* family in the park. Left, making a point. Right, a child of the Northwest.

slaves, and mulattoes (mixed black and white stock) and Indian/black mixtures were added to the population. But that was about as complicated as things got.

The 19th century saw severe changes in the ethnic make-up of Argentina. Through a concerted effort, the vast majority of the Indian population was wiped out by the Argentine army, thus opening up territory for European settlement. Also, after the abolition of slavery, the black population faded

from view (see "The Case of the Afro-Argentines").

New hands: These changes coincided with the beginning of a period of massive immigration from Europe. Inspired by European liberalism, Argentina sought to develop its economy and fill out as a nation, so immigration was encouraged by government policy. Argentina was seen as a land of opportunity, and the Europeans arrived in droves. Between 1857 and 1939, over 3.5 million laborers were added to the population. These newcomers were predominantly Italian (about 45 percent) and Spanish (about 30 percent), but others came from

France, Poland, Russia, Switzerland, Wales, Denmark, Germany, England and elsewhere. In the early-20th century, there were arrivals from Syria and Armenia.

By 1914, the foreign-born population was 30 percent of the total, and in some of the larger cities, the foreigners outnumbered the natives. These new hands were put to work filling positions in the expanding agricultural industry, in cattle-raising and processing, and in the developing economies of the cities.

With the Depression, there was a halt to the influx. After the Second World War, more started to come in, but they were mostly from surrounding countries, where work was often hard to find.

In recent years, there haven't been too many people coming from outside, but there have been patterns of internal migration. As industries start up in different regions, people will move to fill the jobs. As the rural economy has faltered, there have been large-scale migrations to the cities by those looking for work. The urban economies have not been able to accommodate the increasing population demands, and *villas miserias* (shanty towns) have developed outside the larger industrial areas. Although Argentines as a whole enjoy a fairly high standard of living, conditions in the slums continue to worsen, and the situation will have to be addressed by those seeking to govern the country as a whole.

Distinguishing angst: All these comings and goings are what has created the great Argentine identity crisis. Nonetheless, while they continue to proclaim their lack of a cultural center, the Argentines go about their lives behaving in a way that is uniquely Argentine. It is, in part, this malaise which distinguishes Argentines from their neighbors. The Peruvians and Brazilains don't spend too much time on this sort of soul-searching. The Argentines are still trying to figure out if they're European or Latin American, and they are famous throughout Latin America for not having made up their minds yet.

Demographic factors have stabilized somewhat in recent years. The current Argentine population is around 31 million. Of these, over 10 million live in the greater Buenos Aires area. Over 80 percent of the total is urban. Roughly 85 percent are of

European descent; the remainder are divided among small groups of Indians, those of mestizo stock, and members of small non-European immigrant groups, such as Arabs and Asians.

The official language is Spanish, but it is spoken by many with a zesty Italian lilt. The accent is often hard for visitors to understand, but the ear soon becomes accustomed. Dialects vary around the country.

Although there has been a fair amount of intermarriage of nationalities, many groups in Argentina have kept themselves distinct. Across the country there are communities that over the years have strived to keep an ethnic purity, for example, the small Welsh

enclaves in Patagonia, and the German and Eastern European villages in the north. Many communities maintain their own social services, such as hospitals, schools, and athletic clubs. Newspapers come out in a variety of languages.

Mother England: One relatively small but tight community is that of the Anglo-Argentines. It was to a large extent British capital that built the Argentine railway and banking systems in the second half of the 19th century. Their money also went to develop the cattle industry, with modern methods of refrigeration, packaging, and transportation. British breeds of cattle were imported to upgrade the national stock. Some Englishmen bought gigantic tracts of land in the south to raise sheep, and their economic and social monopoly made southern Patagonia seem, for a time, an extension of the British Empire.

The first British settlers came in to administer the building of the industrial infrastructure, and their services helped to make Argentina one of the world's 10 richest countries by the early-20th century. That position has been lost, but the Anglo-Argentine pride in their contribution to the nation still holds.

Today, the community remains quite cliquish. Sons and daughters are educated in

Tribal ways: There is not much left of the original pure Indian population of Argentina, but small pockets remain, mostly in the far north and south. Exact population figures are disputed, but current estimates range from 100,000 to 600,000. Figures are further confused by the difficulty of establishing ethnic purity.

Reservations were created by the Argentine government for certain groups, but the land given was largely barren, and poverty is severe in these communities. Few of the tribes practice traditional lifestyles, but certain ceremonial elements have been maintained. Some still speak their native dialects as first or second languages. Quechua,

schools modeled after the British system, with names like St. Andrew's and St. George's—even fulltime rugby coaches are hired from England. Polo and cricket are played weekends on the manicured lawns of the exclusive Hurlingham Club outside Buenos Aires. However, the Anglo-Argentines do feel that their loyalties lie with Argentina, and the fight with Mother England over the Malvinas (Falkland) Islands placed a heavy social burden upon them to demonstrate this.

Left and above, immigrants from Russia and Holland in the early 1930s.

which has similar dialects in Bolivia and Peru, is still spoken in the northwest, where the Colla are the largest Indian group. Chiriguan, Choroti, Mataco, Mocovi and Toba are spoken in the Chaco area; the Chiriguan are the principal tribe of Mesopotamia. The Araucano-Mapuches and the Tehuelche were the major groups of Patagonia and the pampas although there are very few pureblooded descendents left today. The indigenous groups of Tierra del Fuego, the Yamana and Ona, were exterminated by settlers at the turn of the century.

City versus country: There is one clear distinction one should make when talking about Argentines, and that is the one between *porteños* (residents of Buenos Aires) and the rest of the nation's population. This schism is as old as Argentina, and the difference is insisted upon by persons on both sides of the division. *Porteños* will maintain, only half in jest, that there are really no Argentines, besides themselves, worth mentioning. Buenos Aires is, after all, the seat of the nation's culture, heritage, etc, is it not? With a mixture of pity and resentment the rest of the population seems resigned to this egocentric designation. Those of the interior have their own ways of doing things, and they don't need the *porteños* to help them along. A brief, informal survey provides a

course, other cities in Argentina, but none of them could be considered a major cosmopolitan center.

Occasionally, inhabitants of the interior will make a foray into the Big City, but after a few days of movies, bright lights and crowded streets they are more than ready to get back to the clean air and quiet of their home terrain.

Porteños, on the other hand, rarely venture out to see the rest of their country. Many middle-class families have small weekend houses on the outskirts of Buenos Aires, and upper-class families have their *estancias* or "camps" to visit, and there are the occasional ski trips out west for the comfortably-off, but

set of characteristics ascribed to the two sides. The *porteños* think they are sophisticated, glamorous and cultured while the country folk are unsophisticated, ugly, superstitious and ignorant. Those of the interior believe themselves to be humble, commonsensical, and more in touch with the land, and regard the *porteños* to be aggressive, pretentious, high-strung and ignorant creatures.

Much of this can be explained in the framework of the standard conflict between city dwellers and country folk. The difference here is that there is just one city pitted against the rest of the country. There are, of

that's about the extent of the adventuring.

Tactile-defensives beware: Geographical factionalism aside, there are some qualities which, in the realm of broad generalization, could be said to be shared by all Argentines. One characteristic that binds them to other Latin cultures is their relaxed approach to life and time frames; if something doesn't get done today, it will surely get done tomorrow. When waiting for an Argentine to keep an appointment, whether for a cup of coffee or an important business meeting, allowance should be made for benign tardiness. It's part of a way of life.

There is a sentimental streak, captured in

the melancholy strains of the tango, that runs through all Argentines. This often exhibits itself in the warmth of personal contacts and a high degree of tactility. In conversation, people are always touching each other lightly on the arm or slapping each other on the back. The intimate and colloquial *vos* form, rather than the formal *usted*, is used to address nearly everyone. Greetings and goodbyes always involve a lot of hugging and kissing. Visitors should be aware of the etiquette of introductions: even at first meeting, unless one is introduced under highly formal business circumstances, kisses on the cheek are in order. Women kiss women, and women kiss men; only men don't kiss men,

practice, in other cultures, of shipping kids off to school at the tender age of 18.

The sense of family is an extended one, and children will often grow up with cousins as their best friends. This closeness frequently carries on into adulthood. Weekend gatherings of the clan for an *asado* (barbeque) keep all in touch.

Creatures of habit: In terms of life experiences, Argentines tend to be a bit conservative: they don't much like to try new things. New foods, for example; grilled beef is eaten at lunch and dinner, day after day, year after year, and people don't seem to tire of it. Per capita consumption of beef is 220 pounds every year, as against, for example, 78

but after a friendship develops, even this restriction is done away with.

Families here tend to be closely knit. It is not unusual for young people to live at home until they get married, and even then they may only move a few blocks away. Students do not usually move out when they enter university, as they often attend a school in their home towns; this is not the big pack-up-and-leave-the-nest breaking point that it is elsewhere. Argentines view as heartless the

Opposite page: left, Araucanian woman, and right, fertility dance of the Chirimuskis. Above, leather chic from Le Fauve.

pounds in the United States. There aren't many ethnic restaurants here, and those that exist tend to serve food on the safe side: French or German. Spicy and exotic cuisines are not in much demand, and sashimi is not likely to become all the rage. However, as long as the restaurants serve beef, Argentines love to go out to eat. Buenos Aires is reputed to have the third highest restaurant/population ratio in the world, after Paris and Tokyo.

National drinking habits are rather conservative as well. For all the wine that is produced here, consumption seems to be in very measured amounts. Beer is increasingly popular, but is mainly viewed as a means to cut a summer thirst. Much of the aforementioned steak gets washed down with economy-sized bottles of soda pop.

One doesn't see much dancing on table tops here, and it is this widespread reservedness of behavior that makes a trip to the La Boca district of Buenos Aires so much fun. Here one can see Argentines cutting loose. High-spirited crowds mix with the sailors in port, in a free-for-all of dancing, drinking and general spectacle-making. But this is not the norm. In general, Argentines hate to draw attention to themselves. Loud and unusual behavior in public is sternly looked down upon.

with the theme *"Argentina te quiero"* (Argentina, I Love You), to encourage Argentines to see their own country. One of the motives of this campaign is to keep the money of those who can afford to go elsewhere here at home.

Strong opinions: There are a couple of topics on which Argentines conduct heated public debate, where making an emotional display is no embarrassment; one is sports and the other is politics.

Soccer, or football, is the big national sport, and team allegiances are strong. At a fairly early age, most Argentines must decide where those allegiances lie. Matches draw large crowds, and the enthusiasm of

Even when it comes to vacations, Argentines are creatures of habit. Although their country has a variety of destinations nearly unparalleled, year after year people will return to the same resort for their summer holidays. Foreigners, even on a short visit, will often see more of this country than a native will in a lifetime.

Listening to accounts of the adventures to be had out there, an Argentine will sigh and say that, yes, maybe next year he'll go to see the whales at the Valdés Peninsula, or the glaciers of Lago Argentino, but one way or the other he probably won't make it. The government has started a major campaign,

fan support has gotten increasingly out of hand in recent years.

Argentines are a highly opinionated bunch, and one subject on which anyone will have strong opinions is politics. The population is one of the most politicized in South America. Anyone will readily tell you what political party he belongs to and why, what party he voted for in the last election and why (these matters are sometimes separated for reasons of expediency), and what the main issues are.

There is an impressive level of awareness of the issues at both national and global levels. Harsh realities of recent years have made everyone an expert on economics. Anyone on the street can tell you just what he thinks about the implications of government policy in relation to the International Monetary Fund.

During his presidency, Raúl Alfonsín increasingly involved Argentina in both inter-American affairs and the activities of the Non-Aligned Movement.

Although voting is mandatory in Argentina, people don't seem to mind the obligation. A high percentage of them would probably continue to vote, even if the law were rescinded. People here view with horror the large-scale apathy of voters in other countries. They find it hard to believe that

logically, to form a full circle rather than a linear progression; the two extremes start to look a lot alike on certain issues. There are severe splits even within single parties, the most notable being within the Justicialist (Peronist) Party. Most parties have youth branches, which offer younger members a chance to get involved. This makes for some colorful names, perhaps the best being Intransigent Youth.

No matter what a person's party membership is, he will often end up explaining his persuasion in relation to Peronism. The effect of this party's ideologies has been so pervasive that it has become the basis for putting everything else in perspective. You

turnout is so low in the United States, for example, when so much rides on a single election. The general opinion seems to be that, at the very least, one should go to the polls to vote against a party that in power has made unpopular moves; punitive or protest voting is a common phenomenon amongst the electorate.

There is a broad range of political parties in Argentina, including many regional and provincial ones. They range from the ultra conservative to the ultra left, and seem, ideo-

Left, a meeting of generations. Above, two faces of *porteño* youth.

may love them or you may hate them, but where you stand is to be explained through them.

Evita Duarte Perón holds a special place in Argentine political thinking. Even those who do not agree with the precepts of Peronism as a whole give her credit for initiating several large steps forward in national policy. Feminists hold her in very high esteem, pointing out that she was behind her husband's moves to give women the vote, to protect the rights of women workers, and to legalize divorce (this last was held invalid, soon after her husband's fall in 1955, and the right to divorce was only reinstated in 1987).

Evita is viewed by many as the original Argentine feminist, and many today take strength from her example.

Observed rites: While Argentines have a constitutional guarantee of religious freedom, Catholicism is the state religion. It is mandated that the president of the republic be Catholic, although there are periodic moves in congress to change this.

Nominally, about 90 percent of the population is Catholic, but strict faith does not seem to have a firm grip on the national psyche. The church is kept in its role as an institution, and its teachings seem more an incentive for periodic observances than a model for day to day living.

debate in Congress, divorce was legalized, but many couples who have been living in a de facto state of marriage with second or third partners, feel that the process of legal disentanglement from original contracts is too complicated and costly to be bothered with.

There is a standing law that all children in Argentina must be registered upon birth with Christian names. This can present problems for immigrants wishing to maintain an ethnic heritage from the mother country. If the proposed name has a Spanish translation, this must be used, at least for official purposes. The stringency of the application is up to the presiding judge; if he doesn't mind

Annual pilgrimages to holy sites such as Luján draw thousands of participants, and special occasions, like the 1987 visit by the Pope bring the country to a near standstill. However, weekly attendance at mass is a much less pressing matter for many.

The influence of the Church has been lessening over a long period. Towards the end of the 19th century, schools and the rites of burial and marriage were secularized. But elements of the faith continue to play a role in the political scene. The legalization of divorce has been an extremely divisive issue for years.

In 1987, after repeated votes and hard

that the desired name isn't one of a verifiable saint, then it can squeeze by. Once the new name is on the books, it is open for use by others to follow. The list of usable names is reportedly much longer in Buenos Aires than elsewhere.

Riding around on city buses, a visitor may periodically see his fellow passengers make the sign of the cross; a church has been passed. In some sections of town, this may happen every few blocks. One gothic secular structure in Buenos Aires, which looks for all the world to be a church, invariably gets a misguided devotional response from out-of-towners.

The further one goes from Buenos Aires, the more the versions of Catholicism take on the characteristics of folk religion. Pilgrimages are made and offerings brought to local shrines revering unofficial saints. Miracles are averred to have taken place in all sorts of out of the way spots. A quasi-religious cult of devotion has grown up around the person of Evita Perón. Flowers are placed before her tomb daily. In the northwest region of the country, festivals such as an annual Carnival can be seen to contain certain elements not wholly Christian in origin.

Villa Freud: The popularity of psychiatry in Argentina has taken on a force strong enough to qualify it as a secular religion of economic lines. As part of the sweeping benefits granted to the work force through Peronism, psychiatric clinics have been established by many industries.

Explanations for this phenomenon usually center around the much talked-about national identity crisis. Analysis has helped to lessen anxieties, real or imagined, about not belonging to a greater whole. Also, as the standard of living has slipped, and other problems have come to plague the nation, people have come to feel more disoriented than ever.

The study and practice of psychology was heavily suppressed during the years of the *Proceso*. Military authorities viewed the

sorts. A small group of pioneers, who were devotedly reading the works of Freud, got a boost from European-trained practitioners who came over in the 1930s and 40s. Ever since then, psychoanalysis has become increasingly popular. Buenos Aires is said to have a higher number of psychiatrists per capita than the state of New York, and one barrio of the city has been nicknamed Villa Freud in recognition of its heavily doctored population.

The field is practiced across all social and

Left, the aprés ski set at Bariloche. Above, Argentine rocker Charly Garcia.

field as somehow subversive, and books on the subject were even removed from public and private shelves. University departments were drastically reduced or closed down altogether. Since 1983, however, the field has seen a strong resurgence, and it seems to be the vogue subject for university study. In coming years, the per capita ratio of psychologists can be expected to increase even further.

Tea ceremony: Young visitors to Argentina will often ask where they can meet Argentines of their age. A coffee house wouldn't be a bad place to start. Here and in bookstores, young intellectuals congregate to discuss politics and art. There are also many small clubs that feature local bands playing everything from punk rock to jazz. The sí portion of the Clarín daily paper which comes out on Friday, has a complete listing of goings-on. Popular rock groups include Virus, Soda Stereo, Los Redonditos de Ricotta, Hemorrageo Cerebral and the Charly Garcia Band.

One of the best ways to get a feel for the youth of Argentina today is to get invited to someone's house. Small gatherings in tiny apartments are a favorite form of entertainment and relaxation. The evening will usually consist of lots of talk and little else. The talk will often center around politics—a

good way to round out your knowledge of the various youth parties and movements, of which there are many.

Inevitably, someone will have brought along a guitar and maybe a bongo drum or a flute. A sing-along will start. The songs, too, will often be of a political nature, some of them hold-overs from decades past, singing the praises of the working man or the generally downtrodden. As the evening proceeds into early morning, the host will begin to pass around the *mate*, strong herbal tea, served in a hollow gourd, and sipped through a communal straw.

This Argentine version of a tea ceremony

has a magical way of increasing the feeling of camaraderie in a small group. The visitor should beware; ignorance of the finer points of the ritual will inevitably make for much scrutiny and merriment on the part of the practiced hands.

The history of Argentine counter-culture in recent years has had its own twists and turns. Argentina experienced a hippie period that paralleled that in the rest of the world, but its development was cut short by the arrival of the military regimes in the 1970s. During the *Proceso*, it was too dangerous to appear overtly leftist. Now that democracy has returned, many seem to be picking up the thread. This is even true for many who were too young to remember the original movement. Hair is getting longer on many young men; beads, beards, and a love and peace attitude are reminiscent of earlier times.

Combine all this with the highly politicized nature of Argentine society, and you get a feeling of energy from the youth that is encouraging. People seem to be coming out of shells, after years of holding their creativity and public expression in check. Political singers are extremely popular at many levels of the society. One of Latin America's biggest stars is the Argentine communist Mercedes Sosa. Her concerts have been packing people in for several decades.

Sidewalk poetry: Women who don't take kindly to being accosted on the streets may have a rough time of it here. Verbally passing judgment on women in the street is practically the male national sport, elevated, some say, to an art form. They've even given it a name: *piropo*. This is not a matter of a few crude words thrown out in passing; poetry, albeit hasty and primitive, is supposed to be involved.

The subject is not really expected to take the man up on his implied interest. Most of these *calle* Casanovas probably wouldn't know what to do with an aggressively positive response. The man's ego is satisfied through this simple exercise, and he figures it hasn't done the target any harm.

There are, of course, men who are out looking for more, but that is beyond the confines of the game of *piropo*, and with time one learns to distinguish the two.

Left, a moment's uncertainty. Right, a butcher takes a breather.

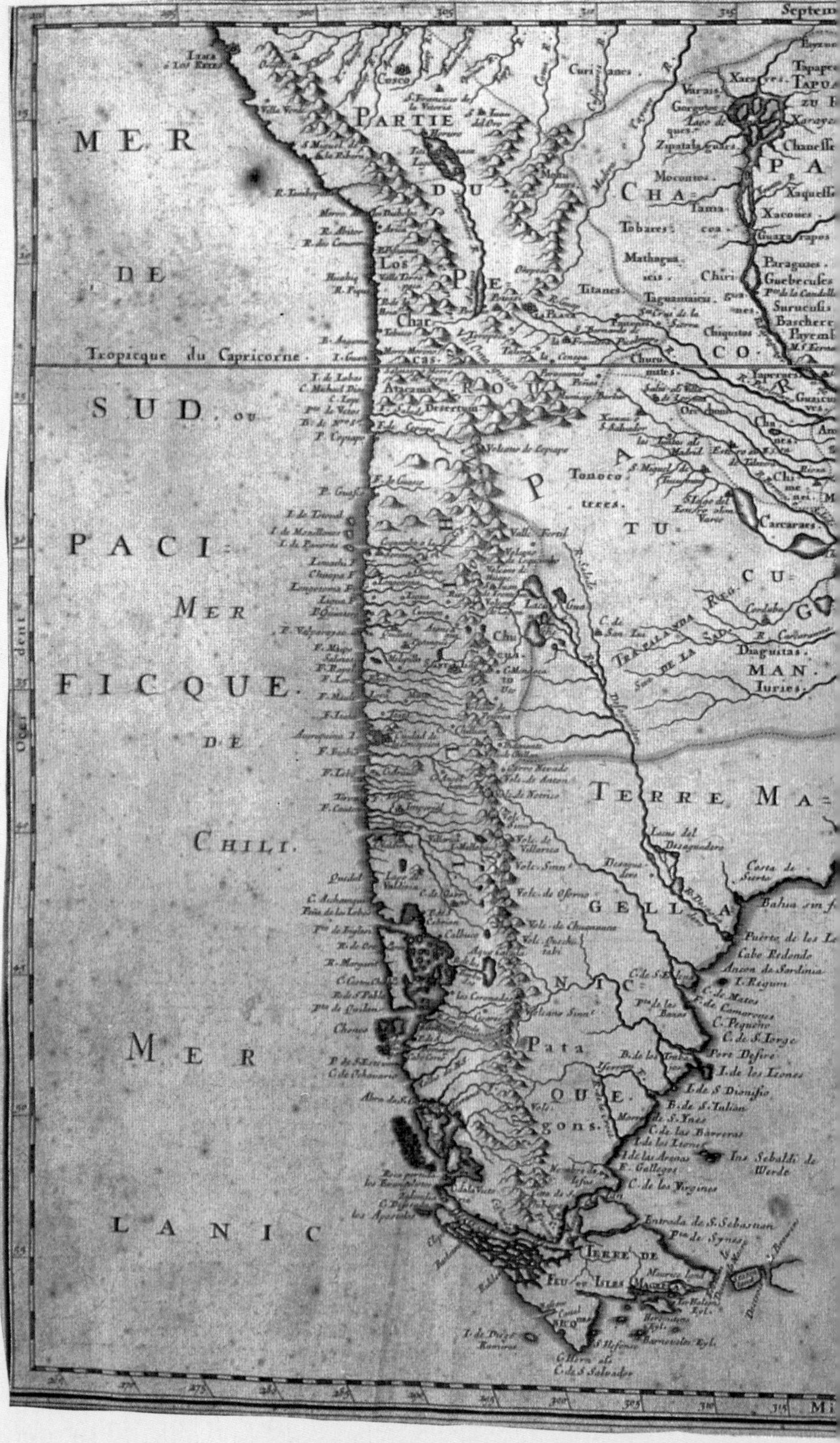

MER

DE

SUD, ou

PACI-

Mer

FICQUE.

DE

CHILI.

MER

LANIC

PARTIE

DU

PE

ROU

Tropique du Capricorne.

PA

TU

CU

MAN.
Iuries.

TERRE MA-

GELLA

NIC

Pata

QUE.
gons.

TERRE DE
FEU ou ISLES

CHA

CO.

Cosco

Ins Sebald de
Werde

Occident

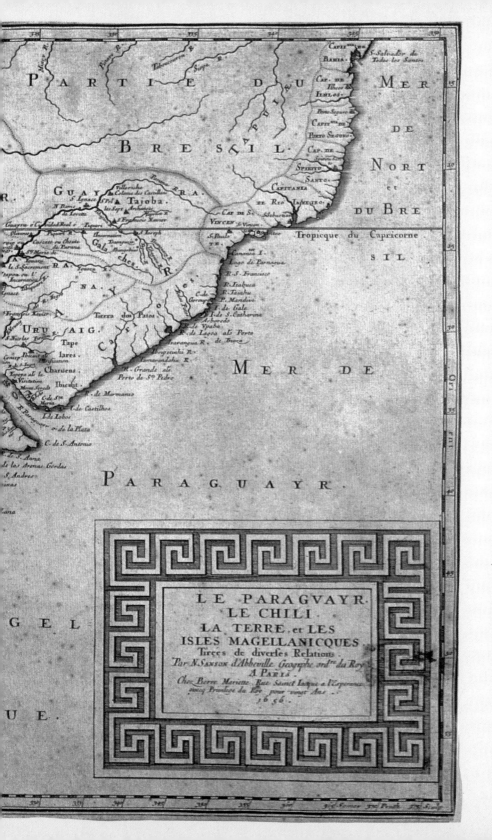

DESCRIPTIONS OF ARGENTINA: 1800-1920

Today's traveler to Argentina follows in the wake of a tremendously diverse group of characters which has probed and prodded the country for her secrets, climbed every mountain, witnessed the major events in her history and invariably compared the customs and mores of her people, so similar yet so different from themselves.

While Magellan and Darwin are the most familiar names of those who have visited Argentina, a surprising number of others have felt compelled to publish their travel diaries. Perhaps these visitors were encouraged to share their experiences because many in Europe and the United States were curious to know what it was really like in the reaches of Patagonia and Tierra del Fuego and among the wild gauchos of the pampas.

The reader of travel literature, especially of the 18th- and 19th-century variety, discovers many of the wonders of Argentina that no longer exist. These fabulous tales do need to be approached somewhat cautiously because many of the western travelers did not speak the language nor necessarily understand the events unfolding before them. Nonetheless, these accounts do provide the color and flavor that is sometimes missing from published scientific diaries. Additionally, their perspectives are noteworthy in providing a more complete picture of the Argentines and their country.

As one might expect, the early traveler faced a broad spectrum of perils that, in the case of Argentina, included robbery, Indian attacks, diseases such as yellow fever and syphilis, lack of food and shelter, and painful modes of transportation.

The dangers, though, seemed to be far outweighed by the joys the voyager experienced. Unexpected hospitality in the most out of the way places, chance encounters along the road, the sight of Tehuelche natives and gauchos displaying their equestrian skills, and the exhilaration of visiting places few had seen before were some of the

Preceding pages: 17th-century map of the Southern Cone. Left, morning tea in an upper-class salon.

high points the foreigner might come across.

The city of good airs: The 19th-century traveler would often commence his or her itinerary in Buenos Aires. Charles Darwin, in 1833, described the city as "large and I should think one of the most regular in the world. Every street is at right angles to the one it crosses, and the parallel ones being equidistant, the houses are collected into solid squares of equal dimensions, which are called quadras". Writing 10 years later, Colonel J. Anthony King commented that, "The market place of Buenos Ayres is made the center of all public rejoicings, public executions, and popular gatherings. It is in the market place that Rosas (the 19th-century dictator) hung up the bodies of many of his victims, sometimes decorating them in mockery, with ribbons of the Unitarian colour (blue), and even attaching to the corpses labels, on which were inscribed the revolting words, 'Beef with the hide.'"

J.P. and W.P. Robertson wrote a series of letters from South America which they published in 1843. What first impressed them were the methods of transportation in the city. "Nothing strikes one more on a first arrival in Buenos Aires than the carts and carters. The former are vehicles with large wooden axles, and most enormous wheels, so high that the spokes are about eight feet (two meters) in diameter, towering above both horses and driver; he rides one of these animals...The first sight you have of these clumsy vehicles is on your landing. They drive off like so many bathing-machines to your hotel, a dozen carters, just like a dozen porters here, struggling in rude contention for the preference in carrying shore passengers and their luggage."

By the turn of the century, Buenos Aires had become the noisiest and brashest city in Latin America, as wealth poured into the country and chilled beef was exported to Europe.

Thomas Turner, who lived in Argentina from 1885 to 1890, was greatly amused by some of his compatriots who visited the capital totally unprepared, expecting to find a wild and uncivilized place. They arrived "so thoroughly imbued with these silly notions that the outfits they have brought with them have been better suited to the necessities of the Australian bush or the Canadian backwoods than to the requirements of the life they were likely to experience in Argentina. Where they should have brought dress suits and dancing shoes, they came provided with a whole defensive arsenal and a supply of coarse apparel."

G.L. Morrill, an American minister who wrote about Buenos Aires in his *To Hell and Back: My Trip to South America* (1914), had this to say about the cosmopolitan nature of the Argentine capital: "An afternoon walk shows the city very much like Paris in its

tine outback, and whose book *Rough Notes Taken During Some Rapid Journeys Across the Pampas and Among the Andes* is one of the best travelogues on Latin America, was well aware of and prepared for the violence he faced. Head wrote that, "In crossing the pampas it is absolutely necessary to be armed, as there are many robbers or saltadors, particularly in the desolate province of Santa Fe. The object of these people is of course money, and I therefore always rode so badly dressed, and so well armed that although I once passed through them with no one but a child as a postilion, they thought it not worth their while to attack me. I always carried two brace of detonating pistols in a

architecture, fashionable stores, cafés and sidewalks filled with little tables where males and females flirt and gossip. There are newspaper kiosks and flower girls selling violets on the corners. The side streets are crowded with cars and carts and the main avenues with taxis which rest in the center or rush up and down either side. At nights it is a big white way with electric lights blazing a trail to the light-hearted cafés and theatres."

Perils: Dangers on the road were certainly plentiful for both traveler and native alike. Francis Bond Head, an English mining engineer who spent two very tempestuous but enjoyable years, 1825-26, in the Argen-

belt, and a short detonating double-barreled gun in my hand. I made it a rule never to be an instant without my arms, and to cock both barrels of my gun whenever I met any gauchos."

Darwin, the mild-mannered scientist, concurred with Head when he wrote that, "A traveler has no protection besides his firearms and the constant habit of carrying them, is the main check to a more frequent occurrence of robbery."

Head, whose apt moniker was "Galloping Head," describes the dangers Indians posed quite clearly. "...a person riding can use no precaution, but must just run the gauntlet, and take his chance, which, if calculated, is a good one. If he fall in with them, he may be tortured and killed, but it is very improbable that he should happen to find them on the road; however, they are so cunning, and ride so quick, and the country is so uninhabited, that it is impossible to gain any information.

Along with the violence one might have encountered in the wild west atmosphere were the unfortunate disasters along the way. "Changing horses for the last time, we again began wading through the mud. My animal fell, and I was well soused in black mire—a very disagreeable accident, when one does not possess a change of clothes," said Darwin.

A woman traveling alone faced another sort of problem. The American Katherine S. Drier described what she had to contend with in Buenos Aires in 1918. "Before leaving for Buenos Aires everybody in New York told me that the Plaza Hotel was the only hotel in Buenos Aires, and that of course I would make it my headquarters during my sojourn there. But my information had been given me by men, and neither they nor I expected to find that the Plaza did not take women unaccompanied by their husbands or supposed husbands. Not even sisters accompanied by their brothers, or wives whose husbands have to travel, or widows, are made welcome. Much less re-

Darwin also noted that the wild animals of the pampas could prove problematic. "It is very difficult to drive animals across the plains; for if in the night a puma, or even a fox, approaches, nothing can prevent the horses dispersing in every direction; and a storm will have the same effect. A short time since, an officer left Buenos Aires with five hundred horses, and when he arrived at the army he had under twenty."

Left, Spaniards on the hunt in Puerto Deseado, 1586. Above, boleadora-wielding pampean Indians.

spectable maiden ladies!"

Tehuelche and Puelche: The native Americans were of constant interest to the traveler of the 1800s, although by the 1870s they were becoming rarer and rarer as the campaigns to conclude the "Indian problem" reached their peak. One intrepid individual, the Jesuit Thomas Falkner, spent almost 20 years living among the Puelche and Tehuelche tribes of southern Argentina beginning in the 1730s until the religious order was expelled from the country. His account, *A Description of Patagonia*, was used as a guide by Darwin a century later.

Meeting an Indian could be a highpoint of

a journey, as Lady Florence Dixie related in her *Across Patagonia* (1881). "We had not gone far when we saw a rider coming slowly towards us, and in a few minutes we found ourselves in the presence of a real Patagonia Indian. We reined in our horses when he got close to us, to have a good look at him, and he doing the same, for a few minutes we stared at him to our hearts' content, receiving in return as minute and careful a scrutiny from him."

Of the Indians themselves, many of the travelers remarked on their positive characteristics, especially among the doomed Tehuelche. Julius Beerbohm, who wrote *Wanderings in Patagonia or Life Among the*

into consideration, to the general run of civilized white men."

One of Galloping Head's fondest wishes was to spend time with the native American. "His profession is war, his food simple, and his body is in that state of health and vigor that he can rise naked from the plain on which he has slept, and proudly look upon his image which the white frost has marked out upon the grass without inconvenience. What can we 'men in buckran' say to this?

Country life: The gauchos were often perceived as being as wild as the Indians, and just as interesting. Additionally, the gauchos and others living in the countryside were noted for their hospitality. Colonel King

Ostrich-Hunters (1879), had much to say about the original inhabitants of Argentina. "The Tehuelches are on the whole rather good-looking than otherwise, and the usual expression of their faces is bright and friendly. Their foreheads are rather low but not receding, their noses aquiline, their mouths large and coarse, but their teeth are extremely regular and dazzlingly white...in general intelligence, gentleness of temper, chastity of conduct, and conscientious behavior in their social and domestic relations, they are immeasurably superior not only to the other South American indigenous tribes, but also, all their disadvantages being taken

writes that, "whether in health or sickness, the traveler is always welcome to their houses and boards, and they would as soon as think of charging for a cup of water, as for a meal of victual or a night's lodging."

Darwin, too, was greatly struck by the cowboys he met. "The gauchos, or countrymen, are very superior to those who reside in the towns. The gaucho is invariably most obliging, polite, and hospitable. I did not meet with even one instance of rudeness or inhospitality." And once, when Darwin inquired whether there was enough food for him to have a meal, he was told, "We have meat for the dogs in our country, and therefore do not grudge it to a Christian."

But traveling in the countryside was generally not a very comfortable affair. Galloping Head presents a none too appealing description of his night's accommodations. "We arrived an hour after sunset—fortified post—scrambling in the dark for the kitchen—cook unwilling—correo (the courier) gave us his dinner—huts of wild-looking people—three women and girls almost naked ('They be so wild as the donkey,' said one of the Cornish party, smiling; he then very gravely added, 'and there be one thing, sir, that I do observe, which is, that the farther we do go, the wilder things do get!')—our hut—old man immovable—

tals, the people often relied on an assortment of folk medicine. Darwin was appalled at the remedies and only felt able to mention the following: "One of the least nasty is to kill and cut open two puppies and bind them on each side of a broken limb. Little hairless dogs are in great request to sleep at the feet of invalids."

Many were impressed by the skills the gauchos demonstrated as they worked their horses, threw bolas to fell ostriches, or lassoed cattle. Darwin mentioned a sight to which he was witness. "In the course of the day I was amused by the dexterity with which a gaucho forced a restive horse to swim a river. He stripped off his clothes, and

Maria or Mariquita's figure—little mongrel boy—three or four other persons. Roof supported in the center by crooked poles—holes in roof and walls—walls of mud, cracked and rent...Floor, the earth—eight hungry peons, by moonlight standing with their knives in their hands over a sheep they were going to kill, and looking on their prey like relentless tigers."

In the country, far from doctors and hospi-

jumping on its back rode into the river till it was out of its depth; then slipping off over the crupper, he caught hold of the tail, and as often as the horse turned around, the man frightened it back by splashing water in its face. As soon as the horse touched bottom on the other side, the man pulled himself on, and was firmly seated, bridle in hand, before the horse gained the bank. A naked man on a naked horse is a fine spectacle; I had no idea how well the two animals suited each other. The tail of a horse is a very useful appendage."

Earth and sky: The size of the country and the rough paths made the traveler's trip a

Left, Indian settlement by the Sierra de la Ventana. Above, Darwin's research vessel, the H.M.S. Beagle.

very long one, indeed. E.E. Vidal, an early-19th century traveler, quotes the unnamed author of *Letters from Paraguay,* who describes his trip from Buenos Aires to Mendoza, at the foot of the Andes, as taking 22 days in a large cart drawn by oxen. "We set off every afternoon about two, and sometimes three hours before sunset, and did not halt till about an hour after sunrise." Having a sufficient supply of water was one of the obstacles the writer faced in his journey. "We were obliged to halt in a spot, where even the grass seemed to have been burned to the very roots, and nothing was presented to the eye but barrenness and desolation...We had but one small jar of water left, our thirst seemed to increase every moment." Nature intervened as a thunderstorm struck the camp. "'Look at the oxen; they smell water.' We all eagerly turned to the poor panting animals, and saw them stretch their heads to the west, and snuff the air, as if they would be certain of obtaining drink could they but raise themselves into the atmosphere. At that moment not a cloud was to be seen, nor a breath of air felt; but in a few minutes the cattle began to move about as if mad, or possessed by some invisible spirit, snuffing the air with most violent eagerness, and gathering closer and closer to each other; and before we could form any rational conjecture as to what could occasion their simultaneous motion, the most tremendous storm of thunder, lightning, and rain I ever witnessed in my life came on. The rain fell in perpendicular streams, as if all the fountains of heaven had suddenly broken loose."

Many travelers commented on the seemingly endless flat pampas. W.J. Holland, an American scientist on an expedition to Argentina in 1912, described the scene from his train compartment. "I have crossed the prairies of Minnesota and the Dakotas, of Kansas and Nebraska, of Manitoba and Alberta; I have traveled over the steppes of Russia; but in none of them have I seen such absolutely level lands as those which lie between Rosario and Irigoyen. The horizon is that of the ocean; an upturned clod attracts attention; a hut looks like a house; a tree looms up like a hill."

Food and politics: The customs of the Argentines, whether of city-folk, gauchos, or Indians, have always been cause for comment. Thomas Turner, describing one well-known and wealthy family at supper in the 1880s had this to say: "Of the domestic habits of the Argentines, their manners at table, e*n famille*, it is impossible to give an attractive description. Their manners at table are ultra-Bohemian. They read the papers, shout vehemently at each other, sprawl their limbs under and over the table, half swallow their knives, spit with true Yankee freedom on the carpeted floor, gesticulate and bend across the table in the heat of argument, smoke cigarettes between the courses, and even while a course of which some of them do not partake is serving—a soothing habit which stimulates expectoration and provokes discussion—use the same knife and fork for every course—fish, entree, or joint, in a word, the studied deportment of the street is, in the house, exchanged for the coarse manners of the tap-room."

Turner was also shocked at the way politics dominated discussions, something that still is prevalent. "Although forbidden subjects are discussed by both sexes with zest and freedom, the staple topic of conversation is politics. Everybody talks politics...Even children talk politics, and discuss the merits of this, that or other statesmen with parrot-like freedom of opinion and soundness of judgement."

Many of the travelers' accounts are tinged with racism and the attitude that the writers' own cultures were most always superior to that of the Argentines. Comments such as, "Most of the corruption which exists in public life is due to the participation of foreigners therein; Italians chiefly", "the Argentine is not old enough yet to have developed the sense of humor," or, "I was becoming accustomed to the polite airs of this town that prints literature mad with Yankeephobia to snarl and bite all over S.A. against North America whose Monroe Doctrine, money, mentality and morality have been Argentina's help in the past and is her only hope in the future," can be found in many first-hand descriptions of Argentina.

At the same time, the wanderers and explorers have passed on the country's lore, which might otherwise have been lost to us.

Right, a 19th-century gentleman farmer.

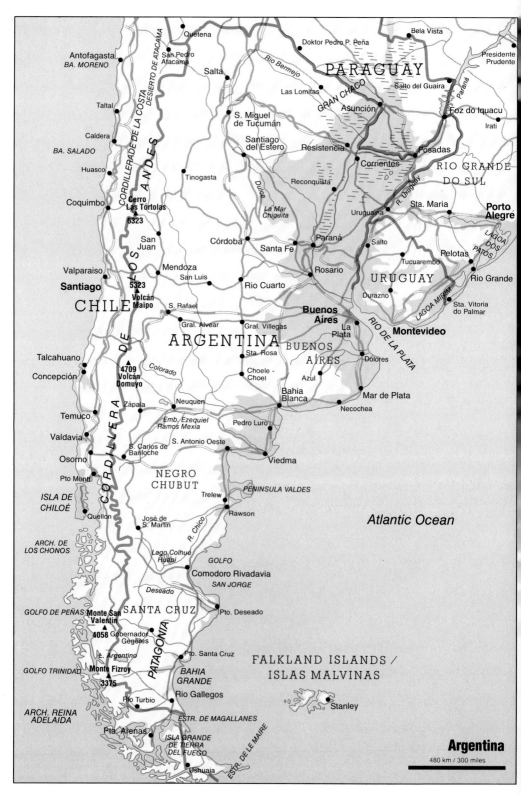

Quetena

Antofagasta
BA. MORENO

Doktor Pedro P. Peña

Bela Vista

Presidente
Prudente

San Pedro
Atacama

DESIERTO DE ATACAMA

Salta

Río Bermejo

PARAGUAY

Salto del Guaira

Paraná

Foz do Iguacu

Irati

Taltal

Las Lomitas

GRAN CHACO

Asunción

CORDILLERA DE LA COSTA

Caldera

BA. SALADO

Huasco

S. Miguel
de Tucumán

Santiago
del Estero

Resistencia

Posadas

RIO GRANDE
DO SUL

ANDES

Tinogasta

Reconquista

Corrientes

Coquimbo

Cerro
Las Tórtolas
6323

Dulce

La Mar
Chiquita

Uruguaiana

R. Uruguay

Sta. Maria

Porto
Alegre

LAGOA
DOS
PATOS

San
Juan

Córdoba

Paraná

Salto

Pelotas

Valparaíso

Mendoza

San Luis

Santa Fe

Rosario

URUGUAY

Tucuarembo

Rio Grande

Santiago

5323
Volcán
Maipo

Río Cuarto

Durazno

Sta. Vitoria
do Palmar

CHILE

LOS

S. Rafael

LAGOA MIRIM

CORDILLERA DE

ARGENTINA

Buenos
Aíres

La
Plata

RIO DE LA PLATA

Montevideo

Gral. Alvear

Gral. Villegas

BUENOS

Talcahuano

Colorado

Sta. Rosa

AÍRES

Dólores

Concepción

4709
Volcán
Domuyo

Choele -
Choel

Azul

Zápala

Neuquen

Bahia
Blanca

Mar de Plata

Temuco

Emb. Ezequiel
Ramos Mexia

Pedro Luro

Necochea

Valdavia

Osorno

S. Antonio Oeste

S. Carlos de
Bariloche

Viedma

Pto Montt

NEGRO

ISLA DE
CHILOÉ

Quellon

CHUBUT

Trelew

PENINSULA VALDES

Atlantic Ocean

ARCH. DE
LOS CHONOS

José de
S. Martin

R. Chico

Rawson

Lago Colhué
Huapi

GOLFO

Deseado

Comodoro Rivadavia

SAN JORGE

GOLFO DE PEÑAS

Monte San
Valentin

4058

SANTA CRUZ

Gobernador
Gregores

Pto. Deseado

CORDILLERA DE

PATAGONIA

L. Argentino

Pto. Santa Cruz

FALKLAND ISLANDS /
ISLAS MALVINAS

GOLFO TRINIDAD

Monte Fizroy
3375

BAHIA
GRANDE

Río Turbio

Rio Gallegos

ARCH. REINA
ADELAIDA

Stanley

Pta. Arenas

ESTR. DE MAGALLANES

ISLA GRANDE
DE TIERRA
DEL FUEGO

ESTR. DE LE MAIRE

Ushuaia

Argentina

480 km / 300 miles

PUTTING TOGETHER THE PIECES: AN ARGENTINE ITINERARY

While it is possible to get package tours to Argentina, this is by far the least preferable way to see the country. The independent visitor can familiarize himself with the points of interest, through the "Places" chapters that follow, and then set about planning an itinerary. And it does take planning, for Argentina is a huge country and destinations often lie far apart. Getting from the deserts of the northwest to the coastal wildlife of Patagonia requires organization, and the likelihood of fitting everything in on one visit of course depends on how much time one has.

Fortunately, Argentina has a solid infrastructure geared for tourism. Comfortable hotels are available in all popular spots, and in even the most remote reaches there are usually at least camp grounds. Planes, trains and buses run on convenient schedules and cars can be rented. In some areas, one might even prefer to get around on foot or horseback. Air passes on the national carriers enable one to cover the larger distances at reduced rates.

In the following chapters the country has been divided up into territories that one is likely to see as a whole: Buenos Aires, the vacation coast, the central sierras, the northeast, the northwest, the western wine country, Patagonia, and Tierra del Fuego. Whatever your point of entry—across the Andes from Chile, down by bus from Brazil or landing at the Buenos Aires airport—it's always possible to move on from Point A to Point B. How much of an adventure you make of it is up to you.

When figuring all these out, it helps to be mindful of the time of year one will be visiting. During the regional high season, reservations may be hard to come by; winter rains may make a park inaccessible; wildlife one will see in a particular spot depends on migration patterns. These chapters will help you decide whether you'd like to be sunning on the beaches of Mar del Plata in January, gliding down the ski slopes of the Andes in August, or eating a *bife de chorizo* in Buenos Aires any time of the year.

Preceding pages: a condor tours his domain; a gaucho surveys his territory; a chilly vantage point.

MI BUENOS AIRES QUERIDO

Some people call Buenos Aires a city of 11 million crazy drivers (earlier accounts report it to be a city of five million crazy drivers). Ask a *porteño* about the local driving habits and he'll say, "Fast, yes, but *skilled*. Not like the Brazilians, who are just fast and crazy." Traffic in the city is seen as one big Grand Prix, approached with machismo and a healthy dose of humor.

Those just visiting will probably not have cars, and so will be at the mercy of other people's driving. This should be looked forward to as an adventure.

Buenos Aires, for all its enormity, is a very easy city to get around. Streets run on a logical grid pattern with regular numbering. The bus system is extensive and efficient. Depending on the exchange rate, taxi fares range from quite reasonable to ridiculously low. But the nicest way to get around Buenos Aires is to walk. This is how one stumbles upon the parks and interesting holes in the wall. The terrain is easy on the walker, as it's flat as a *panqueque*. For whole wide stretches, the largest altitude variation comes at the drainage runs at the intersections. While taking your stroll, just be aware that pedestrians aren't accorded too many rights in this town. *Suerte!*

Preceding pages: early morning along 9 de Julio Avenue, Buenos Aires. Left, guard at the Casa Rosada.

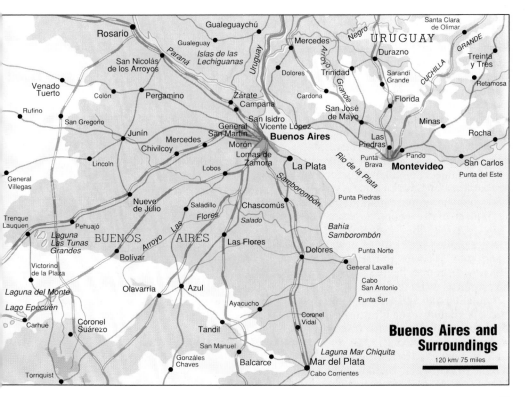

Buenos Aires and Surroundings

120 km/ 75 miles

CITY OF CONTRADICTIONS

Buenos Aires is more than chic shopping districts, good restaurants, high culture and handsome European-looking people. It is a city that began as a center for contraband and has continued its tradition of subterraneous life. There are at least two sides to most things in Buenos Aires, and they are usually at odds with each other.

The *porteños* (people of the port) have not looked outward towards the port for several centuries. They are much more interested in themselves. One of the first questions a visitor will be asked is what he or she thinks of Argentina. It is not unusual to hear a resident complain bitterly about the city and at the same time furiously defend it against criticism from outsiders. Likewise, *porteños* look to Paris for trends in style and admire the European way of life, yet few would choose to live anywhere else than Buenos Aires.

The intensity of opinions about Buenos Aires applies to almost any given issue. Every story has at least two versions, except perhaps one—everyone agrees that the Malvinas (Falkland) Islands are Argentina's. Try asking a *porteño* who Rosas was, or why the masses burnt down five colonial churches in 1955. You will surely get a taste of the fervor of Buenos Aires.

History in Buenos Aires is alive. Not only are men who died 200 years ago still the subjects of shouting matches, but architecture, street names, statues and innumerable museums are constant reminders of the country's past. The famous Argentine poet, Jorge Luis Borges, called it "a city of nostalgia" and wrote "it seems to me a tale that Buenos Aires ever began; I consider it as eternal as water and air."

Founding and settlement: In fact, it had a beginning, even if historians still dispute the date and the discoverer. What is certain is that in 1516, Juan de Solís disembarked here in his search for a route to the Indies. Buenos Aires lies at the mouth of one of the world's largest rivers, which Solís named Mar Dulce (Sweet Sea). The western banks lead open onto the pampas—flat, treeless land, with extraordinarily rich black top soil, ideal for agricultural planting. Solís also gave the river another name, the Lion's Sea, because of its brown tone and its vastness. It was later that this estuary acquired its present name of Río de la Plata.

Pedro de Mendoza was the next European to arrive. In 1536, under royal Spanish auspices, he established the first settlement (some say in what is today Lezama Park). He encountered the fertile pampas, as well as its inhabitants—hostile aborigine Indians. After five years of continual attacks by the Indians, the group moved upriver to Asunción, Paraguay. Mendoza left two important legacies: the city's name, Nuestra Señora de Santa Maria del Buen Aire, and hundreds of horses and cows that were to multiply and later become the foundation of the Argentine economy.

Mix of old and new.

Finally, in 1586, Juan de Garay, a *mestizo* from Asunción, returned with about 70 men and established a permanent settlement. A fortress was built facing the river, and the town square, Plaza de Mayo, was marked off to the west. At the far end of the plaza they built the Cabildo (the Town Council) and on the northern corner, a small chapel. Although new buildings have been constructed on the ruins, the plaza maintains this basic structure and is still the center of the city's activities.

Buenos Aires was the last major city in Latin America to be founded. It was not only geographically cut off from more developed trade routes, but, under Spanish law, the use of its ports for European imports and export of precious metals from Potosí and Lima was prohibited. Logically, the English, Portuguese and French took advantage of the lack of Spanish presence on the Río de la Plata, and illegal trade relations flourished. The settlement was able to survive in large part due to this contraband.

Manufactured goods were exchanged for silver brought from northern mining centers, and for cow hides and tallow. Construction materials also began to be imported, since the pampa had neither trees nor stones. Homes were originally built of adobe and straw.

Faced with competition in the region from other European nations, in 1776 Spain declared what is now Argentina, Uruguay, Bolivia, Paraguay and the northen section of Chile a viceroyalty. Buenos Aires was made the site of the central goverment. With its new judicial, financial and military role, the city burgeoned as a regional power. Functionaries, lawyers, priests, military personnel, artisans and slaves arrived, and the small village began its transformation into a major cosmopolitan city. In Latin America, only Lima and Mexico City exceeded the economic development at the time.

The *porteños* were accustomed to a certain economic and political independence from Spain. When, alone, they were able to repel two British invasions in 1806 and 1807, pride in the city's military prowess, and what later was to be called nationalism, ran high.

Independence and development: In 1810 the city's residents took advantage of Spain's preoccupation with Napoleon, and won an increased amount of autonomy for themselves. However, it was not until 1816 that independence was declared for the whole country.

In the subsequent decades, the government of Buenos Aires was consumed with the struggle for control over the rest of the country. The Federalists, represented by Juan Manuel Rosas, the governor of Buenos Aires from 1829 to 1852, believed each province should maintain considerable power and independence. The Unitarians, who came to power when General Urquiza overthrew Rosas, sought the dominance of Buenos Aires over the rest of the country. The tension between residents of the interior of the country and the *porteños* still exists, but at a social, rather than political, level.

A delightful juxtaposition.

Finally, in 1880 the dispute was resolved in a small street battle, and the city became a federal district, rather than simply the capital of the province of Buenos Aires. This was also to be a decade of intense change for the city. Under President Julio Rocas, the mayor of the city looked to Europe and especially Paris as a model for change in Buenos Aires. Hundreds of buildings were constructed in imitation of the latest Parisian styles. New neighborhoods were created for the wealthy by filling in huge sections of the river, particularly in the northern parts of the city, where Retiro, Recoleta, and Palermo lie.

It was also in the decade of the 80s that the massive immigration from Europe began, principally from Italy and Spain although also from Germany, Poland and Britain, as well as Lebanon and Syria and later Russia. By 1910 the city had reached a population of 1,300,000. Public service such as the tramway, running water, schools and police protection were well under way.

The city's literature, opera, theater and other arts were becoming known around the world. Suddenly, Buenos Aires was on the map as the Paris of Latin America for upper-class European and North American tourists.

In the last 20 years the city has lost pace with other major cosmopolitan cities. The results of political and economic instability can be seen in the old cars, buildings in disrepair, and the lack of construction. Where buildings have sprung up, there is little regard for maintaining the beauty of the old city, and virtually no urban planning for a new city.

The incongruous architecture of some areas of Buenos Aires may disappoint those who had imagined a picturesque European city. But it's the real city; a city in crisis, a city whose future is undefined and a city that reflects the special character of its residents.

Mix of old and new: To understand Buenos Aires, one must venture beyond the downtown area. One must walk the streets of residential areas, ride **A view from the port.**

buses, hang out in cafés, dine on parrilladas and pizza and, above all, talk to the people. Their conflicting and emotional feelings about the city and the whole country are contagious.

Buenos Aires is not only enormous in relation to the population of the rest of Argentina, but is also one of the largest cities in Latin America. The Federal District occupies 77 square miles (200 square km) and the entire metropolitan area spans over 1,121 square miles (2,915 square km). Approximately 10 million people or one third of the country's population, live in the city and surrounding areas. Three million reside within the Federal District.

Buenos Aires is marked to the north and east by the Río de la Plata and, on a clear day, one can see all the way across the mud-colored river to the Uruguayan coast. To the south, the city limit is marked by the Riochuelo, a shallow channel constructed to permit entrance to the major ports.

The city's landscape is varied. There are wide boulevards and narrow cobblestone streets. The downtown area boasts charming boutique windows, outdoor cafés, simple but elegant restaurants, and grand old cinemas and theaters. In residential districts, old ornamental apartment buildings, with French doors that open onto plant-filled balconies, stand side by side with modern six to 12-story buildings, most with sliding glass doors that open onto balconies. Sycamore and Tipuana trees line the streets, providing shade for little boys playing soccer in the streets. There are innumerable parks and plazas, where one may feel comfortable jogging, or simply sitting quietly near the old men playing *truco* (a card game) or chess in the summer.

A city of barrios: There are 46 barrios in Buenos Aires, each with its own special history and character. With few exceptions, the neighborhoods have a Roman grid structure surrounding a central plaza with a church. Most barrios also have a main street for commerce, with a two-story shopping mall, as well as a butcher, baker and vege-

A father and son enjoy an afternoon coffee.

Tigre

San Fernando

PILAR

ESCOBAR

Del Viso

TIGRE

SAN

FERNANDO

BECC

El Talar

San Isidro

Don Torcuato

SAN

ISIDRO

Villa de Mayo

BOULOGNE

GENERAL

SARMIENTO

VILLA JOSÉ

L. SUAREZ

FLO

José C. Paz

Campo de Mayo

General Sarmiento

(San Miguel)

VILLA

BALLESTER

GENERAL

SAN

MARTIN

Reconquista

Genera

San M

Bella

Vista

Arroyo Las Catonas

VILLA

BOSCH

VILLA

DEVO

Caseros

MORENO

MORÓN

DISTRITO

VERS.

VI

RE

Moreno

Reconquista

Merlo

Morón

General

San

Martín

San Justo

CHIC

DISTRITO

FEDER

Libertad

MATANZA

MERLO

Pontevedra

Laferrere

Arroyo el Pantanoso

Autopista

TTE.

General

Marcos Paz

Matanza

MARCOS PAZ

Aeropuerto

Internacional de

Ezeiza

ESTI

ECHEVERF

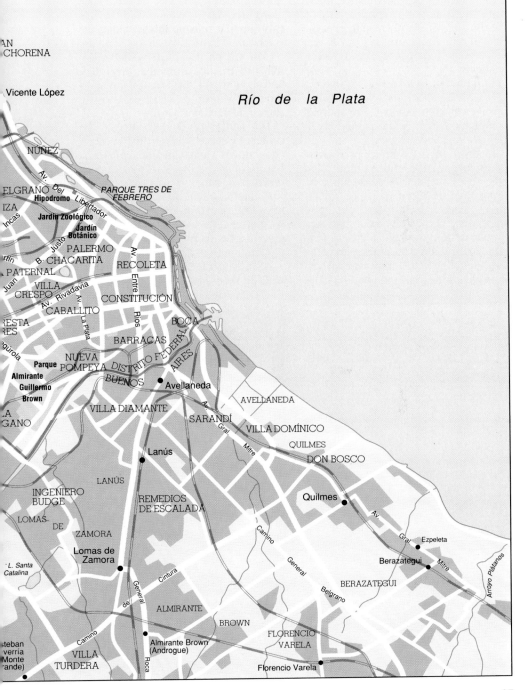

AN
CHORENA

Vicente López

Río de la Plata

NÚÑEZ

ELGRANO
Av. Del
Hipodromo
Libertador
PARQUE TRES DE
FEBRERO
IZA
Incas
Jardín Zoológico
Jardín
Botánico
tín
Justo
PALERMO
B. CHACARITA
RECOLETA
Av.
PATERNAL
Juan
VILLA
CRESPO
Av. Rivadavia
Entre
CONSTITUCIÓN
Av. La Plata
CABALLITO
Ríos
RESTA
RES
BOCA
gürola
BARRACAS
NUEVA
Parque
POMPEYA
DISTRITO FEDERAL
Almirante
BUENOS
Guillermo
AIRES
Brown
• Avellaneda
LA
GANO
VILLA DIAMANTE
AVELLANEDA
SARANDÍ
Av. Gral. Mitre
VILLA DOMÍNICO
QUILMES
DON BOSCO
• Lanús
LANÚS
INGENIERO
BUDGE
REMEDIOS
DE ESCALADA
Quilmes •
Av. Gral. Mitre
Ezpeleta
LOMAS
DE
ZAMORA
L. Santa
Catalina
Lomas de
Zamora •
Camino
General
Berazategui •
Cintura
Belgrano
BERAZATEGUI
Arroyo Plátanos
ALMIRANTE
de General
BROWN
FLORENCIO
VARELA
teban
verría
Monte
rande)
VILLA
TURDERA
Camino
Roca
Almirante Brown
(Androgue)
Florencio Varela •

table and fruit stand. A sports club, a movie theater, a pizzeria, and an ice-cream parlor also form part of the typical barrio.

Needless to say, the social atmosphere in these barrios is much warmer than in the busy downtown area, where pedestrians, as in most big cities are on the run and will barely stop to give the time of day. In a barrio, a lost traveler will be accosted by helpful and curious residents.

To grow up in a barrio is to have a special allegiance to it. Soccer teams from each club compete in national competitions that create natural rivalries among many districts.

In order to get a sense of Buenos Aires' layout, it is useful to simplify and talk about major blocks of the city. From Plaza de Mayo, two diagonal avenues extend to the northwest and southwest. The central track between the two is the most populated area of the city. To the south is the oldest part of the city, including San Telmo and La Boca, where working and some middle class people live. To the north, are the barrios of Retiro, Recoleta and Palermo, where the wealthy moved when yellow fever hit the southern district in the 1870s.

A fourth zone may be delimited to the west. With the establishment of two railway lines—the Once line that runs along Rivadavia Avenue, and the Retiro line that runs northwest along the river—new barrios began to spring up.

(Do not be deceived by the many maps of Buenos Aires that are tilted, and show west at the top of the map as though it were north. The Río de la Plata runs southeast, not west.)

The center of Buenos Aires: The center of Buenos Aires is truly the city's "downtown", and while most *porteños* live in outer barrios, everyone comes downtown, either to work, to eat, or to find entertainment. Residential barrios have their own mini-commercial areas, so that except to visit friends, many *porteños* never cross the city; they simply bee-line it to downtown.

As in every big city, there are hurried, well-dressed business people in the

Left: left, the Casa Rosada, and right, the mix of architecture fronting the Plaza de Mayo.

center of Buenos Aires, but there are also Argentines here enjoying the bookstores, the movies, the theater, the roundtable discussions and conferences on every imaginable topic, the plazas, the shopping and the political and cultural street life. Some streets, like Florida, Corrientes and Lavalle are for strolling, and are filled with leisurely visitors who have come to walk, watch and be watched.

A two hour jaunt starting at the Plaza de Mayo, along Avenida de Mayo and back down Corrientes and Lavalle to Florida Street, provides a quick introduction to the government buildings as well as the commercial, financial and entertainment districts.

Plaza politics: Buenos Aires began with the **Plaza de Mayo**, today a strikingly beautiful plaza for its tall palm trees, elaborate flower gardens and central monument, set off by the surrounding colonial buildings. The plaza has been and continues to be the pulsating center of the country. Since its founding in 1580, as the *Plaza del Fuerte* (for-

tress), many of the most important historical events have had physical manifestations here.

The most eye-catching structure in the plaza is unquestionably the **Casa Rosada** (Pink House), the seat of the executive branch of the government. Flanking it are the Bank of the Argentine Nation, the Metropolitan Cathedral, the City Council and the *Cabildo* (Town Council).

The Casa Rosada was originally a fortress overlooking what is now the **Plaza Colón**, but was at that time the river's edge. When the Indians' attacks subsided, the plaza became **Plaza del Mercado**, a market place and social center. The name and role of the plaza changed again with the British invasions of 1806 and 1807, when it became the **Plaza de la Victoria**. Finally, following the declaration of independence, the plaza assumed its present name, in honor of the month of May in 1810 when the city broke away from Spain.

The date also marks the first mass

The city's graceful Cabildo.

Mapa

Cancha de Polo

Av. Bulrich
Demaria
Juncal
Darragueyra
Av.
PALERMO
Santa
Cruz
Bonpland
Fitz Roy
Av. Juan B. Justo
Godoy
Darragueyra
PALERMO
Serrano
Gurruchaga
Malabia
Nicaragua
Soler
Uriarte
Honduras
Avenida
J. A. Cabrera
J. Alvarez
Lavalleja
Cordoba
Arganaraz
Castillo
Loyola
de
Israel
Guardia Vieja
Av. Corrientes
Estado
Lambare
Rio de Janeiro
Sarmiento
PARQUE DEL CENTENARIO
Campichuelo
Rio de Janeiro
Av. Diaz
Ambrosetti
Bartolome Mitre
Av.
Acoyte
Rivadavia
PARQUE RIVADAVIA
CABALLITO
Av. J. B.
Jose
Av. Pedro Goyena
AV. JOSE M. MORENO
Directorio
Av.
BOEDO
Bell Ville
Santander
Balbastro
Plata
Pavon
de
Juan
Moreno
Rondeau

Av. Sarmiento
del
Rep. India
Cerviño
Ugarteche
Cabello
JARDÍN ZOOLÓGICO
Plaza Italia
Fe
JARDÍN BOTANICO
Av. Gral. French
Juncal
Arenales
Caning
Charcas
Salguero
Paraguay
Bulnes
El Salvador
de
Honduras
Gorriti
A. J.
Figueroa
F. A.
Guardia Vieja
Lavalle
Tucuman
San
Luis
Cordoba
Cabrera
Soler
Laprida
Aguero
Billinghurst
AGUERO
Av. Santa
Av. Corrientes
V. Gomez
Salguero
Mario Bravo
Aguero
Velez
ALMAGRO
Rivadavia
H. Yrigoyen
Alsina
Moreno
Belgrano
Venezuela
Av. H. Yrigoyen
Venezuela
Mexico
Estados Unidos
Av. C. Calvo
San Juan
Pavon
Asamblea
Garay
Juan
de
Inclan
Trenta y Tres
Salcedo
Boedo
Plata

Av. Sarmiento
Salguero
Av. Casares
Libertador
Av. Ocampo
Castilla
Av. Pte.
Austria
Museo de Bellas Artes
Av. F. Alcorta
Av. del Libertador
Mto. a Carlos M. de Alvear
Alvear Palace Hotel
Antiguo Convento de los Recoletos
Basílica Menor de Nuestra Señora del Pilar
Cementerio de la Recoleta
Jockey Club
Av. Gral. Las Heras
PARQUE
Pacheco de Melo
Diaz
RECOLETA
Juncal
Pueyrredon
Azcuenaga
P. de Melo
Av. Callao
López
Juncal
Arenales
Plaza V. López
Arenales
Av. Santa Fe
Teatro Nacional Cervantes
Paraguay
Plaza Gral. Lavalle
Cordoba
Palacio de Justicia
Viamonte
Tucuman
Lavalle
Calao
Obelisco
9 DE
Museo de Arte Moderno
Corrientes
Uruguay
Sarmiento
Cangallo
BALVANERA
Mto. a los Dos Congresos
Bartolome Mitre
Plaza del Congreso
Palacio del Congreso Nacional
Alsina
Plaza de Miserere
Rivadavia
H. Pichincha
Matheu
Moreno
Pte.
Belgrano
MISERERE
Catamarca
Saavedra
Juluy
Venezuela
Mexico
Chile
Estados Unidos
Pichincha
Matheu
Sarandi
Combate de los Pozos
Independencia
Unidos
Calvo
Humberto I
Rios
Virrey
Peña
Av.
Carlos
Saavedra
Juan
San
URQUIZA
SAN CRISTOBAL
Oruro
Pavon
Av. Juan
Entre
P Echague
Inclan
Chiclana
Oruro
Salcedo
Brasil
PARQUE PATRICIOS
PATRICIOS
Monteagudo
Echague
Catamarca
Juluy
Pichincha
Matheu
Santa
Rios
Caseros
PARQUE AMEGHINO
Cruz
Luca Labarden
Patagones
Luna
La Rioja
Rondeau
Garcia
PARQUE PATRICIOS

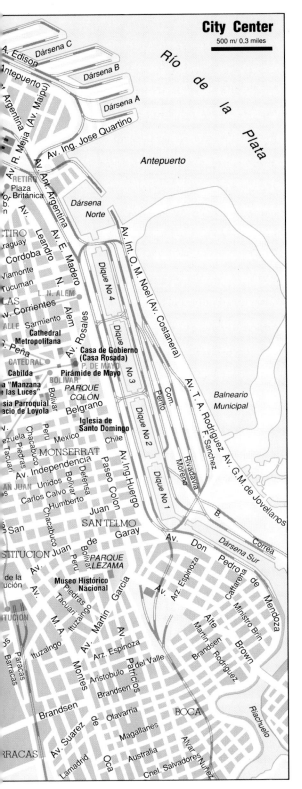

Río de la Plata

A. Edison
Dársena C
Antepuerto
Argentina (Av. Maipú)
Dársena B
Dársena A
Av. R. Mejia
Av. Ant. Argentina
Av. Ing. Jose Quartino
Antepuerto
RETIRO
Plaza
or Británica
b.
n
Av.
Dársena
Norte
TIRO
Leandro
raguay
Av. E. Madero
Av. Int. O. M. Noel (Av. Costanera)
Cordoba
N.
Viamonte
Tucuman
L. N. ALEM
LAS
v. Corrientes
Alem
ALLE
Sarmiento
Av. Rosales
Cathedral
Metropolitana
Peña
Casa de Gobierno
(Casa Rosada)
CATEDRAL
P. DE MAYO
Cabilda
Pirámide de Mayo
a "Manzana
BOLIVAR
Dique No 4
Dique
e las Luces"
PARQUE
COLON
sia Parroquial
acio de Loyola
Belgrano
No 3
Balneario
Municipal
Av. T. A. Rodríguez
Av. G.M. de Jovellanos
ezuela
Peru
Mexico
Chile
Iglesia de
Santo Domingo
Taclari
Chacabuco
Piedras
MONSERRAT
Av. Ing.Huergo
F. Sanchez
Av. Independencia
Paseo Colon
Dique No 2
AN JUAN
Unidos
Bolivar
Defensa
Moreno
s
Carlos Calvo
Rivadavia
Humberto
Juan
B.
San
SAN TELMO
Garay
Dique No 1
Com.
Perito
STITUCION
Juan
de
PARQUE
LEZAMA
Av.
Don
Pedro
de
Dársena Sur
Correa
Mendoza
Museo Histórico
Nacional
Cartagena
de la
ución
Piedras
Garcia
Av.
Arz. Espinoza
Ministro Brin
TUCION
M. A.
Martin
Brown
Paracas
Ituzaingo
Av.
Arz. Espinoza
Alte.
Barracas
Montes
del Valle
Martin Rodriguez
Brandsen
Aristobulo
Patricios
Brandsen
Brandsen
de
Olavarria
BOCA
Riachuelo
Magallanes
Alvar
Suarez
Australia
Cnel. Salvadores
RRACAS
Lamadrid
Oca
Nuñez

rally in the plaza, on this occasion to celebrate independence. Subsequently, Argentines have poured into the plaza to protest and celebrate most of the nation's important events. Political parties, governments (de facto and constitutional), and even trade unions and the Church, call people into the plaza to demonstrate a symbolic power.

Salient events in the history of **Plaza de Mayo** include the 1945 workers' demonstration, organized by Eva Perón to protest her husband's brief detention. Ten years later, the airforce bombed the plaza while hundreds of thousands of Perón's supporters were rallying to defend his administration from the impending military coup. In 1982, Argentines flooded the plaza to applaud General Galtieri's invasion of the Malvinas/ Falkland Islands. A few months later, they were back again, threatening to kill the military ruler for having lied to the country about the possiblities of winning the war with the British. More recently, in 1987, the plaza was jammed with some 800,000 *porteños* demonstrating against a military rebellion, and again at the end of 1989, protesting President Menem's pardon of convicted generals.

But the most famous rallies have been those of the Mothers of Plaza de Mayo, whose Thursday afternoon protests in demand of information on the whereabouts of their "disappeared" children, and punishment of those responsible for the kidnappings, still go on today. Their presence in the plaza is perhaps the best illustration of the symbolism of occupying space here. During the last years of the military regime, young people accompanying the Mothers would chant at the menacing army and police units, "Cowards, this plaza belongs to the Mothers..."

The Pink House: Leaders traditionally address the masses from the balconies of the **Casa Rosada**. This building was constructed on the foundations of earlier structures in 1894. Sixteen years earlier, President Sarmiento had chosen the site for the new government house. There are several versions of why he had it painted

POLITICS IN THE STREETS

Buenos Aires, Easter Sunday, 1987. For hundreds of thousands of citizens, the traditional mid-day meal was canceled. A sector of the military had organized an uprising and, in response, *porteños* flooded the Plaza de Mayo to symbolically defend democracy. President Raúl Alfonsín addressed the crowds. He instructed them to wait for him in the plaza while he went to the military barracks to negotiate a solution. There were drum rolls, whistles blowing, political banners and Argentine flags waving. The crowds, jumping in unison, chanted *"El que no salta es un militar,"* (If you're not jumping, you work for the military). Another song ended "this afternoon, the people are in the streets." That afternoon the rebels surrendered, and few doubted that the mass rally was the key factor that had persuaded them to change their minds.

This was not the first, and surely will not be the last, rally in Buenos Aires. A large part of politics in Buenos Aires happens in the streets. Rallies, marches, political graffiti or simply citizens gathered together in

Florída Street to discuss the issues at hand form part of a tradition. The amount of physical space occupied, the location of one's banner, the slogans chosen, all form part of a language used by the protesters to communicate among themselves and to those not present. One sector may be shouting "Dear Raúl, the people are with you," while another chants back "La gloriosa jotape" (the Peronist Youth song). A third group tries to reconcile the two with "The people united, will never be defeated."

At least since the Peronist government of 1945, most major historical events have had physical manifestions in the streets. An important date in the history of this phenomenon was October 17th, 1945, when Evita called the workers to Plaza de Mayo to protest Perón's detention. Thousands of people marching over the bridges from the south constituted what historians now consider the birth of the working class as an integral part of the political system. Perón later institutionalized the practice with innumerable rallies, in which he spoke to the crowds from the balcony of the Casa Rosada, and the people chanted their response, accompanied by kettle drums (*bombos*).

In a country where there have been no guarantees that one may exercise the right to vote, and negotiations behind closed doors have been the norm, street protests have been, for many, the principal form of expressing opinions. During military governments that followed the overthrow of Perón, rallies were often met with repression. Yet in other periods the marches have taken on a festive atmosphere.

When rallies became too dangerous, graffiti took their place. This was especially true during the exile of Perón, when groups of young people organized with cars, painting material, scouts and even lawyers on call in case of an arrest.

Since then, graffiti has become part of the fabric of political life. During the military government, slogans such as "Down with the dictatorship," and "Where are the disappeared?" were countered by paramilitary phrases like "Death to the subversives." Today, graffiti varies from "IMF out of Argentina" to "Family yes, Divorce no" and, of course, the standard "Vote for..."

To get a feel for what is happening in Argentina one may, of course, read the local newspapers and magazines. But reading the graffiti on the walls of Buenos Aires, or any other Argentine city, is an equally effective way to tune in to the political climate and the issues of the moment.

pink, the most credible of which is that it was the only alternative to white in those days. The special tone was actually achieved by mixing beef fat, blood and lime. Some insist that Sarmiento chose pink to distinguish the building from the White House. Still others say that pink was selected as a compromise between two feuding parties whose colors were white and red.

There is a small museum inside the Government House that contains antiques and objects identified with the lives of different national heroes. The museum is in the basement.

Grenadiers Regiment guards the Casa Rosada and the President. This elite army unit was created during the independence wars by General San Martín, and they wear the same blue and red uniforms that distinguished them during those times. At 7 p.m. each day, soldiers lower the national flag in front of the Government House. On national holidays the Grenadiers often parade on horseback, and they accompany the President during all his public appearances.

The other major historic building in the Plaza de Mayo is the **Cabildo** (Town Council), located at the western end of the plaza. This is perhaps the greatest patriotic attraction in Argentina. School children are brought here and told the story of how their forefathers planned the nation's independence in the Cabildo.

The town council has been on this site since the city's founding in 1580, although the present building was constructed in 1751. Originally, it spanned the length of the plaza with five great arches on each side. In 1880, when Avenida de Mayo was built, part of the building was demolished. And once again, in 1932, the Cabildo was further reduced, now to its current size, with two arches on either side of the central balconies.

The Cabildo also has an historic museum, exhibiting furniture and relics from the colonial period. The city government runs an outdoor theater in the interior patio in some seasons.

Across Avenida de Mayo, to the north, is the **Consejo Municipal** (City Council), an ornamental old building known for its enormous pentagon-shaped clock in the tower.

Church and state: The **Metropolitan Cathedral** is the next historic building on the plaza. It is the seat of Buenos Aires' archbishopric, and lies at the north-western corner of the plaza. The Cathedral's presence in this highly political plaza is appropriate. The Catholic Church has always been a pillar of Argentine society, and since the city's founding, the Church has shared the Plaza de Mayo. In a mural at the northern end of Avenida 9 de Julio, two symbols are used to illustrate the founding of the city: a priest and a spade, representing the military.

The Cathedral was built over the course of several decades and was completed in 1827. It was built, like the Cabildo and the Casa Rosado, upon the foundations of earlier versions. There are 12 severe neo-classical pillars in the front of the Cathedral that are said to represent the 12 apostles. The carved

triangle above reputedly portrays the meeting of Joseph and his father Jacob. This section is generally considered to be the work of architects. Yet a theory persists among some that it was created by a prisoner, who was then set free as a result of its beauty.

Inside, are five naves with important art relics. The oil paintings on the walls are attributed to Rubens. There are also beautiful wood engravings by the Portuguese, Manuel de Coyte.

For Argentines, the most important aspects of the Cathedral is the tomb of General Jose de San Martín, liberator of Argentina, Chile, Peru, Bolivia and Uruguay. San Martín, who actually died during his self-imposed exile in England, is one of the few national heroes revered by Argentines of all political persuasions.

At the northeastern corner of Plaza de Mayo is the **Banco de la Nación Argentina** (National Bank of the Argentine Nation). The old Colón Theater was on this site before it reopened on Lavalle Plaza in 1908. The imposing marble and stone Bank was inaugurated in 1888.

The Plaza de Mayo has a central pyramid that was constructed on the first centennial of the anniversary of the city's independence. Among other purposes, it serves as the centerpiece for the Mothers of Plaza de Mayo's weekly rounds.

Ornamental lunch: The view from Plaza de Mayo down Avenida de Mayo to the National Congress is spectacular, and the 15-block walk a wonderful introduction to the city. The avenue was inaugurated in 1894 as the link between the Executive Branch and the Congress, most of which had been completed by 1906. It was originally designed like a Spanish avenue, with wide sidewalks, gilded lamp posts, chocolate and fitter shops, and old Zarzuela theaters. Today, however, there is a super-positioning of influences with local adaptions that complicates descriptive styles. As in much of the city, "neo-classical", "French" "Italian" and "art nouveau" are terms that do not ad-

Left, the obelisk sits at the center of the city's nightlife. Below, life imitates art.

equately describe the special combination of influences seen here. Nor is there a traditional coherence from one building to the next; ornamental buildings stand side by side with others that are simple and austere.

There are several well-known restaurants along the way. One of the oldest is **Pedemonte**, dating back to the turn of the century. This is a favorite lunch spot for government functionaries and politicians linked to activities in the neighboring executive branch.

Further down, in the 800s, is the **Tortoni Café**, a historic meeting place for writers and intellectuals. Apart from the famous customers said to have frequented the café, the ornamental interior makes the place worthy of at least a quick glimpse. Marble tables, red leather seats, bronze statues and elaborate mirrors create a regal atmosphere. A jazz band plays in a back room at night (while tangos are sung from 10 p.m. on Fridays).

Traditional Spanish restaurants are also a prominent feature of Avenida de Mayo. At the 1200 block, one block to the left, is **El Globo**, one of the best, known for its *Paella Valenciana* and *Puchero* (boiled stew). There are similar restaurants one block to the right towards Rivadavia.

World's widest avenue: You could not have missed **Avenida 9 de Julio** at the 1,000 block, the world's widest avenue, according to the Argentines. It is 460 feet (140 meters) from sidewalk to sidewalk, and everything about it is big—big billboards, big buildings, big *Palo Borracho* (drunken trees) with pink blossoms in the summertime, and, of course, the big obelisk.

The military government of 1936 demolished rows of beautiful old French-style mansions in order to build this street. Much of the central block is now occupied by parking lots. The only mansion to survive was the **French Embassy**; its occupants refused to move, claiming it was foreign territory. There is a sad view of its barren white wall facing the center of town, testimony to the tragic disappearance of its

Café social life.

DINING OUT IN BUENOS AIRES

It is not easy to dine out in Buenos Aires. Not, that is, if one is an organized and trusting soul. Much of what one sees—or at least expects—turns out to be something else, or falls far short of what is promised. The city is full of eating establishments, ranging from the most sophisticated restaurant to the simplest fast-food joint, but unless one is determined to go entirely native and eat only what the true blue Argentine eats, confusion is likely to rear its head sooner or later.

There are two ways to eat in B.A: eat Argentine or go international. The former is simple but requires years, even a lifetime, of rigorous training. It is not easy for the unsuspecting visitor, reared on a wide variety of foods, to plunge headlong into a diet of nothing but broiled beef day after day. More than one tourist has been known to break down and threaten suicide if offered just one more portion of *asado*. This tantrum may be combined with pleas for a piece of fruit or some vegetable.

Turning to the international cuisine is usually not the ideal answer. There are excellent restaurants by local standards, but these standards do not have much in common with those of New York, San Francisco, Brussels or Lyon. It must be understood that, by and large, French cooking in B.A. is Argentine French cooking—very tasty, perhaps, but quite different in most cases from the sort of fare one gets in France. The same goes for Italian, Spanish, Chinese and most other ethnic foods prepared here. If you are willing to accept the *porteño* idea of a Bearnaise sauce and to not complain that the tarragon used on your chicken is Russian tarragon, not the real McCoy, then you will get on well. You can even get along splendidly, if you visit one of the few reliable establishments around town, such as **Monmartre**, **Tomo Uno**, **Francis Mallman** or **El Gato Que Pesca**, which make herculean efforts to come clean with their clientele.

However, you are in Argentina, so first you wish to try what Argentines normally eat. This comes down, basically, to beef: grilled, broiled, fried or boiled, but beef nevertheless. At least once a day and sometimes twice. Beef is easy to find here, almost every city block has at least one restaurant, and the betting is ten to one that it will contain a *parrilla* (grill). Off the *parrilla* one can opt for a rib steak, a rump steak, a strip rib, or a number of other variations. There will also be a complete and extensive variety of sausages and offal, some of which are rarely if ever seen on a respectable U.S. or European menu. Do not be put off. Much of it is delicious, all of it is palatable, and some of it is truly exciting.

A brief rundown of some of the terms you will encounter: a *bife* is a steak, but it can come in many shapes. The most common are the *bife de costilla* and the *bife de chorizo*, the former is a T-bone, and the other has nothing to do with the spicy local sausage, but rather is a largish, thick steak cut from the underside of the rib roast. *Asado* is a general term meaning roast, but it is most frequently used in the sense of an outdoor barbeque. *Tira de asado* is a thin strip of rib roast if prepared on the grill, but is much thicker, with more bone, when done on the *asador* (vertical spit).

Chorizo is a spicy sausage, *salchicha* is a long, thin, slightly less spicy sausage, and *morcilla* is a blood sausage. A *parrillada mixta* is a mixed grill which, in addition to most or all of the above, will probably contain *riñones* (kidneys), *mollejas* (sweetbread), *chinchulin* (the lower intestine, truly delicious when well crisped), *ubre* (udder) and *higado* (liver). Chicken is frequently included as well. A *parrillada mixta* is usually sufficient for two normal Argentines or four to five innocent tourists.

Apart from beef, in many of the better *parrillas* (steak houses) one can usually find chicken, lamb, and kid on the menu. French fries and salads are the standard side dishes. Beef with the local red wine is a hard combination to beat. An order of coffee to go with the meal, if firmly and repeatedly expressed, will generally get results but is considered little less than heresy.

Desserts are not an Argentine strong point, in spite of a national sweet tooth. *Dulce de leche* is a milk jam, overpoweringly sweet but great if that's the way you like things. This can come alone or may be served with a flan (baked custard). *Queso y Membrillo* (or *Batata*) is a combination of cheese with quince preserve (or sweet potato preserve) and can be very good indeed. Fruit salad and canned peaches are two other fixtures on most menus, and that is about that. Just one last mention: *empanadas* or turnovers, very much like Cornish pasties, can be fried or baked, and come with a variety of fillings, mostly beef based. *Empanadas* should not be missed.

neighbors.

The **Obelisk**, which marks the intersection of Diagonal Norte, Corrientes, and 9 de Julio, was built in 1936 in commemoration of the 400th anniversary of the first founding of the city. One assumes that because of its phallic appearance, it was the subject of much public joking. Three years after its creation, the City Council voted 23 to three to tear it down. But apparently even the order was not taken seriously, since it still stands today.

Avenida de Mayo ends at Plaza Lorca, two blocks before reaching the Congress building.

Pizzas, pigeons and politics: The next block is **Plaza de los dos Congresos** (Plaza of the two Congresses). It happens to be the zero kilometer mark for maps of the entire country. The plaza is a wonderful place for people-watching on warm summer evenings. Old and young eat pizza and ice-cream on the benches among the pigeons, enjoying the civilized atmosphere. There is a dramatic fountain with galloping horse and little cherubs, and, at night, classical music booms out from below the falls. There is a monument above the fountain that honors "two congresses"—the 1813 assembly that abolished slavery, and the 1816 congress of Tucumán that declared the country's independence.

The Congress Building houses the Senate, on the south side, and the House of Representatives on the north (Rivadavia entrance). Congressional sessions are open to those with press credentials or a pass provided by a member. The interior is decorated with appropriate pomp: large paintings, bronze and marble sculptures, luxurious red carpets, silk curtains and wood paneling. The building also boasts an extensive library.

Across Rivadavia is a new modern wing of the **House of Representatives**. Construction began in 1973, but halted with the military coup of 1976. With the return to democracy in 1983, building resumed, and the wing was inaugurated in 1984.

On the corner of Rivadavia and Callao is the old art nouveau **Molinas Café**. The building dates from 1912, and since that time it has been famous as a meeting place for congressmen and their staffs.

Rivadavia is a key street in Buenos Aires. It divides the city into two; street names change at its crossing and numbering begins here as well. *Porteños* claim that they not only have the widest street in the world, 9 de Julio, but the longest, Rivadavia, which continues west into the countryside and out towards Lujan.

About 12 blocks out from Rivadavia is the neighborhood known as **Once**. This is the cheapest shopping district in town, particularly for clothes and electronic goods.

Eating places near the Congress include **Quorum**, located exactly behind the Congress, on Riobamba Street. This is a big meeting place for congressmen. Another famous restaurant in the area is **La Cabana**, at Entre Ríos 436. La Cabana is unfortunately recognized as one of the best meat eating spots in the city and therefore is somewhat overpriced and touristy. They have wonderful salads and baby beef.

The street that never sleeps: Four blocks down Callao (the continuation of Entre Ríos) is **Corrientes Avenue**, another principal street in the lives of *porteños*. It is often introduced to foreigners as the "street that never sleeps" or the "Broadway of Buenos Aires."

Indeed, there are neon lights, fast food restaurants, and movie theaters on Corrientes. But the atmosphere is exceedingly intellectual, rather than gaudy like New York's Broadway. There are little bookstores everywhere, *kioscos* (newspaper stands) with a wide selection of newspapers, magazines and paperbacks, and old cafés where friends gather for long talks. The selection of international and national films also reflects the serious interests of the moviegoers.

The bookstores are traditionally one of Corrientes' greatest attractions. They are single rooms, open to the **The Congress building.**

108

street, selling both secondhand and new books. Some patrons come to hunt for old treasures, or the latest bestseller. Others use the book stores as a meeting place. The stores stay open way past midnight, and, unlike many other Buenos Aires shops, one may freely wander in and out without being accosted by aggressive salespeople.

Having a coffee: Another endearing feature of Corrientes and adjoining streets is the café life. There are hundreds of old cafés, with tall, wood-framed windows that are left open when it's warm. A small table next to the window permits the lone thinker to gaze at the street life, and to write or read in a relaxed atmosphere. But going out for coffee in Buenos Aires is also a social encounter. Even if it is a *licuado* (fruit and milk shake) that you finally indulge in, "having a coffee" means an intimate moment with a friend. And without a doubt, the nicest aspect of these coffee breaks is that the waiter will never hurry you. A traditional café for young intellectuals is **La Paz**, on the

corner of Montevideo and Corrientes.

Free culture: One of the first points of interest walking east again on Corrientes is the **San Martín Municipal Theater** at 1532. This chrome and glass building was inaugurated in 1960. It is the largest public theater in Argentina, with five stages and an estimated half a million spectators each year. There is a never-ending agenda of free concerts, theater, film festivals, lectures and musical performances here. Passers-by inevitably join the groups of people outside the theater reading the list of upcoming events.

In the block behind the theater, at Sarmiento 1500, is the San Martín Cultural Center, a sister building with an equally important flurry of cultural activity. The **City Tourism Bureau** is on the fifth floor, where one can pick up a free invitation to city tours.

The tradition of free concerts, seminars and other cultural activities, is one of the most striking aspects of life in Buenos Aires. If anything, the activity has gained momentum in recent years,

Hunting for bargains along Corrientes.

despite the economic crisis, and has undoubtedly been bolstered by the new freedoms under democracy. For visitors, both these centers are a wonderful introduction to the contemporary cultural scene in Buenos Aires.

Plaza Lavalle is another center of activity in the area. It is two blocks north of Corrientes at the 1300 block. The **Federal Justice Tribunals** are at one end of this historic plaza, and the internationally renowned Colón Theater is at the other. The plaza first served as a dumping ground for the unusable parts of cattle butchered for their hides. In the late-19th century, it became the site of the city's first train station, which later moved to Once.

The Colón Opera House: The **Colón Theater**, Buenos Aires' opera house, occupies the entire block between Viamonte, Lavalle, Libertad and Cerrito (part of 9 de Julio). It is the symbol of the city's high culture, and part of why Buenos Aires became known in the early-20th century as the "Paris of Latin America."

The theater's elaborate European architecture, its acoustics, which are said to be near perfect and the quality of performers that appear here, have made the opera house internationally famous.

Three architects took part in the construction of the building before it was finally finished in 1907. The original blueprint, however, was respected. It is a combination of Italian Renaissance, French and Greek syles. The interior includes great colored glass domes and elaborate chandeliers. The principal auditorium is seven stories high and holds up to 3,500 spectators. There is a 60 feet by 110 feet (18 meters by 34 meters) stage on a revolving disk that permits rapid scenery changes.

Over 1,300 are employed by the theater. In addition to opera, the National Symphony Orchestra and the National Ballet are housed here. In a recent rehaul that cost millions of dollars, a huge basement floor was added—creating storage space for the sets, costumes and props and working space for the various departments.

The poets' hangout, Café La Paz.

The Colón's season runs from May through October. Tours are available during this period.

Pedestrian thoroughfares: Crossing 9 de Julio one enters the **Mini-centro**, an area restricted to vehicles during working hours. The other restricted zones are Rivadavia, Leandro Alem and Córdoba.

Here, it is worth going across to **Lavalle street**, since Corrientes is at its best between Callao and 9 de Julio. Lavalle, like Florida several blocks down, is a pedestrian street. At night, it is filled with young couples strolling on their way to or from the movies. In a four block stretch, there are 18 movie theaters on this street. There are also pizza parlors, cafés, restaurants, including **La Estancia**, and several shopping malls, most of them specializing in clothing.

Avenida Florida, also closed to motor vehicles, is the principal shopping district downtown. The promenade is packed with people, as well as *kioscos,* folk musicians, pantomimists and others passing the hat. There is a leisurely pace here, and because of the crowds, it is not a good thoroughfare for those in a hurry.

Most fun of all are the heated political debates that are unleashed on this avenue. Sometimes they are intentionally provoked by party activists that have set up campaign tables. Sometimes they are started by groups of old men who seem to have made these sorts of discussions their pastime. In other instances, spontaneous arguments break out on the issue of the day. In all cases, people often gather round to hear the central players shout their opinions. Even for those unable to follow the conversation, it is worth pausing to observe these frequent episodes, for they are a wonderful introduction to Argentine politics.

The shopping on Florida is slightly more expensive than in other districts outside of downtown. As elsewhere, most shops are one room boutiques, many in interior shopping malls that exit onto adjacent streets. They sell

The opulent Colón Opera House.

clothes, leather goods, jewelry, toys, and gifts. Leather continues to be the best buy for foreigners.

One of the most famous malls is the **Galeria Pacífica**, between Viamonte and Córdoba. It is part of a turn-of-the-century Italian building that was saved from demolition because of the frescoes on the interior of its great dome. These were done by five Argentine painters: Urruchua, Bern, Castagnino, Spilimbergo and Colmeiro.

Books, burgers and art: The **At-eneo Bookstore** is at 340 Florida. It is probably the largest bookstore in the country.

There are also cafés along Florida, the most traditional of which is **Florida Garden**. Businessmen and politicians gather here for coffee, although simple lunches are served as well. There are also ice-cream parlors, vegetarian restaurants, and hamburger joints along Florida's ten block stretch, for those seeking something standard.

Harrods, one of Buenos Aires' few department stores, is just past Paraguay on Florida. The **U.S. Embassy Lincoln Library** is on the next block. Here one may read the *New York Times* and *Washington Post,* as well as major periodicals and, of course, books in English that may be taken out. The last stop on Florida should be **Ruth Benzacar's Gallery**, at 1000 Florida. Benzacar's is an underground art gallery, dedicated to promoting Argentine contemporary artists.

Below Florida, on the 300 block of Paraguay Street, is **Kelly's**. It is an unlikely name for the best stocked and cheapest Argentine handicrafts store. They sell traditional artisans' goods from different provinces, including double-layered sheepskin slippers (the inside layer is to sleep in), brightly colored wool scarves that are astonishingly inexpensive, leather bags, wooden plates for barbecues, gaucho belts and smaller souvenirs.

South towards Plaza de Mayo is the financial district. Tall banks and exchange houses line the narrow streets. Weekdays, the district is filled with well-dressed business people, and the

The busy pedestrian thoroughfare at Florida.

only vehicles pressing their way through the crowds are the armored bank trucks. Weekends, with booming Lavalle and Florida just blocks away, the financial district is eerily silent.

The Southern Quarter: The expansion of Buenos Aires in the 17th century first occurred towards the south, making the Southern Quarter one of the oldest residential areas of the city.

There are three areas of interest to most tourists: 1) Manzana de las Luces (Block of Enlightenment), 2) San Telmo, historically a fascinating barrio and today inhabited by artists and antique dealers, and 3) La Boca, at the southeastern tip of the city, famous for the pastel colored tin houses where dock workers used to live, and the raucous restaurants where working-class Argentines and tourists come to enjoy themselves.

La Manzana de las Luces refers to a block of buildings constructed by the Jesuits in the early-18th century. The San Ignacio Church, the old Jesuit school and underground tunnels are

bordered by Bolívar, Alsina, Peru and Moreno streets.

The area was originally granted to the Jesuits at the end of the 17th century. In 1767, the Spanish Crown withdrew the gift, in light of what was perceived as the group's increasing power. In fact, of principal concern in this case, as with Jesuit missions throughout the world during this period, were the egalitarian principles practiced by the priests in their social organizations.

Despite the repression against the Jesuits, many of the churches still stand, the oldest of which is the **San Ignacio Church**. This church, also the oldest of the six colonial churches in Buenos Aires, was constructed between 1710 and 1735. It is an impressive baroque structure, at the corner of Alsina and Bolívar.

Walking south on Defensa street one finds the **Estrella Pharmacy**, a 19th-century drugstore with marvelous metaphorical murals on the ceiling and walls, portraying disease and medicine.

On the second floor of the same

Get your token at the nearest kiosk.

building is the **City Museum**, with its rotating exhibitions of aspects of the city's past and present, including photo studies of architecture, as well as more curious shows, such as old post cards of the city.

Across the street is the **San Francisco Basilica** and the **San Roque Chapel**. The main church, finished in 1754, is the headquarters of the Franciscan Order. Parts of the neo-classical building were rebuilt at the end of the 19th century, in immitation of the German Baroque styles in vogue at the time. The chapel was built in 1762.

San Francisco was severely damaged in 1955, as were a dozen other churches, when angry Peronist mobs attacked and set fire to the historic structure. The violence was a response to the Catholic Church's opposition to the Peronist government, and its support for the impending military coup.

Art, architecture and antiques: San Telmo, like Greenwich village in New York, used to be one of the more run-down sections of the city, until history,

architecture, and low rents in the 1960s caught the attention of artists and intellectuals who began to revive the area. Attractive studios, restaurants and antique shops began to replace the decaying tenements. An open-air flea market held Sundays in the central plaza brought in enough tourists to nourish the new business ventures.

While San Telmo is now one of the principal tourist stops, the neighborhood maintains its historic authenticity and its vitality. **Plaza Dorrego**, the sight of the Sunday flea-market, is proof of this. Weekdays, it remains a fascinating spot, where old people who have lived all their lives in the barrio, many of whom still speak with an Italian accent, meet to talk and to play chess and *truco*.

San Telmo emerged in the 18th century as a resting stop for merchants en route from the Plaza de Mayo to the warehouses along the Riochuelo. Next to the Plaza Dorrego was a trading post for goods coming in from the ports. On adjacent streets, *pulperías* (bar/grocery

A rounding out of the national diet of beef.

stores) quickly sprang up to accommodate passersby.

Except for the Bethlemite priests that had established themselves in the San Pedro Church, the area's first residents were Irish, Blacks and Genoese sailors, whose rowdy drinking habits made the *pulperías* famous.

In the early-19th century, important families built their homes along **Defensa Street**, which connects Plaza de Mayo and Plaza Dorrego. During this period, a typical home included three successive interior patios, and only the facade would change, as new architectural styles arrived. They were called *chorizo* (sausage) houses, because of their long shape. The first patio was used as living quarters, the second for cooking and washing, and the third for the animals.

In the 1870s, a yellow fever epidemic hit the area. At the time, it was believed that the fog off the Riochuelo carried the disease. Those who could, fled San Telmo and built homes just west of the downtown area, approaching what is now called Congreso, and in the northern section, now called Barrio Norte.

In the 1880s and subsequent three decades, San Telmo received poor European immigrants, particularly Italians, that were arriving in Argentina. Many of the old mansions and *chorizo* houses were converted into *conventillos* (one room tenements that open onto a common patio), in order to accommodate the flood of new families.

Tango bars: A walk through San Telmo begins at Balcarce and Chile Streets, the northern edge of the barrio. There are several old tango bars nearby, such as **La Casa Rosada**, **La Casa Blanca**, and two blocks back towards Belgrano Avenue, one of the oldest, **Michelangelo**.

Crossing Chile on Balcarce, one comes to a two block long cobblestone street called **San Lorenzo**. To the right are a number of beautiful old houses. Many are now nightclubs. Others, with interior patios, have been converted into apartments, studios and boutiques. One may stroll in without worry of

trespassing. At 317 San Lorenzo, there is such a building. It has brick and wood ceilings dating back at least 200 years.

The next block is Defensa Street. Because this street was the main route to downtown, many of the old mansions are situated along it, some now in decay. The famous **Viejo Almacen** tango bar is two blocks away, at Balcarce and Independencia. The building is at least 150 years old, and used to function as the British Men's Hospital.

Balcarce Street continues across Independencia and is one of the prettiest streets in San Telmo for strolling. The next block is **Guifra Alley**, where many of the old *pulperías* used to be.

The next block on Balcarce is **Carlos Calvo**, another narrow cobblestone street, especially charming due to its numerous colonial houses that have been restored.

Good restaurants: To the right on Calvo are several picturesque restaurants, including **The Comite** and **La Casa de Esteban Lucas**, on the corner of Defensa and Carlos Calvo. Down the

hill to the left, on Carlos Calvo, is the famously expensive **El Respecho**. This is one of the few colonial buildings that has been maintained intact, without major renovations over the years. Heavy colonial furniture and ornate wall decorations create a sense of old Buenos Aires. Even the menu was created with history in mind.

Half a block past Carlos Calvo on Balcarce is the old home of the Argentine painter **Castanigno**, whose murals from the 1950s may be seen on the ceiling of Galeria Pacifica on Florida Street. Since the artist's death, his son has converted the building into an art museum.

Halfway down the block on the right is an old *conventillo* that has been renovated and now serves as an art center. There are two stories of studios that open onto a central plant-filled patio. Visitors may wander through and watch the artists at work. Weekends are the best time to visit.

Humberto 1 Street is the next block. Turning to the right, one comes upon

the old **San Pedro Gonzalez Church**. The church was built by the Bethlemite priests in 1770.

Across the street is the **National Council of Education**. Next door, there is a small plaque that calls attention to the site of an old *pulpería*, run by a woman named Martina Cespedes. During the British invasion, the woman and her many daughters enticed British soldiers into their bar one by one, tied them up and turned them over to the Argentine army. Although one of her daughters reputedly married a British victim, the mother was rewarded for her brave deeds with the title of Captain of the Argentine Army.

Sunday flea market: Finally, we are upon **Plaza Dorrego**, the center of San Telmo's commercial and cultural life. It is the site of the Sunday fair, featuring junk jewelry, secondhand books, antiques and some handicrafts. Surrounding the plaza are several restaurants, bars and antique shops that are fun to wander through. One of the prettiest is the old *chorizo* house, **Paisaje de Defensa**, a block south of the plaza. Another charming shopping mall on Defensa is **Galeria del Sol de French**. It was redone in a colonial style, with flagstone floors, narrow wooden doors, bird cages and plants hanging from wrought iron hooks along the long patio.

For those who enjoy open-air food markets, a block past the plaza, on Carlos Calvo, there is a large municipal market.

Lezama Park is just four blocks south of Plaza Dorrego on Defensa. Many believe that this little hill was the site of the first founding of the city. Later it was the home of Gregorio Lezama, who converted it into a public park. By the end of the 19th century, it was an important social center, with such amenities as a restaurant, circus, boxing ring and theater.

Today, the park is somewhat run-down, and the view is no longer attractive due to the surrounding construction and heavy traffic. However, the old mansion still holds nostalgic memories and has been converted into a **Historical Museum**.

A conventillo house.

La Boca: The working-class neighborhood of La Boca is at the southern tip of the city, along the Riochuelo Canal. The barrio is famous for its sheet-iron houses painted in bright colors, and for its history as a residential area for Genoese sailors and dock workers in the 19th century.

La Boca came to life with the mid-19th century surge in international trade and the accompanying increase in port activity. In the 1870s, meat salting plants and warehouses were built, and a tramway was constructed that facilitated access to the area. With the expansion of the city's ports, the Riochuelo was dug out to permit entrance of deepwater ships. Sailors and longshoremen, most of whom were Italian immigrants, began to settle in the area.

The sheet-iron homes that can still be seen throughout La Boca and across the canal in Avellaneda were built from materials taken from the interiors of abandoned ships.

The idea was taken from the Genoese. The style, as well as the bohemian colors, so unusual in Buenos Aires, became a tradition in La Boca.

One painter's influence: The famous painter Benito Quinquela Martín also influenced the use of color in the neighborhood. Quinquela was an orphan, adopted by a longshoreman family of La Boca at the turn of the century. An an artist, he dedicated his life to capturing the essence of La Boca. He painted dark stooped figures, set in raging scenes of port action.

In one work (that Mussolini reputedly tried unsuccessfully to buy from him with a blank check), an immense canvas splashed with bright orange, blues and black, men hurriedly unload a burning ship.

Neighborhood residents took pride in their local artist, and were influenced by his vision of their lives. They chose even wilder colors for their own homes, and a unique dialogue grew between residents and artist.

Quinquela took over an alleyway, known as **La Caminita**, decorated it with murals and sculpture, and estab-

ormal and
nformal
omantic
xpression.

THE SULTRY TANGO

Argentina has, in reality, two national anthems: one is its formal ceremonial hymn, and the other, *"Mi Buenos Aires Querido"* (My Beloved Buenos Aires), is a tango, the country's most authentic form of popular music. Today, most of the legendary clubs and music halls that gave birth to the tango exist only in lyrics and in the memories of old timers who recall dancing its intricate steps during its pre-World War II golden era. Nonetheless, the tango is in the midst of a revival. The spectacular musical production *Tango Argentino,* acclaimed during its 1986 presentations in the United States and Europe, and the growing success of contemporary *tanguista* Astor Piazzola are only two of the signs that the tango's special magic is being rediscovered.

What are the origins of this sensual and melancholy music, so intimately identified with Argentina and its nerve center and capital, Buenos Aires? The story begins just as the last century was ending. The whole Río de La Plata region, in Uruguay as in Argentina, began to receive great waves of European immigrants, along with thousands of returning criollos, recently discharged veterans of the 50-year-long civil wars that followed independence from Spain. Most of these settled in and around the growing ports of Buenos Aires and Montevideo. The mixture of Italian, Spanish, East European and Jewish newcomers mingled with the local population, itself a combination of Spaniards, Blacks and indigenous Americans. Each of these groups had its own distinct musical heritage.

In the rough-and-tumble world of the predominantly male immigrants, warweary ex-soldiers and working poor, the pulsing rhythms of the candomble that arrived with African slaves mixed with the haunting melodies of Andalusia and Southern Italy and the locally popular *milongas.* Sometime during the decade of the 1880s, a fusion of all these cultural elements occurred and something new—the tango—was born.

Exactly when and exactly where is both a mystery and a controversy, but one thing is certain: its debut did not take place in 'polite company'. The most important gathering place for popular classes of this period was the brothel. Located in the semi-rural areas of Buenos Aires around Retiro (now the site of the northern train terminals) and Pal-

ermo, and in the port areas of La Boca and 25 de Mayo Street, as well as on streets around the Plaza Lavalle brothels were the epoch's cultural melting pots. In the parlors, as customers awaited their turns, musicians played and sang suggestive and often obscene lyrics that gave the tango its early fame for ribaldry. Because of the marginality of the context, only fragments of the earliest tango lyrics survived, and their authors remain anonymous or known only by colorful nicknames. It wasn't until 1896 that Rosendo Mendizabal, a mulatto pianist, put his name to *El Enterriano,* making it the first signed tango.

But the men who spent their nights listening to tangos in the brothels also lived by day in the populous tenements that were concentrated in the older southern areas of Buenos Aires. Inevitably, the tango began to spill out into the patios, to be played by the neighborhood organ grinders, and to become part of other popular cultural forms, such as the much-attended theatricals called *sainetes.* By the time the new century was

Tanguistas perform at a street fair.

being welcomed, the tango had entered a second stage in which its audience included all but the still disapproving upper classes.

During these early years, the configuration of a tango orchestra varied greatly. As many of the musicians were of modest means, they relied on whatever instruments could be provided by those who hired them or could be rented. Guitars, violins, flutes and the less transportable piano were joined by that most special of all tango instruments, the bandoneon, a close relative of the accordion.

In the century's first decade, Buenos Aires, and with it the tango, experienced a transformation. The growth of the agro-export economy brought closer contacts with Europe, and wealthy Argentines, after visiting the clubs and cafés of Europe, looked for similar entertainments at home. A number of the old bawdy clubs, bars and brothels responded to the new demand and more elegant cabarets appeared.

Another source of change was the arrival of the recording industry. By 1913 a limited number of local recordings were being made, and in 1917 Victor Records captured the young voice of Carlos Gardel singing "*Mi Noche Triste*" (My Sad Night). It was, in many ways, the end of one era and the beginning of another.

Carlos Gardel was the tango's first international superstar. A look at his career shows the most important developments of the genre in its golden era. Despite the debate among aficionados, it seems most likely that Gardel was born in Uruguay, the tango's other home base, sometime around 1881. What transformed Gardel into a star, as they transformed the tango into music with a far wider appeal, were recordings, radio and the new talking moving pictures. Gardel went to France in 1929, where he made films at Joinville, and in 1934 he signed a contract with Paramount, for which he was to make five films. By the time of his death in a plane crash in Colombia in 1935, Gardel had become the personification of the tango. When the boat bearing his body arrived in the port of Buenos Aires, hundreds of thousands gathered to say goodbye to the *"pibe de Abasto"* (kid from the neighborhood of Abasto, the area around the old Central Market. In 1984 the municipality renamed the local subway stop after Gardel).

The tango's ebbs and flows in popularity were always tied to broader social conditions. In the late 1930s it dipped, only to hit a new peak under the Peronist governments of 1945 and 1955, when with a heightened nationalism and increased worker earnings, new clubs and dance halls boomed. By the end of the 1950s the tango had entered a crisis, in part because its popular followers suffered political defeats, in part because of the onslaught of new forms of music, mainly rock, and in part because the great names of tango were disappearing from the scene. New names, with new ideas about how to both rescue and revive the tango have appeared, creating controversy, at times acrimonious, between defenders of the old guard and promoters of the new. Unquestionably, the most important of the neo-*tanguistas* is Astor Piazzola, whose training as a classical musician and jazz experience has helped him produce a series of daring experiments in musical fusions, to growing acclaim in the United States and Europe.

eping
dition
ve at a
nce hall.

lished an open-air market to promote local artists. The brightly painted homes and colorful laundry hanging out to dry provide the background to this charming one-block alley. There are small stands, manned by the artists themselves, where watercolor paintings and other art are sold to tourists.

A stroll through La Boca begins at La Caminita. Heading north from the river on the alley, it is worth walking around the block and back to the riverside in order to get a sense of the normal residential street. The tin houses were not created for tourists; they are, in fact, comfortable homes. Most have long corridors leading to interior apartments, and are graced by wood paneling. The cobblestone streets are graced by tall Sycamore trees, and elevated sidewalks are a manifestation of frequent flooding.

La Vuelta de la Rocha, where La Caminita begins, consists of a small triangular plaza with a ship's mast. It overlooks the port area, which may be more accurately described as a decay-ing shipyard. More boats lie half sunken on their sides than upright and functioning. Depending on which way the wind is blowing, the visitor may be accosted by the rude odors of the canal, so polluted that reputedly there is no life in its waters. Residents blame the old slaughterhouses upriver, which, in the past, dumped wastes into the canal.

East along Pedro de Mendoza, the avenue parallel to the canal, is the **La Boca Museum of Fine Arts** (1835 Mendoza). The top floor was used by Quinquela as an apartment studio. Many of his most important paintings are here, and one may also see the modest apartment he used in his last years. The museum is a fun stop, if only to get the view of the shipyard from the window of the studio, the same shipyard depicted in his paintings.

Rowdy cantinas, rowdy soccer: Just past the Avellaneda Bridge is **Nicochea Street**, where rowdy cantinas form a sharp constrast to the sedate restaurants in other areas of Buenos Aires. These were originally sailors' mess halls, and

the high spirit recalls the jazz clubs of New Orleans.

Brightly colored murals of couples dancing the tango, speakers set out on the sidewalk blaring loud music, and somewhat aggressive doormen who compete for the tourists, may combine to frighten off those who are not prepared. But the scene is not as seedy as it might appear. Families from the interior of the country are there for a festive night out. Old people are singing their favorite tunes and dancing amidst balloons and ribbons. And the idea that a night out on Nicochea Street is a celebration of sailors returning home is definitely preserved. Much of the action on Nicochea Street is concentrated between Brandson and Suarez streets. Two blocks west is Almirante Brown Avenue, the main thoroughfare in La Boca. The avenue holds no particular charm, except for its excellent pizzarias. *Porteños* from all over the city come to La Boca to eat *pizza a la piedra*, a thin dough pizza baked in a brick oven, *faina*, a special chick pea

dough that is eaten on top of the pizza, and *fugazza*, an onion and cheese pizza. One of the most well known pizzerias is **Rancho Banchero**, at the corner of Suarez and Almirante Brown Avenue.

La Boca is also famous for its soccer team, Boca Juniors, where Diego Armando Maradona played. When Argentina won the World Cup in 1986, Maradona stole the show with his winning goals. He now plays in Italy, although his adoring fans continue to follow his career, and his Neapolitan exploits make front page news in Buenos Aires.

The Northern Quarter: The northern district, which includes Retiro, Recoleta and Palermo barrios, is the most expensive residential and commercial area of the city. Elegant mansions built at the turn of the century immediately remind the visitor of Paris, although the architectural styles are actually a mixture of different influences.

Until the end of the 19th century, this area was unpopulated, except for a slaughter house where the Recoleta

Plaza now lies. Much of the area was under water. In the 1870s, following the yellow fever plague, many of the wealthier families from the south moved north.

Great changes came in the 1880s when President Rocas began a campaign to turn Buenos Aires into the Paris of Latin America. Prominent Argentines had traveled to Paris and were deeply influenced. They brought back materials and ideas for the transformation of Buenos Aires into a cosmopolitan city.

Rocas' policies were and still are controversial. Critics supported a more nationalistic policy, oriented toward the development of the interior of the country. Yet, unquestionably, the so-called "Generation of the 80s" was responsible for making Buenos Aires the great city that it became.

A tour of the area begins at the eastern edge of the city, where Florida Avenue ends in Plaza San Martín.

Standing at the top of the hill in **Plaza San Martín**, amidst the spectacular old palms, jacaranda, tipus and palo boracho trees, there is a wonderful view of the barrio of Retiro. Across the Avenue at the bottom of the hill, Leandro Alem, is the old **Retiro Train Station**. Next to the station is the **British Tower**, renamed following the Malvinas/Falklands War as the Air Force Plaza. The Sheraton Hotel is also in view, and still further to the south, a series of highrise glass and chrome office buildings known as the **Catalinas**. The Catalinas were completed in the late 70s, and except for a few buildings like the Rolero, a tall round structure on Libertador Avenue, the Catalinas are the only large-scale additions to the downtown area since the 1940s.

From Plaza San Martín, one may also see the **Kavanagh Building**, just to the right, built in 1936 and reputedly Latin America's first highrise. Next door, is the **Plaza Hotel**, where such notables as Isabel Perón, the Shah of Iran, and Fidel Castro have stayed.

On the other side of the plaza are two fantastic old mansions. One is the

A moment of calm in the Plaza San Martín.

Anchorena family's residence, built in 1909. It was later used as the Foreign Ministry until that was moved, in 1984, to Reconquista Street. Another beautiful private residence, constructed in 1902, is at Maipu and Santa Fe. It is now used as a social club for military officers, and as an arms museum.

Chic shoppers: Before setting off to the Recoleta, those interested in shopping may want to detour to **Santa Fe Avenue,** one of the principal commercial districts. The busiest area is between Callao and 9 de Julio avenues. Here, there are innumerable shopping malls, replete with little boutiques selling clothing, shoes, chocolates, leather goods, linens, china and jewels. But perhaps the greatest attraction is watching the young *porteñas* from Barrio Norte, decked out in the latest Parisian styles, and simply out for a sunny stroll.

The **Recoleta**, often referred to as Barrio Norte, is adjacent to Retiro on the northern side. A 20 minute walk from San Martín Plaza to **Recoleta** Cemetery provides a pleasant introduction to what some *porteños* call their golden years (1880 to 1920). Many of the city's most sumptuous palaces may be found along Tres Arrollos and Alvear Avenues.

The **French Embassy** at 9 de Julio and Alvear is hard to miss, not only because of its luxurious appearance, but because it is the only building left standing in the middle of the wide avenue. Two blocks further, at 1300 Alvear, is the **Carlos Pellegrini Plaza** where two other great mansions, the **Brazilian Embassy** and the exclusive **Jockey Club** are located.

Some of the best quality and most expensive shops are situated along **Alvear**. At 1777 and 1885 there are elegant malls, ideal for window shoppers. Parallel to Alvear is **Quintana Avenue**, another expensive shopping district.

Quintana ends at the **Ramon Carcano Plaza** and the Recoleta Cemetery. Here, it is worth stopping for croissants and coffee at **La Biela**, or one of the numerous sidewalk cafés overlooking the plaza. Under the shade of a giant rubber tree, one has a view of the entrance to the famous Recoleta Cemetery, the handsome American baroque **Pilar Basilica**, the convent, now used as a cultural center, as well as a series of well-kept parks and gardens.

Recoleta is without a doubt the most fashionable plaza in the city. The coffee is twice as expensive in the cafés, but nobody cares. Young students gather here on warm summer evenings to see and be seen. On sunny afternoons, neighborhood mothers take over the central promenade with dozens of baby strollers and little blond toddlers. The adjacent grassy areas belong to the pure-bred dogs and their owners, who also have their social gatherings.

This civilized plaza, ironically, has a wonderfully gory past. It used to be the sight of a *hueco de cabecitos*, a dumping ground for heads of cattle slaughtered for their hides. As in the case of other *huecos*, a little stream flowed past the area, where other wastes were also thrown. The meat was not consumed,

and black women were reputedly employed to drag away the carcasses.

The stream was piped underground in the 1770s and the Recoleta priests began to fix up the area, converting it into an orchard and vegetable garden. Until the 1850s, the Río de la Plata ran up to the edge of the plaza, covering what is now Libertador Avenue. Under Rosas' administration this area began to be filled in. It was not until the 1870s that the population, principally the wealthy, started to migrate to this northern barrio.

The **Basilica of our Lady of Pilar** was built between 1716 and 1732. Subsequent restorations have been faithful to the original Jesuit simplicity of its architects, Andres Blanqui and Juan Primoli. Much of the building materials were brought from Spain, such as wrought iron gates and stone. It may be recalled that there are no rocks in Buenos Aires, since it forms part of the Pampa, and it was not until much later that stones were transported from an island in the Delta.

Among the historic relics contained in the church is a silver-plated altar, believed to have been brought from Peru. Like many other colonial churches, during the British invasions, it was used as a hospital by the foreign soldiers.

Evita's final resting place: The **Recoleta Cemetery** is the burial ground for the rich and famous, and the most expensive property in the country. Entering the gates, one has the sense of walking into a city in miniature, and, in fact, it is an architectural and artistic history of Buenos Aires from its inauguration in 1882. The great leaders and their enemies are buried here.

The history of the place should be indisputable, since the tombs and cadavers are material proof. Yet the schisms of the rest of Argentine society are reflected here, not only in terms of the conflicting architectural styles, but, astonishingly, in who is actually here and why.

For example, one of the most visited tombs is that of Evita Perón. Neverthe-

The colonial grace of the Pilar church.

less, a tourism functionary adamantly denied that she is buried here, explaining that she is not of the "category" of people buried in the Recoleta. In fact, she is 30 feet (nine meters) under ground to keep her enemies from stealing her body, as occurred in 1955.

Parks and patriachs: Down the hill from the Recoleta is Libertador Avenue, and on the far side, before one reaches Figueroa Alcorta Avenue, there are a series of parks and gardens that are great for joggers interested in seeing more than the pretty woods and fields of Palermo. On the way down the hill, is one of the most spectacular of Buenos Aires' monuments, a mounted statue of **General Alvear**. A large roller coaster and Ferris wheel, from the nearby Italpark, provide a strange backdrop to this grand sculpture.

Across the street, on Libertador, there is the **Museum of Fine Arts**, which has an excellent collection of Argentine and foreign paintings and sculpture.

Almost at the end of this row of plazas is the **Chilean Embassy**. Behind it is one of the prettiest public gardens in the area. Nearby is the reconstructed home of Independence Wars hero, General San Martín, and a series of statues sits in front of the building, representing different friends of the liberation fighter.

Palermo Chico, a neighborhood of the rich and famous, is just around the bend. In fact, one must weave around several bends in order to get a sense of this exclusive neighborhood. It is a cozy nest of palaces, set off from the rest of the city by its winding streets that seem to exclude those from outside its boundaries. Movie stars, sports heroes, and diplomats make up this unusual community.

The area was built up together with the Recoleta area in the 1880s. Many of the old French-style mansions are now used as embassies, since the original owners have been unable to maintain such an exorbitant standard of living. There are also many new wood and brick homes with classic red tile roofs,

which, except for the well-kept gardens, can hardly compete with the great stone palaces.

The rest of Palermo is known for its parks and gardens, although there are other quite beautiful residential sections. There are hundreds of acres of exotic vegetation that include the strange juxtaposition of pines and palms. There is an equally eclectic array of entertainment.

There are few cities in the world with such an infrastructure for recreation, and this is undoubtedly a key to understanding *porteños*. Here, the frenzy of the city subsides and *porteños* refuel with the oxygen from the sumptuous vegetation. There are families picnicking, men working out with their buddies, young couples in the grass who have escaped the stern supervision of their parents, and, of course, lots of babies. The park is a constantly changing scene of people, bicycles and dogs.

Sports and snacks: A pleasant, but lengthy jaunt through Palermo may begin in Palermo Chico. The heart of

the park area, **Parque 3 de Febrero**, is six blocks further down Figueroa Alcorta Avenue from the tip of Palermo Chico.

The park includes 1,000 acres (400 hectares) of fields, woods and lakes. There are several points of interest near and within it. Approaching Sarmiento Avenue on Figueroa Alcorta, one passes the National Cavalry on the right, and immediately afterwards, the **KDT Sports Complex**. A small entrance fee (usually around one dollar) permits access to excellent sports facilities. There are tennis courts, a running track, an indoor pool, and a café with a terrace overlooking the track. Many simply come, however, to sprawl out on the well-trimmed grass to begin work on their tans before hitting the beaches of Mar del Plata or Punta del Este.

The **Japanese Botanical Garden** is across the avenue. Extraordinarily lush gardens, with fish ponds spanned by white, wooden walking bridges, provide one of the most beautiful places to stroll in the city.

Tomando sol.

126

The intersection of Figueroa Alcorta and Sarmiento, the wide avenue that crosses the park, is marked by an enormous statue of **General Urquiza**, who became president when he overthrew Rosas in 1852. To the right on Sarmiento there is the **Municipal Planetarium**, open to the public, and a small man-made lake. To the left on Sarmiento is **Iraola Avenue**, which leads one to the heart of Palermo's parks and lakes. There are paddle boats for rent, a storybook pedestrian bridge that leads to rose-lined gravel paths with stone benches every few yards. There are ice-cream vendors, men who sell warm peanuts, sweet popcorn and candied apples, and still others who specialize in *choripan* (sausage sandwich) and soda. An indoor/outdoor café, called **Green Grove**, overlooks the most crowded area of the lake.

Iraola weaves around the lake and back to Libertador and Sarmiento, where another large monument marks the intersection. This one was a gift from the Spanish community, and is surrounded by a pretty fountain pool.

Kiddies and creatures: The back entrance to the zoo is on the corner. The main entrance is on Las Heras Avenue. The **City Zoo** is pleasant, and has a variety of monkeys and birds native to South America. The real attractions, however, are the hundreds of local children racing from one cage to the next.

Across from the zoo's main entrance, on Plaza Italia, is the **Rural Society**, an association of large-scale farmers. The Society sponsors all kinds of activites, including dog, horse, cattle and even automobile exhibitions, all of which are open to the public.

Plaza Italia is at the intersection of Las Heras, Santa Fe, and Sarmiento avenues. The plaza holds no special charm except that it is the sight of so much activity. Weekends in the area are especially fun. On adjacent blocks, there is a street fair, known as the "hippie market," since the individual stands are often run by young "bearded-and-sandalled" types, and they themselves make the ceramic mugs and ashtrays,

Many porteños rely on the services of professional dog-walkers.

leather shoes, belts and handbags, the jewelry, and embroidered and tie-dyed clothes sold at the fair. On the last block, the stands are dedicated to secondhand books and magazines.

The plaza is often used by political parties, particularly leftist ones like MAS (Movement Toward Socialism) and PI (Intransigent Party). They set up information tables, and organize political/cultural events, like puppet shows and street theater, which people coming to and from the zoo, the Rural Society or the street fair, pause to watch.

The other center of attention in the neighborhood is the **Hipodromo**, the horse race track. Its main entrance is on Santa Fe, just past Plaza Italia, although it is possible to sneak a hurried view over the wall, from the back side in the park.

Side trips: From Buenos Aires there are innumerable possibilities for day trips to small towns in the pampa and north along the river to the delta and its many islands. Here are three suggested all-day outings:

Tigre: Tigre is an old town situated at the mouth of the Delta. Fruit brought by boat from the northern provinces is deposited here en route to Buenos Aires. But the principal economic activity revolves around the summer tourists and weekenders who come to fish, row, water ski and cruise the winding channels that flow past hundreds of little islands.

While it is only 17 miles (28 km) from downtown Buenos Aires, the air is clear, the vegetation subtropical, and the rhythm of activity less hurried. Those who live year-round on the islands rarely venture into the big city. They go into Tigre or simply buy their food off a grocery boat that swings by once a day. There is almost no crime, and it is said that the dogs never get sick because of special immunities gained from drinking the brown river water.

After touring the charming plant-filled residential area of the town, one heads for the main drag along the riverside, **Paseo Victorica**. Old English rowing clubs and *parrilla* restaurants

Some of the grandiose sculpture along Libertador Avenue.

line the street. There are several small docks, where *lanchas* (taxi boats) depart. Several larger ferries have two hour cruises. They leave from the dock next to the train station. One even has a restaurant on board. Boats may also be rented for floating parties, and there is a ferry that crosses over to the Uruguayan beaches.

The town is easily accessible from Buenos Aires. There is a train from Retiro, and a bus, no. 60, that begins at Constitution, passes through downtown, and ends at the Tigre Hotel.

Lujan: Lujan is one of the oldest cities in the country and today is visited by Argentine tourists because of its religious importance. It is situated 40 miles (63 km) west of Buenos Aires, along the Lujan River. Trains leave from Once and take two hours, stopping at every little town in the pampa along the way.

The **Basilica de Lujan** is a magnificent gothic structure, built over the course of 50 years and completed in 1935. The great attraction is a statue of the **Virgin of Lujan**, which dates from 1630. Each December 8th, hundreds of thousands of young Catholics make a pilgrimage from Buenos Aires to celebrate the *Fiesta de Nuestra Señora de Lujan*.

The Lujan River runs through the city, and in colonial times, boats heading to the northwest were checked here for contraband. When there have been no recent rains, the river is a place of recreation for residents and tourists.

There are several museums in Lujan. The **Complejo Museo Grafico Enrique Udaondo** is in a beautiful old colonial building, and exhibits relics relating to the customs and history of the country. In an annex is the **Museum of Transportation**. There is also the **Museo de Bellas Artas**, in Florentino Ameghino Park, dedicated principally to contemporary Argentine art.

On national and religious holidays there are gaucho competitions on horseback that are spectacular. Most of the competitors are in fact descendants of gauchos and now work as farm hands, although costumes and saddles

Pleasure-boating in the delta, near Tigre.

are saved for these special occasions.

A highly recommended restaurant is **L'Eau Vive** (Constitucion 2106), run by a group of women missionaries. The specialty of the house is trout. It's closed on Mondays and Tuesdays, and reservations are suggested.

For those driving, there is a fun stop on the way to Lujan. It is an open-air zoo called **Mundo Animal** (Animal World). Llama, sheep, horses, cows and deer will follow your car begging for food. Lions, monkeys and other wild animals are in special areas where one is not permitted to get out of the car.

La Plata: La Plata is the capital of the Province of Buenos Aires, and despite being only 35 miles (56 km) south of Buenos Aires, it is representative of many provincial cities in Argentina. Life is less frantic, the city is clean and orderly, and boasts independent political and cultural activities.

From **Constitution Train Station**, there is a two hour train to La Plata. South of the city, one passes through an industrial belt populated by poor and working class people. A number of shanty towns line the tracks.

Some 24 miles (38 km) from Buenos Aires, where routes 1 and 14 split, is an *estancia* that used to be owned by the Pereyra family. It was expropriated by Perón and transformed into a recreational park, where working-class people who live in the area can come to relax.

On an adjacent part of the property is a zoo, where the animals run wild, and visitors can drive safari-style through the countryside.

Nine miles (14 km) further south is **Ciudad de los Niños** (Children's City), a marvelous recreational center for children, built by Evita Perón in the early '50s.

A few more miles down Route 1 is the city of **La Plata**, founded in 1882 by Dr. Dardo Rocha. The city was conceived by Pedro Benoit, and takes the logical form of a rectangle with the horizontal/vertical streets that are numbered and diagonal avenues.

Order and cleanliness permeate the atmosphere of the tree-lined streets, public squares and parks.

The **Provincial Legislature** is located off Plaza San Martín, as is the **Government Palace**, and the **Paisaje Dardo Rocha**. The gothic **Cathedral of La Plata** is on the Mariano Moreno Plaza. Across the plaza is the **Municipal Palace**. One block away, between 9th and 10th streets, is the **Teatro Argentino**.

There are a series of pretty parks in the center of the city called **Paseo de Bosque**, with lakes, a zoo that is actually much more complete than the Buenos Aires zoo, an observatory and a theater, **Teatro Martín Fierro**. La Plata is famous for its **Museum of Natural Sciences**, which was founded in 1884. This museum has many fascinating geological, zoological and archaeological exhibits, and is located in the **Paseo de Bosque**. The **Museo Provincial de Bellas Artes**, at 525 51st Street, has an excellent collection of Argentine paintings and sculpture. The large **University of La Plata** is only blocks away.

Left, a bit of preserved heritage. Right, inner peace at the La Plata cathedral.

GAMBLERS AND GAMBOLERS:
THE VACATION COAST

If your interests on a vacation tend at all toward the sociological and anthropological, then when on a vacation to Argentina, this is the place to come. Here along the extensive Atlantic coast, in an array of resorts for all tastes and bank accounts, one can see the Argentines at play. Although their country is enormous, and has an astonishing variety of appealing destinations, few Argentines seem interested in exploring it. Instead they head for the beach. Year after year, they return to the same spot, often to the point of renting the same changing cabana every time.

This fostering of a second home leads to a real sense of community in each resort. Families who may live far apart during much of the year, see each other each summer, watch each other's kids grow up, and keep up with the community gossip.

Along these beaches, the older folks pass the day playing the card games of *truco* and canasta, while the young swim and play paddle ball and volleyball. Young women prance about in their *cola-less* bikinis (this translates roughly into tail-less; the backsides of these suits are strikingly short on fabric) and everyone seems relaxed and happy to escape the mania of city life.

There is a fierce sense of pride among Argentines for their riviera. Keen competition exists among all the resorts of the South Atlantic, and some of Argentina's hot spots consider themselves rivals of such places as Punta del Este, in Uruguay. Fashions are kept up to the minute, and many fads actually start here. Those of the smart set insist on being seen here at least once during the summer season.

So if your exposure to Argentine society has been mostly to those living under the pressures of *porteño* life, it's not a bad idea to visit the coast, where everybody is smiling. It's not a bad spot to take a vacation either.

Preceding pages: an off day near Mar del Plata. Left, net maintenance is part of a fisherman's job.

MAR Y SIERRAS

When the first European explorers sailed off this coast in the early-16th century, they looked upon a landscape very similar to the one that a visitor can see today. The difference, of course, is that today there is the occasional outcropping of settlements, urban nuclei rising from the very edge of the pampa, with their low white houses and the occasional skyscraper.

This scenic coastline is popularly known as the **Atlantida Argentina**. The area is also sometimes referred to as **Mar y Sierras**, Sea and Hills, a frank description of this stretch, where fertile rolling hills come right to the edge of the sea.

The main strip of the popular Argentina vacation coast extends from San Clemente del Tuyú to Mar del Plata, the hub of the Atlantida area. Though founded late in the 19th century, Mar del Plata was at first a resort for well-to-do *porteños*, i.e. for those residents of Buenos Aires who could afford the 250-mile (400-km) journey to the then solitary cliffs near Punta Mogotes. Early on, this journey was made by train, and later by car. Only in the mid-1930s did Mar del Plata really start to boom and swing. This was due mainly to two developments: the opening of the Casino, with its 36 roulette tables (in those days the largest gambling place in the world), and the paving of the Ruta Nacional 2, which brought Mar del Plata to within four hours by car from Buenos Aires.

With the construction of still another road along the coast (Ruta Provincial 11), other smaller seaside resorts started to sprout up north and south from Mar del Plata. Before too long, each of these places acquired a character of its own; some were preferred by the elderly, others by youth, some by those who like rock music and some by the lovers of smooth tango dancing.

How to get there: If an excursion to

The Mar del Plata Golf Club.

the vacation coast was a small adventure until 30 or even 20 years ago, mainly because of the muddy condition of access roads to most of the smaller villages, today there is nothing more comfortable and pleasant than a trip to any spot along the Atlantida Argentina. This trip can be made by bus or plane. Only Mar del Plata and Miramar are directly connected to Buenos Aires by railway with first class services. The trains are equipped with dining, cinema and bar cars, and make the journey in four hours. What's more, they cost about the same price as taking the bus. A growing number of vacationers use the air services, which are inexpensive, and frequent in summer. Most flights connect the Buenos Aires city airport, Aeroparque Jorge Newbery, with Mar del Plata's Camet airport, but an increasing number of services with commuter-type planes now serve smaller resorts along the coast. Resorts with such services include Santa Teresita, Pinamar, Villa Gesell, Miramar and Necochea. The two principal airlines are Aerolineas Argentinas and Austral, but some of the smaller operators, like LAPA, offer a special pickup and delivery service, whereby a customer is delivered by microbus from door to door.

Fishermen's retreats: The Atlantida Argentina is, generally speaking, all the Atlantic coast belonging to the province of Buenos Aires, though the popular spots run from San Clemente del Tuyú to Villa Gesell and then south from Mar del Plata, along the endless and solitary shoreline to Monte Hermoso, near the seaport of Bahia Blanca.

San Clemente del Tuyú is located near the northern point of **Cabo San Antonio**, the most easterly point of continental Argentina. It is adjacent to Bahia Samborombon, the muddy mouth of the Rio Salado and other, smaller rivers of the pampa. The bay is rich with fish that come to feed here.

San Clemente del Tuyú has a sea aquarium, tennis courts, soccer fields and many other open-air sports facilities, as well as several well-equipped campsites. But the place is most popu-

A colorful fishing fleet.

lar among fishermen, who, starting in October, like to catch the *corvina negra* or *corvina rubia,* a delicacy used in soups and stews.

From San Clemente, the paved Provincial Road 11 runs straight south, coming first to **Las Toninas** and then **Santa Teresita**, the biggest town along this stretch of coast. **Costa del Este**, **Aguas Verdes**, **La Lucila del Mar**, **Costa Azul**, **San Bernardo** and **Mar del Ajó** are the other towns along this fairly developed northern stretch. Most visitors to this area come to swim, sun bathe and walk along the narrow beach beside the high sand dunes, but many others come to fish. One of the most popular pursuits is shark fishing, with catches reportedly ranging up to three feet (one meter). This, however, is simply for sport; when it comes to mealtime, most of these visiting fishermen retire to one of the area's countless tiny seafood restaurants, many of which specialize in Italian fare. South from Mar de Ajó, the beach becomes increasingly solitary. The spaces be-

tween settlements become wider, and one can find more stretches of isolated pristine shore.

Old wrecks and lighthouses: Along this part of the coast, one can see many old lighthouses (*faros*) made of iron and brick. One of these, **Faro San Antonio** lies north of San Clemente del Tuyú. Another is near Punta Medanos, at the southern tip of Cabo San Antonio, and still others can be found halfway to Mar del Plata (**Faro Querandi**), on the southern outskirts of Mar del Plata (**Faro Punta Mogotes**) and at Monte Hermoso.

Some of these towers are over a century old, and are worth a visit from both an architectural and historical point of view. Many of them have shared in the area's long and fascinating history of maritime adventures and misfortunes. In a walk along the beach one will frequently encounter the stranded and disintegrating hull of some old windjammer or steamer.

Pines and shade: Probably one of the most lovely of all the urban areas along

the Atlantida Argentina is the one that comprises Pinamar, Ostende, Valeria del Mar and Cariló.

Pinamar is a very fashionable spot. It is bordered by a pine forest, and the scent of the pines mixed with the salty sea air gives the town a bracing atmosphere. There are no sand dunes at Pinamar, which makes access to the beach easy, even by car. The town has a wide variety of sports facilities, including an attractive golf course amid the pines. Accommodations range from four-star establishments down to modest, inexpensive pensions. It should be noted that although hotels of all categories are available all year round, most people come for two weeks or a full month and therefore choose to rent a flat at prices which are much cheaper than that of the most humble pension. These apartments of one, two or three bedrooms may be rented on the spot, or in advance in Buenos Aires.

The greater Pinamar area includes **Ostende** and **Valeria del Mar**, where some very high dunes are to be found. A gambling casino, formerly located in Pinamar, is now south of Valeria. South of that, **Cariló** is a country club-style community dotted with elegant villas and shaded by pines. About 12 miles (20 km) south of Cariló lies **Villa Gesell**. It is especially popular with young people, due to its plethora of bars, discotheques and skating rinks. Villa Gesell also has several excellent campsites.

The main attractions between Gesell and Mar del Plata are the shady campsites at **Mar Chiquita** and **Santa Clara del Mar**, both located at some distance from the beach.

Pearl of the Atlantic: Shortly before **Mar del Plata**, the landscape changes dramatically. Approaching the city on the coastal Ruta Provincial 11, the high cliffs of Cabo Corrientes and the downtown skyscrapers built upon this rocky peninsula seem to grow from the sea like a fata morgana. It is a truly striking first impression. As one gets closer, secondary impressions should not disappoint the visitor, either.

Below: left and right, the girls of summer.

This city is proudly called *La Perla del Atlantico* (the Pearl of the Atlantic) by its half-million residents. Accommodations range from first class hotels to apartments available for short-term lease all year round. The city has well-groomed plazas, parks, seaside boulevards and several golf courses. Beyond the beaches and the sun, lies perhaps the biggest attraction for the city's two million summer visitors, the colossal **Casino** where one can try his luck at roulette, poker, *punta banca*, and a variety of other games.

Another major pastime in Mar del Plata is to see and be seen. All of fashionable Buenos Aires feels obliged to be seen here at least once a year. During the peak of the season, the boutiques and galleries of **Calle San Martín** and the adjacent streets bustle late into the night with the tanned and the beautiful.

A visit to Mar del Plata would not be complete without a sampling of a few of the area specialties. First, a visit to the fishing port, with its red and yellow boats along the quays is a must. A nest

of restaurants in the area serve good, fresh fare. Next, one must be sure to try one of the famed *alfajores marplatenses*. These biscuit sweets are filled with either chocolate or caramel, and are a favorite for afternoon tea. And lastly, the visitor should avail himself of the opportunity to buy well-made inexpensive woolens here. The sweaters, gloves and other items are made by the locals during the winter months.

Solitary beaches: From Mar del Plata, the coastal road runs past the Punta Mogotes lighthouse toward Miramar. The scenery along this 25-mile (40-km) stretch is completely different from that at the northern end of the Atlantida Argentina. Instead of dunes and sandy beaches, the sea is met by cliffs. The road runs along the very edge, offering the traveler a splendid view of the sea, and the spectacle of Mar del Plata disappearing into the distance.

Some smaller resorts line the road to **Miramar**, a rather quiet beachfront town with much less social life than Mar del Plata. However, Miramar does offer room for many outdoor sports like bicycling, horseback riding, tennis, jogging or just walking.

Between Miramar and **Necochea** the seaside resorts become sparser. In fact, along this 50-mile (80-km) of shore there are only three places with facilities for vacationers: **Mar del Sur**, **Centinela del Mar** and **Costa Bonita**.

Scarcer still are the developed beaches south of Necochea. **Claromeco**, about 93 miles (150 km) to the south, is one of the most attractive.

One place to be warmly recommended is **Monte Hermoso**, some 435 miles (700 km) south of Buenos Aires near Bahia Blanca. Visited by Darwin during his voyage on the *Beagle*, and since then well known for its wealth of fossils along the shore, it has a broad beach of fine, white sand, shady campsites and a venerable lighthouse. The peace and quiet of this site promise a relaxing getaway for the traveler.

It is here, at Monte Hermoso, that the Argentine vacation coast comes to an end.

Left, an afternoon's catch. Right, a stroll near the Mar del Plata casino.

THE TRANQUIL
CENTRAL SIERRAS

The province of Córdoba could in many respects be considered the heartland of Argentina. It lies about midway between the Andes and Buenos Aires and the Atlantic coast. Beyond geography, Córdoba represents much that Argentina is known for. Approaching Córdoba from the east, one will drive across miles and miles of the stunningly flat pampa before reaching the gentle waves of the central sierras. Along the open plains or in the hidden valleys one may stumble upon a variety of characteristically Argentine scenes: a vast herd of the country's famous grass-fed cattle, or an animated scene of gauchos branding cattle in a rough-hewn country paddock, or a farm specializing in the breeding and training of world class racing horses and polo ponies. Aside from the chance encounters, there is much that the traveler can set out to see and do here. The city of Córdoba holds some of Argentina's finest examples of colonial architecture, both secular and religious. Many of the area's quaint villages have resort facilities, and summer visitors have their choice among several culture and music festivals. One town of German immigrants even holds an Oktoberfest. The pace of life here is relaxed and the people are friendly. The area's other inhabitants range from the wily puma to the edible armadillo.

Preceding pages: church facade in Córdoba. Left, ceiling of the Córdoba cathedral.

CÓRDOBA'S COLONIAL CHARM

The city of Córdoba dates back to Argentina's colonial times. One of the oldest cities in the country, it was founded by Jeronimo Luis de Cabrera in 1573. Cabrera came from Santiago del Estero in the north, following the Dulce River, and settled his people by the Suquia River. It is interesting to note that when information about these new, not yet settled areas was recounted in Peru by the early adventurous surveyors, some of the characteristics that have made Córdoba touristically attractive were already mentioned. It was told that these lands had low mountains, plenty of fish in the many streams and rivers, an abundance of wild birds and animals (South American ostriches, deer, pumas, armadillos, otters, hares, partridges and much more) beautiful views, and weather like Spain.

In these few words lay the allure, the attractiveness, the charm of the Córdoba region, the same charm which draws Argentines to visit the hundreds of little towns, inns, and campgrounds every year.

When Cabrera arrived in the Córdoba region in 1573, it was populated by three main Indian groups; the Sanavirones in the northeast, the Comechingones in the west and the Pampas in the plains.

Though a few confrontations did take place between Spanish and Indians, the latter were labeled "peaceful and cooperative" by the Spaniards, this commentary dictated by the contrast of these groups with other very bellicose tribes of the northwest, south and east of the country.

The Pampas were nomadic groups who roamed the plains (now called pampas). The Sanavirones and Comechingones lived in caves or crude adobe houses surrounded by thorny bushes and cactus fences. They were organized in tribes led by *caciques* (chiefs) and their subsistence was hunt-

The cathedral exterior.

ing and gathering and agriculture. Their religion centered around the sun and the moon. There were three or four main languages and many dialects in the area.

There is no consensus as to the original population numbers but it is estimated that there were between 12,000 and 30,000 Indians in the area at the time of the Spanish Conquest.

The discovery by the Spaniards of metal sources and stone for quarrying in the mountains more than justified in their eyes and in the eyes of Spain the foundation of a new city.

One hundred years after its foundation, Córdoba manifested the characteristics which are still seen as its trademark. The little village had flourished religiously and culturally. By that time it boasted an astonishing number of churches, chapels and convents erected by the Jesuits, the Franciscans, the Carmelites and others; it had a Jesuit-run university, the oldest in the country, erected in 1621 (now called the Universidad Nacional de Córdoba); the local economy was supported by a variety of agricultural products (corn, wheat, beans, potatoes, pears, peaches, apricots and grapes) and by an extensive and ever-growing wild cattle herd.

The tree: In Córdoba one finds the stark juxtaposition of the impossibly flat pampas with the rolling sierras, the first mountain chain one encounters moving west towards the Andes. As one approaches across the plain, the hills appear as great waves breaking on a beach.

There are three chains of mountains in the western part of the province of Córdoba, all of which run parallel to each other, from north to south. They are the Sierras Chicas in the east, the Sierras Grandes in the center and the Sierras del Pocho (which turn into the Sierras de Guasapampa) in the west. The highest peak in the province is Champaqui, which reaches a height of 9,517 feet (2,884 meters).

The Sierras de Córdoba are neither as high nor as extensive as many of the other mountain formations east of the

The Jesuit church, with university students in the foreground.

Andes. Their easy accessibility, coupled with their beauty, their dry weather, magnificent views, good roads, and the myriad of small rivers and water courses have established Córdoba's reputation as an ideal spot for rest and recuperation.

Most of the rain falls in the summer and is heavier in the eastern section where the hills look very green and lush. In truth the vegetation on these hills is mostly of the *monte* type, bushes and low thorny thickets. Towards the piedmont of the eastern hills, larger trees grow in greater abundance. Among these trees, the friendly algarrobo deserves special mention. From prehistoric times up to the present it has been used by the local populations as a shade-giving tree, as a fruit tree and as a source of wood for fence posts and for fire. It is also one of the trees most resistant to drought, and because of all these virtues, it is sometimes simply called "the tree" by the locals.

Bird songs: The fauna of the region is not as rich as when the Spaniards first arrived, but is still plentiful enough in some hidden areas to support seasonal hunting. Pumas or American lions still roam the hills but are few and isolated. Guanacos are not a common sight around most of the vacation resorts but can be seen toward the higher western areas. Hares abound and are hunted and eaten, as are partridges and vizcachas. Several types of snakes can be found, including rattlesnakes and coral snakes, but the steady invasion of most places in the mountains by residents and visitors has decreased their numbers. Foxes are also occasionally seen. The countless species of birds in the area are a source of attraction and delight for many people.

Córdoba has a continental climate. Though the summer, with its hot days and cool nights, is the favorite season for most visitors, the winter is not without its charm. Because the rains are seasonal, occurring in spring and summer, the views change dramatically.

Across the flats: The easiest access to the city and province of Córdoba is

One of Córdoba's central walkways.

from the south and east. Leaving from Buenos Aires, the visitor has the choice of traveling by plane, bus or train.

The train service (Ferrocarriles Mitre) is comfortable, especially the Pullman section or the overnight sleeping compartments, but it is the slowest form of transportation. The buses are faster, offer a wider variety of schedules and are all new, spacious and comfortable units. There are several companies that make the Buenos Aires-Córdoba run with options to stop in Rosario and a few other large towns (the "express" takes about 9 to 9 1/2 hours). The two principal airlines, Aerolineas Argentinas and Austral, have several daily flights to Córdoba which take about an hour.

If the trip from Buenos Aires is made by land, there are two main ways to go to Córdoba. The shortest is via Rosario, a city of 1,000,000 inhabitants located 185 miles (300 km) from Buenos Aires, using Route 9. The other choice is using Route 8, a slightly longer but quieter and quainter road. In both cases, the visitor will pass through miles and miles of pampas (plain, flat and very rich terrain) dotted with small towns and huge plots planted with corn, wheat, soya and sunflower. Everywhere there are enormous herds of cattle (Aberdeen Angus, Hereford, Holando-argentina) and horses. The roads are quite good and offer the basic commodities (hotels, small restaurants, cafés, gas stations) in almost every town along the way. Córdoba can also be easily reached from the west (either Santiago de Chile or Mendoza) by plane and bus and from the north (Santiago del Estero, Salta, Tucumán, Jujuy) by plane, bus and train.

Spanish grid: The city of **Córdoba** is one of the largest in the country, with a population of approximately 1,000,000. The basis of its economy is agriculture, cattle and the automotive industry. Its key location in the country, at the crossroads of many of the main routes, established its early importance and fostered its rapid growth. Although Buenos Aires, with its excessive

The Candonga church, in the Córdoba hills.

absorption of power and people, has always tended to overshadow the rest of the country, Córdoba and its zone of influence is the strongest nucleus of resistance found in the vast interior of Argentina.

Córdoba, like most Spanish-settled cities, was designed with a rectangular grid of streets, with the main plaza (in this case Plaza San Martín), the cathedral and the main city buildings in the center of the town. It is therefore easy for the traveler to find on a map the different sites of historical, architectural or artistic interest located within the city.

Because many of the early buildings of Córdoba were either religious or educational, time and progress have spared a great number of them, giving visitors and residents a rich treasure-trove of colonial chapels, churches, convents and public buildings amid the modern surroundings.

The city offers a series of information pamphlets for visitors and these can be obtained at the different tourist offices (main office is located at Tucuman 25, Córdoba).

Church circuit: The religous *circuito* (circuits being the different and usually recommended tours) covers most of the oldest colonial religious buildings. Either alone or with a guide the traveler can visit:

1. **The cathedral**: Though its site was decided early in 1577, the final consecration took place in 1784, after collapses, interruptions and changes. These delays account for the many artistic styles visible in the architecture. As it has been described by the architect J. Roca, the cathedral has a classic Renaissance portico and a baroque dome and steeple, with influences of indigenous origin. A large wrought iron gate completes the picture.

The interior of the church is divided into three big naves, separated from each other by wide, thick columns (which replaced the smaller original columns as those were not strong enough to support the building). Many of the murals were sketched and exe-

A river through the sierras.

cuted under the direction of Emilio Caraffa. Manuel Cardenosa and Augusto Orlandi did the enlargements.

The bright stained-glass windows with religous motifs suffuse the interior light with beauty and warmth.

The main altar, made of silver, is from the 19th century; it replaced the original baroque altar which is now in the church of Tulumba.

The cathedral is located across from **Plaza San Martín**.

2. **The Jesuit complex**: This complex is located on the spot where there was originally a small shrine, dating from 1589. It is located on Caseros Street, two blocks from the cathedral.

The group of buildings is made up of the church, the Domestic Chapel and the living quarters. Originally it also encompassed the Colegio Maximo and the university, both of which are now national institutions.

The church dates to the 17th century. One of its outstanding details is an arch, made of Paraguayan cedar and in the shape of an inverted boat's hull, com-

pletely fitted with wooden pegs. The church interior is lined with cedar beams and the roof is made up of beams and tiles. The tiles were joined with a special glue, which after 300 years is still tightly weatherproof. Many of the baroque altars, including the cedar altar, date to the 18th century and the Carrara marble work on the walls is from the 19th century. The paintings of the apostles in the main nave are by the Córdoba painter Genaro Perez.

The Domestic Chapel (with its entrance on Caseros Street) is also from the 17th century. Here, too, the ceiling was constructed of wooden beams, and canes tied with rawhide, which were placed between the beams and then plastered and covered with painted cloth.

The Jesuits and their work occupy a special place in the history of Argentina and the rest of South America, up to the point of their expulsion in 1768 by the Spanish Crown. Córdoba has its share of their legacy, and for those interested in Jesuit lore and work, visits to the

The golf club at La Cumbre.

Santa Ana Chapel in the city, and the towns of **Alta Gracia**, **Colonia Caroya**, **Estancia La Candelaria** and **Jesus Maria** are recommended.

3. **The Church and Monastery of the Carmelite Nuns** (also called Las Teresas) was founded in the early-17th century. It was heavily renovated during the 18th century and many of the buildings date to this later period. The main altar has a large baroque sculpture of Saint Teresa of Jesus and the wooden choir is an example of fine woodwork. In the monastery there is a religious art museum, in which many of the objects once belonging to the cathedral are now exhibited. The entrance is on Independencia Street and the complex is located opposite the cathedral.

4. **The Church and Convent of Saint Francis**: The land for the church was given to the Franciscan Order by the founder of the city, Jeronimo L. de Cabrera. The first chapel was built in 1575; this original chapel and a second one which replaced it no longer exist. The current structure was initiated in 1796 and finished in 1813. Within the complex, a room named *Salon de Profundis* belongs to the original construction. With stone walls and extensive artisanal woodwork, this Church constitutes a unique example of *mudejar* art in the city.

The church is located at the corner of Buenos Aires and entre Rios Streets and is only two and a half blocks from the cathedral.

5. **The La Merced Basilica**: Located in the corner of 25 de Mayo and Rivadavia, only three blocks from the cathedral, the present building was finished in 1826 over foundations from the 1600s.

The main altar, executed in 1890 by the artist Antonio Font, and the polychrome wooden pulpit from the 18th century are two of the outstanding attractions of the interior.

Secular sites: Among the public buildings, the **Cabildo** or City Hall, by the cathedral, is worth visiting. It is now the headquarters of the police force. The arches, with colonial lamps, and

Alta Gracia's old Jesuit complex.

the spacious galleries give one a good feel for colonial architecture.

The balconies of the Cabildo were reserved for seating authorities, in cases of executions, public meetings, bull fights and other major events in the life of the old city.

Also worth mentioning is the **Sobremonte Historical Museum**, an outstanding example of colonial residential architecture. It hosts a very complete collection of Indian and Gaucho artifacts, old musical instruments, ceramics and furniture.

It is located on Rosario de Santa Fe and Ituizango Streets, three blocks from the cathedral.

Near the cathedral, on the Via Peatonal, the traveler can take a break in the cultural tour and enjoy the many cafés or do some window shopping in the innumerable boutiques that dot this downtown area.

Village fests: Once the city of Córdoba has been explored, a trip to the surrounding countryside is highly recommended for those with the time. The local tourism authorities have laid out a number of routes which will lead the dedicated traveler up into the mountains, along paved and unpaved roads to lakes, streams, campsites and spectacular views. While these routes can be done by bus, a car is necessary to really explore the area.

One of the favorite routes, the *Camino de La Punilla*, extends north from the city of Córdoba, through a valley toward **Cruz del Eje**. This route passes through or near most of the small resort towns of the region.

The first stop is **Carlos Paz**, famous for its night life, its casinos, restaurants and clubs, and sports activities centered around Lake San Roque. This town surprises the visitor with its handsome chalets, comfortable hotels and streets packed day and night with tourists (if one visits during the high season).

Eleven miles (18 km) directly north of Carlos Paz is **Cosquin**, a quaint village famous for its Argentine and Latin American folk music and dance festival in the second half of January. Another

nine miles (15 km) north along the narrow but well-paved road brings one to the village of **La Falda**, which holds a festival celebrating the folk music of Argentina's immigrants, along with the Tango, in the first week of February. During other times of the year, golfing, swimming, hiking, horseback riding, and sailing can be enjoyed in these and neighboring towns. Numerous small hotels and pensions are available throughout the region. Students are welcome at the University of Córdoba's vacation center at **Vaquerias**, a short distance outside of La Falda.

About seven miles (11 km) further north lies **La Cumbre**. This town boasts excellent trout fishing from November to April (as do many other towns in the area) as well as facilities for golf, tennis and swimming. Its altitude of 3,768 feet (1,142 meters) makes the climate extremely pleasant and for that reason, as well as for its serenity, it has become known as a writers' haven.

Another nine miles (15 km) along the same road (now one has traveled 66 miles/106 km from Córdoba) will take the visitor to **Capilla del Monte**, a town which celebrates its Spanish Festival in February. One can enjoy hiking, rock climbing, swimming and serenity in this town in the heart of the sierras.

Leaving this northward route and returning to Córdoba, one can head south along the *Camino de los grandes lagos* or *Camino de Comechingones*. This road takes one along the edge of the pampa, parallel to the sierra.

Halfway to Alta Gracia, a strange and unexpected monument looms out of the pampa. This 100 feet (30 meter) high "tomb stone" was built by Baron Bisa in the shape of an airplane wing to commemmorate the tragic death of his wife, Miriam Stephenson, an early Argentine pilot who died in a crash on that spot.

Taba tossing: Arriving in **Alta Gracia**, one finds a charming, prosperous town which welcomes tourists but does not live off them, so one is not overwhelmed by the kinds of crowds or tourist establishments found in Carlos Paz. Life seems to move at a very slow pace here, with shops closing at 12:30 for lunch and opening again at 4:00. There are a number of modest but clean hotels and several decent restaurants. One of the main attractions is the **Jesuit Church and Monastery**, veritable jewels of colonial architecture.

A short excursion into the hills behind Alta Gracia toward **La Isla**, on the **Anizacate River**, takes one over a passable dirt road, past small farms and spectacular views of the beautiful river. With luck, somewhere along this route, or another in the Sierra region, the visitor just might come upon a group of locals branding their cattle and be invited to eat a barbecue (*asado*), drink strong red wine and throw the *taba* (a gaucho game of chance played with the left knee bone of a horse) with some rough looking but friendly country people. Traditionally, when the meal is over, a simple gourd is packed with *mate* (Argentine green tea) and drunk through a silver straw with the same seriousness that New York bankers partake of their cognac after a meal.

Leaving Alta Gracia behind and returning to the main route, one continues on south and enters the Sierras on a well-paved, but winding road. Twelve picturesque miles (20 km) later the **Los Molinos Dam and Lake** appear. This is a favorite spot for the people of the region to practice various aquatic sports. One can eat a decent meal overlooking the dam, high above the lake.

Another 12 miles (20 km) brings one to **Villa General Belgrano**, a town purportedly founded by seamen from the ill-fated Graf Spee, who chose not to return to Germany. The town has a decidedly German character, with its charming chalets and well-kept gardens. As might be expected, the town celebrates an Oktoberfest during the first week of that month. This town and neighboring **Santa Rosa de Calamuchita** are pleasant to visit any time of the year.

For the visitor who wants to stay for an extended period, the Secretaria de Turismo in the city of Córdoba provides excellent detailed maps of these and other routes around the region.

MESOPOTAMIAN MEANDERINGS

As with everywhere else in Argentina, the distances in the northeast are quite large. Here, the major tourist attractions are few and far between. But the two principal sites it does have should not be missed: these are the impressive and thundering falls at Iguazú and the Jesuit ruins at San Ignacio. A hurried visitor may wish to fly to these spots and skip the rest. But for those with more time, the journey overland can be quite worthwhile, providing the relaxation that usually comes with crossing wide open spaces slowly. The best way to do this is in a private car, so one can tarry in selected spots, but public transportation is quite extensive and reliable. Along the way, in the slow-paced and friendly towns, there are churches and modest museums to see. In between the towns, across a variety of terrains, there are national parks containing abundant wildlife. Or one might wish to break up the trip with a visit to a citrus farm or a yerba *mate* plantation, to sample a gourd filled with Argentina's national drink.

Preceding pages: a young dandy with his mount; by the shores of a lagoon. Left, the thunderous veils at Iguazú.

RIVER JOURNEY TO THE NORTHEAST

A tourist can no longer ride the river-boats that used to ply the Paraná between Buenos Aires and Iguazú. The boats have been replaced by the faster road, rail and air connections.

From 1550 to about 1920 the rivers of northeast Argentina were the safest, cheapest and best way to see the country. For more than 350 years, vessels navigated the rivers, carrying goods, settlers, explorers, officials, and in later years, tourists.

Phantom steamer: Everything of any interest in northeast Argentina is on or close to the rivers, so one approach to getting to know this area, on paper at least, would be to take a phantom paddle-steamer and use the river-system to explore this corner of the country. On this hypothetical journey one will embark in Buenos Aires.

Soon after setting sail, the vessel will have to find the navigable mouth of the Paraná, as the river splits up into many channels when it joins the River Plate, forming a huge delta. Suburban **Tigre** is the gateway to this maze of waterways lined with weekend houses, each with its own small jetty. Here people have a restful time fishing, boating or just getting away from the nearby metropolis. The Delta has a life of its own from Mondays to Fridays: there are permanent residents, fishermen, citrus growers and pulp-wood producers, all of whom lead the gentler and slower-paced life of river dwellers. Hotels and guest-houses are available.

Upriver, **Zárate** is the site of a huge road and rail bridge complex, completed in 1979, which at last joined Mesopotamia to Buenos Aires and made obsolete the double ferry connection which was susceptible to interruption by flood and drought water levels and was a fearful hassle.

On then to **Rosario**, a large grain port which was once the second city in the country, though Rosarinos may still debate the "once" bit. It is a large city, with a population of about one million. The turn-of-the-century and art deco architecture in the center of town gives some idea of the history of Rosario. There is one feature of minor interest, the **Monument to the Flag**, which consists of a sweep of steps, an obelisk backed by a series of arches, and an eternal flame.

Heroic sacrifice: Some 20 miles upstream, on the western shore, is the **San Carlos Monastery** at **San Lorenzo**, built at the end of the 18th century and famous for being the site of a battle in the war of independence. Here the Argentine hero San Martín was pinned under his fallen horse. A Sargeant Cabral saved him, but in so doing was fatally wounded. The tree under which he died still stands as a symbol of self-sacrifice.

Rosario is in the province of **Santa Fe**. It is by far the most important city in that province, but it is not the capital, a fact that Rosarinos dislike intensely. This honor goes to **Santa Fe**, a city some way upstream and the next port of

call. First founded in the early 1500s, somewhat north of its present location, it was lost early on to disease and Indian harrassment. The new city was founded in 1573. Today Santa Fe is a pleasant provincial town, steeped in tradition, with all the amenities and little pretense. The ancient but beautiful church of **San Francisco** is surrounded by monastic buildings which house the province's **Historical Museum**.

The floods of 1983 partially demolished one feature of special interest—the suspension bridge built by Eiffel in the mid-19th century. It is hoped this historic structure will soon be restored.

From Santa Fe there is a tunnel under the Paraná River to the town of **Paraná**, capital of the province of Entre Ríos. The eastern shores of the river are along a bank 60 to 100 feet (18 to 30 meters) high. Paraná has fine parks, lovely buildings and churches, and views across the river. Inland, the undulating landscape is dotted with woods of the native acacias and cut by smaller rivers and streams. Santa Fe, on the other shore, sits in lowlands as flat as a pancake, surrounded by lakes, marshes and rivers. Its hinterland is all fenced into square fields, with regularly spaced towns and villages.

Jungle ruins: Upstream near **Cayastá**, on the low bank of a small branch of the river, hidden by vegetation of centuries' growth, old Santa Fe lay in its sleep of oblivion until rediscovered earlier this century. Slowly and gently it is being uncovered. Though it was a small town and all built of adobe (stone of any kind is hard to find in the pampas), there were something like seven churches or religious orders represented here. Today, metal sheds protect the remains from the elements, and boardwalks allow only limited access to the public.

Between **Reconquista** and **Goya** there is still a ferry in operation, and for those interested, the ride across gives one a very good feel for the entire stretch of the Paraná river. It takes from four to six hours and goes along a network of waterways, wending between

The Jesuit ruins at San Ignacio de Miní.

162

islands with wooded shores.

Carnival color: The cities of **Resistencia** and **Corrientes** are linked by a huge bridge. Following the rule of most of the river, Corrientes, on the east bank, sits high, and Resistencia is amongst the swamps. Neither is high on the tourist's agenda, but Corrientes does have a Carnival celebration of note, with floats, music, drums, dancing, fancy-dress and all. This takes place during the last days before Lent, so consult a calendar, as the date for the feast varies.

Inland from Corrientes, the small town of **San Luis del Palmar** has kept its flavor of colonial times and is well worth a visit.

Just past Corrientes one reaches the confluence with the Paraguay river. It is about here, at **Paso de la Patria**, that fishermen from all over the world congregate to try for Dorado, the "fightingest fish in the world." Lodging, boats, guides and equipment are available from July to November.

Incongruous and totally out of the

After a rain in the town of Colón.

blue, the huge church dome at **Itatí** can be seen for up to 15 miles (24 km) across the plains. This dome is said to be the "most something" after St. Peter's. It tops the basilica where many pilgrims converge to venerate the miraculous Virgin of Itatí, housed in the adjoining shrine. She has quite a following. For sheer bad taste it is hard to beat the local *santerías*, which sell plaster statues of the virgin, saints and other religious articles, all gaudy, all grotesque, and all in the cheapest souvenir tradition.

At **Yaciretá** and **Apipe Islands** one can see the work that has started on yet another dam of major proportions. This joint Argentine-Paraguayan project will take a long time to complete. It could prove to be another Aswan, resulting in ecological damage.

Just southwest of **Posadas**, the character of the river changes; the wide and shallow sweeps change to a boxed-in area between steep and high banks in a rolling countryside. From here on up, the river cuts through a basalt flow originating some 800 miles (1,290 km) distant in Brazil. Here even the soil changes; the red lateritic soil of Misiones province deceives one into thinking it is quite fertile, as the vegetation here is very lush. This is, however, a complete hoax, as the vegetation provides for its own growth in the constant fall of leaf litter.

Jesuit missions: **Posadas** is the provincial capital of Misiones, very provincial, with some 150,000 inhabitants and nothing very much to attract the visitor. A bridge has recently been inaugurated which crosses the river to Encarnación in Paraguay. On certain days there is a Paraguayan market operating on the Costanera by the river.

The Jesuits were the real pioneers in Misiones; indeed, it is from their work that the province gets its name. They arrived early in the 17th century, and proceeded to settle and convert the local Guaraní natives. They soon began to be pushed around, first by slave traders in the area and then by the Iberian governments, first Portugal, then Spain. They were finally expelled in

1777 and left behind them the mission buildings and lots of unprotected and slightly Christian souls.

There are 12 known mission ruins in Misiones, but first amongst them is **San Ignacio Miní**. Started early in the 17th century, it was by no means safe from slave raids from the Portuguese colony. At the peak of its existence, it housed some 4,000 to 5,000 Indians. San Iganacio is the most cleaned-up and restored of all the sites. It is best to amble around the ruins at dawn or dusk, when one can be alone and when the light plays wonders on the red stone. It is then that one can commune with the spirit of what was intended in the name of humanity. The surviving Indians are worse off today than they were 200 years ago.

Muddy waters: It is a sad reflection of the short-sightedness of man that all the streams which run into the upper Paraná, save one, are muddy. Clear-cutting, lack of soil protection and the use of slash-and-burn techniques are all chronic problems, and have led to severe ecological deterioration in the area. The Paraná, too, suffers from these ravages in its own headwaters.

Some of the villages of Misiones have a flavor peculiar unto themselves. Wooden houses and churches are made from a mixture of local materials and ideas brought from northern Europe, whence most of the settlers came. Immigrants from Germany, Poland, Switzerland, Sweden and France are settled in this area. This accounts for the fair-haired people seen everywhere.

One finally disembarks in **Puerto Iguazú**, the head point of navigation, now that the Itaipú Dam has closed off the Paraná and since the Iguazú River has its own natural barrier. This small town is fully geared for tourism, with a number of hotels, restaurants, taxis, exchange houses and so on. As a town, it has not much to save it from mediocrity, but it just happens to be the nearest settlement to the **Iguazú National Park** and the world-famous **waterfalls**.

The Devil's Throat: Amidst a spec-

The vortex called the Devil's Throat.

tacular jungle setting, the **Iguazú Falls** lie on the Iguazú River, which runs along the border between Brazil and Argentina. It is said about this magnificent site that Argentina provides the falls and Brazil enjoys the view. Certainly the 600 yards (550 meters) of walks on the Brazilian side give the visitor a panoramic and marvelous view of most of the falls but this is at something of a distance. On the Argentine side, the falls can be approached, viewed, felt and experienced from a number of angles. The lower falls circuit is perhaps the most beautiful thousand-yard walk in the world and should be done clockwise. The trip to **Isla San Martín** is another great experience, for it too allows one to can get right into the heart of the spectacle.

By far the most magnificent walk is the one right across the upper river, from Puerto Canoas to the **Garganta del Diablo** (The Devil's Throat), where the water plunges the entire 240 feet (70 meters) off the basalt flow into the cauldron below. Late afternoon till dusk is the best time to see the Garganta, both for the lighting at that hour and to see the flocks of birds that swoop through the billowing mists on their way back to their nests for the night.

The park has many trails and roads on which one can explore the sub-tropical rain forest surrounding the falls. If one is attentive and lucky, there's a good possibility of seeing some of the exotic wildlife that inhabits the area. At the **Visitors' Center** one can get all the information about the many things to do. The Center distributes lists of the local mammals, birds and plants to aid you in your exploration. The Center also offers slide shows, and the small museum has specimens of some of the animals you might not have time or luck enough to see.

The International Hotel is on the premises of the park, and offers easy access to all the sites. Las Orquideas Hotel lies right outside the park, and there are other accommodations in town.

The Iguazú River is some 600 miles

(900 km) long above the falls and has been dammed. The clearing of the forests in the watershed permits the immediate runoff of the rain, so the river floods, runs dry, runs dirty, 'pulses' (due to industrial energy demands Mondays to Fridays) and, in general, behaves in a way unnatural to the trained eye. But the natural setting is such as to offset any disappointments. The greatest shame for a visitor would be to stay for too short a time; a minimum of three days is recommended for those keen on nature.

Bitter tea: To return to Buenos Aires on the Uruguay River would be impossible, due to the river's rapids. The first obstacle is the **Moconá Falls**, almost inaccessible overland without the mounting of a small-scale expedition.

There are two towns of interest in the southwest of Misiones. **Oberá** has settlers from many European countries vying with each other to improve the clean and neat town.

Apostoles is the capital of the yerba *mate* industry. The Yerba *Mate* tree is

of the Holly genus (Ilex), though there the similarity ends. The leaves of the tree are used by the people of many South American countries to make a strong tea.

The next place worth a visit is **Yapeyú**, originally a Jesuit mission and later a Spanish garrison burnt to the ground by the Portuguese in 1817. Its claim to fame is that the Argentine hero and liberator, San Martín, was born here. His father was a Spanish officer stationed at the garrison. The village has a civic consciousness unknown elsewhere in the country and is kept as "historic" as possible. An ACA (Automobile Club of Argentina) Motel provides accommodations.

Concordia is a large rural city, and is the center of the citrus industry. When the Salto Grande Dam just north of Concordia was planned, the Uruguay River flowed clear, but by the time it was finished the river had become muddy due to deforestation. There is a question as to how long the dam will remain operative; it now effectively serves as a sedimentation tank.

The **Palmar National Park**, half way between Concordia and Colón is worth a visit, but overnight facilities are limited to camping sites in the park and a motel in **Ubajay**, the nearby village. There are a number of interesting walks to be taken in the park, and some rare species of animals to be seen. The wide grasslands of the pampa are here dotted with palm trees, for which the park is named.

Colón is an old meatpacking town. Not too far away is the **Palacio de San José**, the residence of General Urquiza, who is famous for having ousted Rosas, the 19th-century dictator. The house is maintained as a National Historic Monument; its opulence has faded and the paint is peeling but it is impressive.

Just before the rail and road bridge at **Brazo Largo**, which crosses over to **Zárate**, there is a side road east to **Paranacito**, a good place to get a feel for the delta terrain, marshes and all.

A little down-river, but out of sight, is the city of Buenos Aires, where one would disembark.

Left, the San José Palace, former residence of President Urquiza. Right, park ranger at El Palmar.

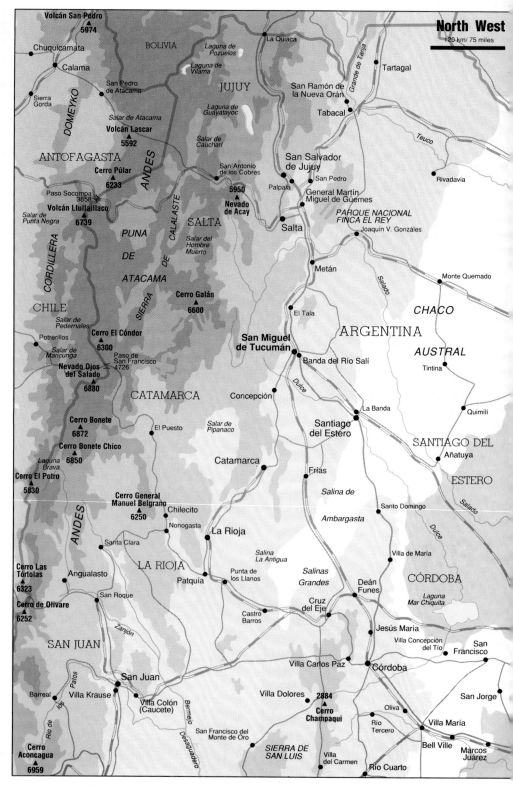

Volcán San Pedro
▲
5974

Chuquicámata

Calama

BOLIVIA

Laguna de
Pozuelos

La Quiaca

Grande de Tarija

Tartagal

San Pedro
de Atacama

Sierra
Gorda

JUJUY

Laguna de
Vilama

San Ramón de
la Nueva Orán

Salar de Atacama

Volcán Lascar
▲
5592

Laguna de
Guayatayoc

Tabacal

Teuco

ANTOFAGASTA

ANDES

Cerro Púlar
▲
6233

San Antonio
de los Cobres

Salar de
Cauchari

San Salvador
de Jujuy

San Pedro

Palpala

Rivadavia

Paso Socompa
3858
▲

Volcán Llullaillaco
▲
6739

Salar de
Punta Negra

CORDILLERA

PUNA

DE

ATACAMA

SIERRA

DE

CALALASTE

▲
5950
Nevado
de Acay

General Martín
Miguel de Güemes

SALTA

Salar del
Hombre
Muerto

Salta

PARQUE NACIONAL
FINCA EL REY

Joaquín V. Gonzáles

CHILE

Cerro Galán
▲
6600

Metán

Salado

Monte Quemado

Salar de
Pedernales

Potrerillos

Cerro El Cóndor
▲
6300

Salar de
Mancunga

Paso de
San Francisco
4726

El Tala

CHACO

ARGENTINA

AUSTRAL

Nevado Ojos
del Salado
▲
6880

CATAMARCA

Salar de
Pipanaco

San Miguel
de Tucumán

Banda del Río Salí

Tintina

Cerro Bonete
▲
6872

El Puesto

Concepción

Dulce

La Banda

Quimílí

Cerro Bonete Chico
▲
6850

Laguna
Brava

Catamarca

Santiago
del Estero

SANTIAGO DEL

Añatuya

Cerro El Potro
▲
5830

Frías

Salina de

ESTERO

Salado

Cerro General
Manuel Belgrano
▲
6250

Chilecito

Santo Domingo

Nonogasta

La Rioja

Ambargasta

Santa Clara

Cerro Las
Tórtolas
▲
6323

Angualasto

ANDES

Salina
La Antigua

Villa de María

San Roque

LA RIOJA

Patquía

Punta de
los Llanos

Salinas
Grandes

Deán
Funes

CÓRDOBA

Cerro de Olivare
▲
6252

Zanjón

Cruz
del Eje

Laguna
Mar Chiquita

Castro
Barros

Jesús María

Villa Concepción
del Tío

San
Francisco

SAN JUAN

Palos

San Juan

Villa Carlos Paz

Córdoba

Barreal

Villa Krause

Villa Colón
(Caucete)

Bermejo

Villa Dolores

2884
▲
Cerro
Champaqui

Oliva

Villa María

San Jorge

Rio de

San Roque

San Francisco del
Monte de Oro

Desaguadero

SIERRA DE
SAN LUIS

Rio
Tercero

Bell Ville

Marcos
Juárez

Cerro
Aconcagua
▲
6959

Villa
del Carmen

Río Cuarto

COLOR AND HISTORY:
THE MAGNIFICENT NORTHWEST

The northwest of Argentina is in large part a desert, and is reminiscent of desert terrains in many other countries. Those who have been to the southwest of the United States may find many similarities; Hispanic culture has left a strong mark here, and one can see adobe homes and modest churches in nearly every community, and the remains of pre-Hispanic culture are everywhere. Variegated barren hills rise all around, large cacti dot the landscape and the deep blue of the sky is only occasionally interrupted by clouds. There are a number of places in the region that don't fit into this category at all, and the scenery ranges from jungle gardens to icy Andean peaks, but wherever you go in the northwest, there's always something interesting to do or see. For those not too anxious to bustle about, the northwest is the perfect area in which to pick a town and settle in for a few days. Here you can sit out on a sunny patio, kick up your feet, munch on *salteñas* and quaff down a few cold bottles of the excellent local beer.

Preceding pages: the church of El Carmen, in Salta; youthful bravado in Casabindo, Jujuy. The bull is spared in this traditional ceremony.

ANCIENT SETTLEMENTS

From a scenic, archaeological, historical, and even geological viewpoint, Northwest Argentina forms a fairly uniform territory presently known as the NOA (Nor-Oeste Argentino). It comprises the provinces of Jujuy, Salta, Tucumán, Santiago del Estero, Catamarca and La Rioja, though the latter provinces are occasionally considered as part of the Cuyo region.

The homogeneity of this vast, largely arid region can perhaps be best understood by taking a glimpse at its pre-Hispanic population. While the wide Patagonian plains and the undulated grasslands of the pampas and Mesopotamia were mostly roamed by nomadic fruit collectors and game hunters, or even fishermen, the NOA has been inhabited for perhaps more than 10,000 years by farmers and animal herders.

This evolution was made possible thanks to the countless rivers and streams which irrigate the valleys of the region. This abundance of water allowed for the development of prosperous permanent settlements, and sometimes extensive cities, whose well-preserved ruins can still be seen along the *Precordillera* (the foothills of the Andes), from La Rioja in the south up north to the *Puna* (high plateau) in Salta and Jujuy. Pre-Hispanic *pucarás* (fortified cities) like Tilcara, Tastil and Quilmes are but some of the dozens of aboriginal towns which bear the attributes of a fairly high architectural design. These sites, though not capable of matching the remains of the Aztecs, Mayas and Incas, still impress the visitor with many surprising, unique and unforgettable features.

Moon Valley: A visit to polychromatic Northwest Argentina should by all means start with two remarkable natural monuments near the border between San Juan and La Rioja provinces: the *Valle de la Luna* (Moon Valley) and the Talampaya Canyon. Both excursions can be made by bus,

beginning in the provincial capitals of either San Juan or La Rioja.

The **Valle de la Luna** is a large natural depression where constant erosion by wind and water through millennia has sculptured a series of sandstone formations of strange shapes and an abundance of colors.

Beyond its beauty, the Valle de la Luna has great geological and palaeontological significance. In prehistoric times (even before the birth of the Andes) this area was covered by an immense lake. Around this, during the triassic period, a rich fauna and flora thrived. A six-foot (two-meter) long reptile, the Dicinodonte, was one of the most typical specimens. In all, 63 different species of fossilized animals have been found and described by palaeontologists.

The small towns of **San Agustín del Valle Fértil**, to the south, **Patquía**, to the east, and **Villa Unión**, to the west, are ideally suited as base camps for those who intend to explore the remote past of the planet.

Pictographs and petroglyphs: Talampaya lies about 50 miles (80 km) west of the provincial road that runs between Patquía and Villa Unión. Although palaeontologically not as significant as the Valle de la Luna, this impressive gorge, with cliffs towering to more than 480 feet (145 meters), was occupied by pre-Hispanic man. Uncounted rock paintings and engravings (pictographs and petroglyphs), including a carving of a human foot with six toes, offer an interesting archaeological contrast to the impressive geological nature of the canyon. The surrounding cliffs harbor dozens of condor nests.

Nearby **Villa Unión** offers the chance to sample the exquisite white wines of the region (the homemade *patero* is especially good). From this town one can make an excursion to **Vinchina**, which has an old water mill and a strange, multicolored, ten-pointed star built by the natives as a ritual site. One can also visit **Jagüe**, a tiny hamlet craddled at the foot of the giant **Bonete Volcano** and situated on the old muletrack which connects the green meadows on the Argentina side with the Chilean mining towns in the southern Atamarca Desert.

Another place well worth a stopover is **Chilecito**. Connected to Villa Unión by the tortuous and colorful **Cuesta de Miranda** pass, this small town lies on the eastern slopes of the majestic Famatina range. Chilecito's attractions include its excellent wines, the very old chapel of Los Sarmientos, a good hotel (Hosteria ACA), two museums and a pleasant climate.

Salt flats and volcanoes: From San Juan, frequent and comfortable bus services carry the visitor to **La Rioja**. This bustling provincial capital has ancient churches, among them the oldest in Argentina (Santo Domingo, built in 1623), and two interesting folkloric and archaeological museums.

A little farther to the north, **Catamarca** offers surprising geographical and historical highlights. Catamarca is a province with the greatest altitude differences imaginable; toward Córdoba and Santiago del Estero in the east, the vast **Salinas Grandes salt flats** are barely 1,300 feet (400 meters) above sea level, while in the west, near the Argentine-Chilean border, the **Ojos del Salado Volcano** reaches the vertiginous height of 22,869 feet (6,930 meters), making it the highest volcano in the world.

Of particular interest for the tourist are the archaeological and historical museums at **San Fernando del Valle de Catamarca**, the provincial capital. Smaller museums are to be found in **Belén**, **Andalgalá**, **Tinogasta** and **Santa María**. These old Indian settlements have more contemporary villages built around the chapels founded by the first European missionaries.

The aridity of the landscape increases from Catamarca toward the dusty flats of Santiago del Estero. This desert region extends across the northeast provinces of Formosa and Chaco, all the way to the shores of the Paraná and Paraguay rivers.

The city of **Santiago del Estero**, the provincial capital, was founded by the

In the Valle de la Luna.

Spanish conquistadors in 1553. It is the oldest continuously inhabited city of the region.

Thermal spas: There is not much to see in this region beyond the algarrobo forests and the cotton fields. However, there is one major attraction: the thermal spas at **Río Hondo**.

Near an artificial lake, which offers a variety of sporting activities, the city of Río Hondo has developed into one of the most fashionable spas in Argentina, with fine restaurants, first-class hotels and even auditoriums suited for conventions. Life here is as bustling in the winter months as it is on the beaches of Mar del Plata in the summer.

While the Termas de Río Hondo are most frequented in the cool season, there are a number of other renowned thermal centers in Argentina which may be visited all year round. Most of them are situated in the NOA region as well. The most popular ones are those at **Rosario de la Frontera** (108 miles/175 km south of Salta), **Termas de Reyes** (14 miles/22 km from San Salvador de Jujuy), and **Copahue-Caviahue**, on the slopes of a dormant volcano, at an altitude of 6,600 feet (2,000 meters), about 155 miles (250 km) from Neuquén, near the southern Lake District. All these, as well as such pleasant and relaxing spots as **Pismanta** (San Juan province), **Cacheuta** and **Los Molles** (Mendoza), **Domuyo** (Neuquén), **Epecuén** (Buenos Aires) and about 40 other mineral springs around the country are rated by many physicians as being extremely therapeutic for a vast range of ailments.

One last point of interest in this desert region is the site of the fantastic meteor craters of **Campo del Cielo**, near Gancedo, where one can see the enormous 33.4 ton El Chaco meteorite on display.

A tropical garden: Not far from Río Hondo the dusty desert gives way to a subtropical spectacle that surprises everybody who visits Tucumán for the first time. Here the almost endless aridity and scenic boredom of Santiago del Estero, Formosa and the Chaco prov-

A trail through Calilegua National Park.

inces is replaced abruptly by a cornucopia of tropical vegetation. It is for this reason that the province of Tucumán-the smallest of the 24 Argentine federal states- is popularly known as the Garden of the Nation.

This climatic and visual contrast is most vividly marked along the Aconquija range, which has several peaks of more than 18,000 feet (5,500 meters). Here the intense greenery is juxtaposed with gleaming snow-capped peaks.

Favored with copious rainfall, the province of Tucumán is one of the loveliest and economically richest of Argentina. On the plains, farming is the major economic activity. Around San Miguel de Tucumán, the provincial capital, one finds the smoky *ingenios* (sugar mills), and industrial factories built since the mid-60s.

The city of **Tucumán** has a unique character. The spacious **Nueve de Julio Park**, the baroque **Government Building** and several patrician edifices, together with a number of venerable churches, are reminders of the town's colonial past. This might best be sensed by visiting the **Casa de la Independencia.** In a large room of this stately house, part of which has been rebuilt, the Argentine national independence ceremony was sworn on July 9, 1816.

Side trips: However, it is not so much the town but its surroundings which make San Miguel de Tucumán worth a break during a tour through the NOA area. Short excursions should by all means be undertaken to **Villa Nougués** and to **San Javier**, high up in the Aconquija range. From here the onlooker gets a splendid view of Tucumán, its outskirts and the extensive sugar cane and tobacco fields surrounding it.

A half-day excursion to nearby **El Cadillal**, with its dam, artificial lake, archaeological museum and restaurants (where fresh *pejerrey* is served) is quite pleasant. It may also be worthwhile to take a guided tour to some of the sugar mills.

Once finished with the sightseeing tours in and around San Miguel de Tucumán, the traveler may choose be-

Harvesting in the great salt flats of the *Puna*.

tween two different roads to carry on toward the north. One choice is the main Ruta Nacional 9, which passes by Metán and the Rosario de la Frontera spa and then winds through dense scrub forest and bushland to Salta and from there to Jujuy. But perhaps the better choice is to leave Tucumán, heading south towards **Acheral**. From Acheral, a narrow paved road starts climbing up and up through dense tropical vegetation, until it reaches a pleasant green valley, which is frequently covered by clouds. The valley is dotted with tiny hamlets, the principle one being the old aboriginal and Jesuit settlement of Tafí del Valle.

Stone circles: Tafí del Valle, situated in the heart of the Aconquija range at an altitude of 6,600 feet (2,000 meters), is considered the sacred valley of the Diaguita natives, who, with different tribal names, inhabited the area. The valley is littered with clusters of aboriginal dwellings and dozens of sacred stone circles. By far the most outstanding attractions at Tafí are the menhirs or standing stones. These dolmens, which sometimes stand more than six feet (two meters) high, have recently been assembled at the **Parque de los Menhires**, close to the entrance of the valley.

From Tafí, a dusty gravel road winds up to the watershed at **El Infiernillo** (Little Hell), at 10,000 feet (3,000 meters) above sea level, and from there it drops down to Amaicha del Valle.

Local tradition has it that at **Amaicha del Valle** the sun shines 360 days of the year. Some hotel owners are said to be so fond of this bit of lore that they reimburse their guests if an entire visit should pass without any sun at all. Whatever the weather, the local hand-woven tapestries and the workshops certainly merit the visit.

Sun-blessed valleys: Upon leaving Amaicha one enters the colorful, sun-blessed **Santa María and Calchaquí valleys**. Together they constituted one of the most densely populated regions of pre-Hispanic Argentina. Shortly after Amaicha, the road splits into two

Drying red peppers for the local cayenne industry.

branches. To the left (or the south) one soon reaches **Santa María**, with its variety of fine artisan products and wines. It also has an important red pepper industry.

However, still better is to go on straight ahead toward the north. Soon after one reaches Ruta Nacional 40, Argentina's longest road, a short approach road leads to the extraordinary archaeological ruins of **Quilmes**. This vast aboriginal stronghold, which once had as many as 2,500 inhabitants, is a paradigm of fine pre-Hispanic urban architecture. Its walls of neatly set flat stones are still perfectly preserved, though the roofs of giant cacti girders vanished long ago. Local guides take the visitor to some of the most interesting sites of this vast complex, its fortifications, its huge dam and reservoir and its small museum.

On goes the journey through forlorn villages like **Colalao del Valle** and **Tolombón** to **Cafayate**. These are where the exquisite white wines made from the Torrontes grape are produced.

Shady patios: Though situated only 160 miles (260 km), (about three-and-a-half driving hours) from San Miguel de Tucumán, Cafayate should be earmarked in advance as a place to spend at least one night.

There is something more to Cafayate than its cathedral, with the rare five naves, its excellent colonial museum, seven *bodegas* (wine cellars), tapestry artisans and silversmiths. It is the freshness of its altitude of 5,280 feet (1,600 meters) and the shade of its patios, overgrown with vines, that really enchant the visitor. The surroundings of this tiny colonial town are dotted with vineyards and countless archaeological remains.

There are two routes which lead from Cafayate to Salta. To the right, along Ruta Nacional 68, the road winds through the colorful **Guachipas Valley**, also called **la Quebrada de Cafayate**. Along this valley, water and the wind have carved from the red sandstone a vast number of curious formations which delight the traveler at every

Baking bread.

bend. It is a pleasant drive of less than four hours (about 112 miles/180 km), and is especially ideal for those who are in a hurry.

The long way: Others, who have more time to spare and who are equally interested in natural beauty and history, should by all means follow Ruta Nacional 40. It snakes along the scenic **Calchaquí Valley**, which is irrigated by the Calchaquí, one of Argentina's longest rivers.

Every one of the many romantic villages along the Calchaquí Valley deserves at least a short sightseeing walk, for one to gain an appreciation of the fine colonial architecture and Hispanic art still largely preserved in this region. A stop at **San Carlos**, not far away from Cafayate, is especially worthwhile. This sleepy spot, with a comfortable ACA Hosteria, is said to have been founded no fewer than five times, first by the Spanish conquistadors as early as 1551, and later by successive waves of missionaries.

Soon after San Carlos the road be-comes even more winding. Through the chimneys of the humble houses lining the way, the tempting smell of traditional dishes is frequently perceivable. The observant traveler may sniff *locro* (stew), *puchero* (soup) or *mazzamorra* (a dessert), as well as fragrant bread being baked in the adobe ovens behind the dwellings.

The route briefly leaves the riverbed and crosses the impressive **Quebrada de la Flecha**. Here, a forest of eroded sandstone spikes provides a spectacle, as the play of sun and shadow makes the figures appear to change their shapes.

Angastaco, the next hamlet, was once an aboriginal settlement, with its primitive adobe huts standing on the slopes of immobile sand dunes. A modern urban center, with a comfortable *hosteria,* stands near by. Angastaco lies amid extensive vineyards, though between this point and the north, more red peppers than grapes are grown.

Molinos, with its massive adobe church and colonial streets, is another

ast food in
Bermejo,
near Salta.

quiet place worth a stop. *Molino* means mill, and one can still see the town's old water-driven mill grinding maize and other grains by the bank of the Calchaquí River.

This is but one example of how ancient traditions live on all along the Calchaquí. At **Seclantás** and the nearby hamlet of **Solco**, artisans continue to produce the famous, traditional handwoven *Ponchos de Guëmes*, red and black blankets made of fine wool that are carried over the shoulders of the proud gauchos of Salta.

Cactus church: By far the loveliest place along the picturesque Calchaquí road is **Cachi**, 108 twisting miles (175 km) north of Cafayate.

Cachi has a very old church with many of its parts (altar, confessionals, pews, even the roof and the floor) made of cactus wood, one of the few building materials available in the area. Across the square lies the archaeological museum, probably the best of its kind in Argentina. With the advice and permission of the museum's director, the traveler may visit the vast aboriginal complex at **Las Pailas**, some 11 miles (18 km) away and partially excavated. This is just one of the countless archaeological sites in the Calchaquí region, which was densely populated during pre-Hispanic times.

Here, as in Cafayate, the visitor may decide to stay for more than just one night. An ACA Hosteria is magnificently situated atop a hill above old Cachi.

So clear is the atmosphere here that the mighty **Mount Cachi** (20,800 feet/ 6,300 meters) seems to be within arms' reach. Inhabitants of this region are said to benefit from the crisp mountain air, and many live to a very old age.

Ruta Nacional 40 at this point becomes almost impassable, though the sleepy village of **La Poma**, 30 miles (50 km) to the north and partly destroyed by an earthquake in 1930, may be visited. But the main tourist route runs to the east over a high-plateau called **Tin-Tin**. This is the native terrain of the sleek, giant *cardon*, or candelabra

A religious procession in Jujuy.

cactus. **Los Cardones National Park** has recently been opened in this area.

Down the spectacular **Cuesta del Obispo Pass**, through the multicolored **Quebrada de Escoipe** and over the lush plains of the **Lerma Valley** the road stretches to Salta. From Cafayate to Salta, via Cachi, without stopovers, it is a demanding eight-hour drive.

It should be noted that in the whole NOA region many roads are impassable during the rainy summer season (roughly from Christmas to Easter). Autumn and spring (April-May and September-November) are the most advisable times for a visit.

Colonial gems: Salta is probably the most seductive town of the Northwest, due both to its setting in the lovely Lerma Valley and to the eye-catching contrast of its old colonial buildings with its modern urban architecture.

For those who don't have much time, Salta is the ideal starting point for many short but satisfying road trips. Less than two hours from Buenos Aires by plane, it offers the possibility of visits by bus,

organized tours or rented car to such destinations as:

— **Cachi**, for a trip of one day or more.

—**Cafayate**, for a day or more.

— **Finca El Rey National Park**, a tropical paradise with many rare specimens of botanical and zoological interest, some 125 miles (200 km) south of Salta, for at least three days.

— **San Antonio de los Cobres**, to admire the well-preserved pre-Hispanic ruins of **Tastil**, by car, or on board the **Tren a las Nubes** (Train to the Clouds), which runs every Saturday from April to November.

— **Humahuaca**, for a day or more.

The city of Salta itself is a fascinating place for the tourist. It cradles such valuable colonial gems as the **San Bernardo Convent**, the **San Francisco Church**, and the **Cabildo** (city hall), with its graceful row of arches. The Cabildo houses a very fine historical museum. The **Archaeological Museum** and the **Mercado Artesanal** (artisans' market), with handicrafts by

some of the tribes living in the vast province of Salta, are two more musts for the tourist. A superb view of the city can be enjoyed from atop **San Bernardo Hill**.

Train to the clouds: Both the Tren a las Nubes and Finca El Rey deserve brief descriptions. The train, fully equipped with dining car, leaves Salta's main station around seven o'clock in the morning and enters the deep **Quebrada del Toro** gorge about an hour later. Slowly, the train starts to make its way up. The line is a true work of engineering art, and doesn't make use of cogs, even for the steepest parts of the climb. Instead, the rails have been laid so as to allow circulation by means of switchbacks and spirals. This, together with some truly spectacular scenery, is what makes the trip so unique and interesting.

After passing through **San Antonio de los Cobres**, the old capital of the former national territory, Los Andes, the train finally comes to a halt at **La Polvorilla Viaduct** (207 feet/63 meters high and 739 feet/224 meters long), an impressive steel span amidst the breathtaking Andean landscape. At this point one has reached an attitude of 13,850 feet (4,197 meters) above sea level.

From here the train returns to Salta, where it arrives, after a ride of about 14 hours, in the late evening. The journey is well worth the time and money (the ticket, by the way, is quite cheap; it may be purchased up to 45 days in advance at the offices of Ferrocarriles Argentinos, the national railway system, in downtown Buenos Aires).

Jungle retreat: Finca El Rey is a natural hothouse, with tropical vegetation as dense and green as one can find almost anywhere in South America. Visitors who come to fish, study the flora and fauna, or just to relax, will find ample accommodations; there is a clean *hosteria,* some bungalows, and even some cabins for students. One can get here by car, bus or plane.

Jujuy: From Salta, a winding but wonderful mountain road called **La Cornisa** takes the traveler, in about an

A cemetery in the Quebrada de Humahuaca.

hour and a half, to **San Salvador de Jujuy**. The visitor is advised to not miss the extraordinary gilded pulpit at the cathedral, carved by the local inhabitants. A few miles from town, one can visit the **Termas de Reyes** spa, located in a narrow valley.

The colorful Quebrada: San Salvador de Jujuy may sometimes lie under a blanket of clouds, but the road from town climbs steadily up, and before long, the sun breaks through. Here, to the north, one enters a wide and most distinctive *quebrada* (gorge), which is dominated by the bed of the Río Grande. This river receives torrential and often destructive rains in the summer. As one carries on up the road, the colors of the valley wall become more and more intense and delineated. One may also notice that the clothing of the Coya people, inhabitants of this high plateau region, is vibrantly colorful.

A first stop is to be made at **Purmamarca**, a tiny village with the striking **Cerro de los Siete Colores** (Hill of the Seven Colors) towering behind the old adobe church. Around the shady square, local vendors offer wood carvings, handwoven carpets and a variety of herbs for every possible ailment.

After a short ride through the Quebrada one comes to **Tilcara**, famous for its huge *pucará* (stronghold), built on a hill in the middle of the valley. Around the main square there are three museums, for archaeology, art and folkloric art. There is also an interesting botanical garden, with specimens from the *Puna* (high plateau).

At **El Angosto**, a few miles north of Tilcara, the Quebrada narrows to less than 650 feet (200 meters) and then opens into a large valley. Wherever the available water is thoroughly used, tiny fields and orchards give a touch of fresh green to the red and yellow shades of the river walls.

At **Huacalera**, with its comfortable hotel, a monument on the left-hand side shows the exact point of the Tropic of Capricorn (23 degrees 27 minutes south of the Equator).

Desert chapels: At last one reaches

the town of Humahuaca, which takes its name from an aboriginal tribe and gives it in turn to the surrounding valley.

Humahuaca lies at an altitude of almost 9,000 feet (3,000 meters). Visitors are advised to walk and move very slowly to avoid running out of breath. It is also advisable to avoid eating heavily; a cup of sweet tea is more beneficial at this altitude.

In Humahuaca one finds stone-paved and extremely narrow streets, vendors of herbs and produce near the railway station, and an imposing monument commemorating the Argentine war of independence. The museum of local customs and traditions is worth a visit. Humahuaca has a comfortable hotel and several good restaurants which serve local dishes. Most travelers pay only a short visit to this fascinating place and return to San Salvador de Jujuy the same afternoon, but a stay of several days is truly worthwhile, as several sidetrips can be made from here.

By renting a pick-up, one can drive

the six miles (nine km) to the extensive archaeolocial ruins of **Coctaca**. The true significance of this site is largely unknown but teams of scientists are studying it, and its secrets may soon be revealed.

Other options are a journey to **Iruya**, a tiny hamlet cradled amid towering mountains, about 47 miles (75 km) from Humahuaca or to **La Quiaca**, on the Argentine-Bolivian border. La Quiaca is the entry point for travelers going into Bolivia.

An even more adventurous trip would be to **Abra Pampa** and from there to the **Laguna Pozuelos Natural Monument**, where one can see enormous flocks of the spectacular Andean flamingo, and vicuña herds grazing near the road. Near Abra Pampa there is also a huge vicuña farm (*vicuñera*).

Here in the heart of the *Puna* or *Altiplano* (a high plateau with an average altitude of 11,550 feet/3,500 meters), a variety of churches and chapels with different architectural styles can be seen. The best examples are at **Casabindo**, **Cochinoca**, **Pozuelos**, **Tafna** and **Rinconada**.

Glowing gilding: Finally, as if left for a happy ending to this excursion through plains and valleys and over mountains, there remains one of the most sparkling jewels of Argentina: the very old **Chapel of Yavi**.

The tiny village of **Yavi**, on the windy and barren high plateau near the Bolivian border, lies protected in a small depression, about nine miles (15 km) by paved road to the east of La Quiaca. Between the 17th and 19th centuries, Yavi was the seat of the Marques de Campero, one of the wealthiest Spanish feudal positions in this part of the continent. Though the chapel here was originally built in 1690, one of the later marquesses ordered the altar and pulpit to be gilded. The thin alabaster plaques covering the windows create a soft filtered lighting which makes the gilding glow.

This precious historical monument makes a fine finishing to a rewarding journey through the northwest.

Left, a typical church of the Northwest. Right, the Train to the Clouds.

THE WINE COUNTRY

In a country full of surprises and little-publicized delights, the west-central region of the Cuyo holds more than its share. Argentina is the fifth largest wine producer in the world, and the Cuyo is the heart of that industry. The vines are nurtured by the melting snows of the Andes, and the mountains themselves add colorful drama to the scene. Every March the grape harvest is celebrated in the *Festival de la Vendimia*, but a visitor at any time of the year can tour the *bodegas* (wine cellars) and sample the excellent wines. The cities of the area are some of Argentina's oldest, and although most have been rebuilt in modern times to repair damage caused by earthquakes, one can still learn a lot about Argentine history in the many regional museums. Nestled high in the Andes is Aconcagua, the tallest peak in the world outside Asia. There are also numerous ski resorts in the area, most notably Las Leñas, which is becoming increasingly popular as an off-season vacation and competition site for skiers from the North. The visitor will find these and countless other pleasures hidden along the winding mountain passes, and tree-lined country roads of the Cuyo.

Preceding pages: riding in to south Aconcagua; a shady road outside Mendoza. Left, a winery owner with his raw materials.

THE CUYO

In the mid-16th century the Spanish colonies along the western coast of South America sought to expand their territories beyond the Andes, to the east, in what is today Argentina. They were driven by reports that these lands held a vast wealth of gold, similar to what had been found further to the north. Several of the early Chilean efforts at settlement were wiped out by repeated Indian attacks. Conquistadors from Peru had better luck, staking their claims to the north. In 1553, Francisco de Aguirre founded Santiago del Estero for the Spanish Viceroyalty of Peru. It is the oldest surviving settlement in all of Argentina. The explorers from Peru went on to found the towns of Tucumán (on a site earlier established by the explorers from Chile), Salta and Xiu Xiu (Jujuy). The Chileans were finally successful in establishing their domain further to the south, in the Cuyo region, parallel to Chile's central valley. Although this side of the range was barren and very arid (Cuyo means desert land in the dialect of the local Indians), it was cut through by rivers flowing from the melting Andean snows.

First cities: The first permanent settlement in the Cuyo was made at Mendoza, a site chosen for its location across from Santiago at the eastern end of the Uspallata Pass, the major access through the Andes in the region. Pedro de Castillo founded the town in 1561, and named it for Hurtado de Mendoza, the governor of Chile. Not long after, the town was relocated several miles to the north.

In 1562, Juan Jufre founded San Juan, to the north of Mendoza, and a third Chilean town, San Luis, was started to the west in 1598.

The Spanish Crown established the eastern Viceroyalty of the Río de la Plata in 1776 to accommodate the growing importance of the port of Buenos Aires. At this time, the Cuyo and the

The central plaza of Mendoza in the mid-19th century.

194

Peruvian holdings to the north passed to the jurisdiction of the new territory. However, the Cuyo remained isolated from the east for many years, and its strongest economic and cultural ties were with central Chile.

The isolation was broken in 1884, with the completion of the transcontinental railway, and today the region is well integrated into the Argentine economy. It is the center of the country's enormous wine industry, and a whole array of fruits and vegetables are grown for eastern markets. The area has also proved to be rich in mineral wealth, if not the gold that the early explorers had hoped to find. The region is the major supplier for the nation's vital petroleum industry, and uranium, copper and lead mines are scattered throughout the mountains. There are several modest hydroelectric projects, and the reservoirs created by the dams have made this a popular recreational area. People also come for the skiing and the civilized pleasures afforded by the hot spring spas and wine *bodegas.*

Shady avenues: Today the Cuyo comprises the provinces of Mendoza, San Juan and San Luis. The largest city is Mendoza, with a population of 600,000. As old as the town is, little remains of its original colonial architecture. The whole region is periodically racked by earthquakes, some of them quite severe. One such quake, in 1861, killed 10,000 and completely leveled Mendoza, and rebuilding was done with an eye to averting further disaster. Another quake, in January of 1985, although it left 40,000 homeless, caused few fatalities.

In spite of Mendoza's relatively modern appearance, it has a long history, of which its residents are very proud. It was from here, in 1817, that San Martín launched his march with 40,000 men across the Andes to liberate Chile and Peru.

The wine industry began in earnest in the mid-19th century, with the arrival of many Italian and French immigrants. Although this remains a substantial part of the economy, it was the development

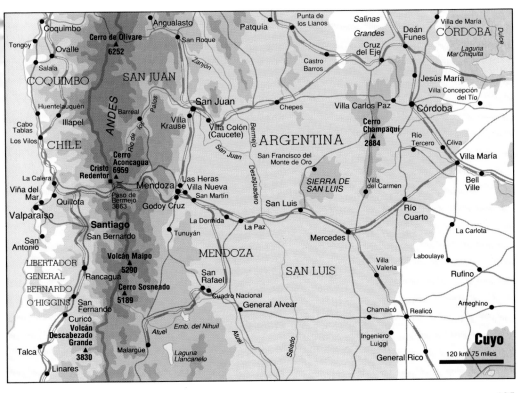

THE WINES OF ARGENTINA

Argentina is the fifth largest producer of wine in the world, with an average of 21 million hectoliters per annum. Almost 90 percent of that wine is produced in the Andean provinces of Mendoza and San Juan, with Rio Negro, Salta and La Rioja producing the rest. Fine wines represent between six and eight percent of production, with jug wine, regional wine and a small amount of special wines (sherries, ports, vermouths, etc.) making up the balance.

Although per capita consumption has declined notably in recent years, it is still high, at approximately 61 liters per year. Wine has been made in Argentina since the time of the Conquest but it has only been in the last 90 years that winemaking has become an important and organized activity; there are not more than four or five wineries with more than a century of uninterrupted production, and only one with more than 140 years of continuous production (Gonzalez Videla, founded in 1840). Some 2,000 wineries now exist throughout the land, though only a handful make fine wine, and even fewer estates bottle or sell under their own brand names.

Argentina possesses a vineyard based almost entirely on European grape varieties. Such noble names as Cabernet Sauvingnon, Merlot, Chardonnay, Chenin, Riesling and Pinot Noir figure prominently. However, due to sloppy or ignorant registration in the early years of the industry, and poor amphelographic control in later times, much confusion still exists as to exactly what grapes are harvested. An organized and scientific examination of many of the better vineyards has shown that many varieties regarded as one thing are actually another. Such is the case with the Argentine Pinot Blanc, which amphelographers have now determined to be Chenin. Much Rhine Riesling is actually Italian Riesling (also known as Tokay Friulano). While this has not affected the quality or the character of the wines, it does lead to some confusion when local wines are compared with those of other countries.

Argentina has traditionally been a red wine country, and in the opinion of visiting foreign experts and local oenophiles, the reds are still superior to the whites (with an exception or two). The most popular and expensive reds are those made entirely or overwhelmingly from the Cabernet Sauvingnon grape, but recently the extraordinary qualities of the Malbec have been discovered. The Malbec is considered only second rank in its native Bordeaux, but it has developed exceptional characteristics in Mendoza. Such internationally famous experts as Hugh Johnson of Britain and Terry Robards and Joseph Schagrin of the United States have pronounced it the premier Argentine red grape. Its wine can be considered unique to Argentina as no other country in the world has managed to obtain the quality which it offers here.

Argentine white wines are largely Chardonnay and Chenin, with some good Rieslings coming along and a few minor wines (Geweurtztraminer, for example) filling out the list. However, just as there is a unique and superior quality wine in the Malbec, so is there a distinguished wine among the Argentine whites. It is not a Mendoza wine, although the grape is harvested there and in San Juan, but comes from the northern-most province of Salta. The grape is the Torrontes, of Spanish origin, but which only develops its full potential in the high Andean valley of Cafayate, about a hundred-odd miles west of Salta city. Torrontes wines are overpoweringly aromatic—much more so than a good Geweurtztraminer, for example—with a rich, gold color, a sturdy body and a first impression of slight sweetness which is later proved false. It is probably the fruitiest wine the Argentines produce. They also bottle a line of sparkling wines of different qualities, some of which are surprisingly good, particularly those made by the Moet and Chandon and the Piper Heisdieck outfits.

Rosé wines, on the other hand, are barely drunk, although some interest has been caused by the introduction of a couple of "blush" wines based on the Cabernet Sauvingnon grape. Brandy and fortified wines such as sherry and port are seldom seen on Argentine tables.

By and large, Argentines drink wine with their meals, but the fastest growing section of the wine industry is the sparkling wine sector, and this is due to the ever increasing fashion of drinking sparkling wine as an aperitif. Far behind, as a second choice, white wine is also drunk before a meal; it is rare indeed to see red wine drunk as an aperitif, although the practice of continuing to drink wine after a meal is fairly common.

Right, barrels of sherry being sunned.

of the petroleum industry in the 1950s that brought real prosperity to the town.

While Mendoza is nowhere near the metropolis that Buenos Aires is, it has its own charms, and a wealth of cultural activity. Transplanted residents from the capital boast a happy conversion to the Mendocinos' more relaxed pace.

The atmosphere of the town is certainly conducive to relaxation. The abundant waters of the region have been put to good use, and the arid landscape has been transformed into a lush oasis. Some of the irrigation canals dug by the original Indian inhabitants are still in use, and many more have been added. The city's low buildings lie along wide, tree-lined streets, where channels of running water keep the temperature an agreeable measure below that of the surrounding desert. Most homes have well-tended gardens and there are parks throughout the city that serve the dual interests of recreation and safety in case of an earthquake. In the midst of the plentiful shade, it is astonishing to realize that all the mil- lions of trees have been planted by the city's residents and developers. Not one of the poplars, elms or sycamores is native to the region.

Beyond and above all this greenery, to the west, lie the Andes, which provide the city with a spectacular backdrop of changing hues throughout the day.

Wild asparagus: Mendoza has a good selection of museums and other sites of interest. The **San Martín Museum**, at Avenida San Martín 1843, houses a collection dedicated to the General and his accomplishments. The **Historical Museum** (Montevideo 544) has a fine collection of artifacts from Mendocino life, and a small San Martín exhibit. Archaeology, anthropology and paleontology buffs will enjoy the **Museum of Natural History** (underground at Plaza Independencia). The University of the Cuyo, in San Martín Park, has an **Archaeological Museum**, with an exhibit of the ceramics of South America, along with a small folkloric collection. The **Municipal Aquarium**, un-

The hard labor of harvesting.

derground at Huzaingo and Buenos Aires is definitely worth a visit.

The city has preserved as an historical monument the ruins of the **San Francisco Church**. Founded by the Jesuits in the 18th century, the church was destroyed by the earthquake in 1861.

Behind the rather unattractive **Government Palace**, is the **Giol Wine Museum**, an extension of the nearby state-owned winery. It is small, but has wine tasting and some interesting old photographs. Some pleasing items can be picked up at the **Artisans' Market**, at Lavalle 97. The main **Tourism Office**, at San Martín 1143, is quite helpful.

The city's two major hotels are the **Aconcagua** and the **Plaza**. The first, built for the World Cup Soccer games in 1978, has airconditioning and a pool, while the second relies more on old style charm to lure its customers.

Those seeking a break from touring can sample the shopping along **Las Heras**, or pull up a chair at one of the shady sidewalk cafés clustered in the city center. Most of these have good fast food, and some offer pitchers of *clerico*, the Argentine version of sangria, made with white wine.

In this desert climate, hot summer days are followed by cool nights, and there are restaurants which offer dining al fresco. **La Bodega del 900**, on the outskirts of town, has a dinner show on its patio, and a small wine museum in its cellar. In any of the finer eating establishments one is advised to try the trout and the wild asparagus.

There are several cafés and nightclubs perched along the foothills to the west. One of the most pleasant of these is **Le Per**, open until quite late, with its patio overlooking Mendoza.

Glory Hill: On the western edge of the city lies San Martín Park, crowned by the **Cerro de la Gloria** (Glory Hill). The park has facilities for a wide variety of sports, including a soccer stadium built for the World Cup. Further up the hill is the **City Zoo**, with shaded walkways wandering among open-air cages.

he melted
nows
escend.

Right at the top of the hill sits an ornate **Monument to San Martín**, complete with bolting horses and Liberty breaking her chains. Bas-relief around the statute's base depicts various scenes of the liberation campaigns. The site also provides an excellent view of Mendoza.

Around the backside of the park is the **Frank Romero Day Amphitheater**, site of many of the city's celebrations, including the grand spectacle of the *Festival de la Vendimia* (Grape Harvest Festival). This takes place every year in March, over three or four days. The first few days there are street performances and parades, and a Queen of the Harvest is chosen. The finale is a somewhat overproduced extravaganza, complete with dancing, fireworks and moving light shows. This is Mendoza's moment to show off its hard-earned wealth.

Bodega hopping: One of the most pleasant diversions in the Mendoza area is *bodega* hopping. Scattered up and down this stretch along the Andes are more than 2,000 different wineries, some small family operations, others huge and state-owned.

All of this cultivation is made possible through an extensive network of irrigation. The area is blessed with a combination of plentiful water, sandy soil, a dry climate and year-round sunshine, which makes for enormous yields.

The first vines were planted in the Cuyo by Jesuit missionaries in the 16th century, but production really took off in the mid-1800s with the arrival of Italian and French immigrants. Many of them simply worked as laborers in the fields, but a knowledgeable few contributed a European expertise that greatly refined the industry.

A number of wineries are right on the outskirts of Mendoza. Tours can be arranged through a travel agent, but a more pleasant way to make the rounds is by getting a map, renting a car and finding them yourself. This provides the opportunity to meander down the lovely country lanes lined with poplars

The pass at Villavicencio.

and wildflowers, and to get a sense of the Cuyo's lifestyle. Local cycling fanatics are out in packs and, with luck, one might even catch a scene of old men playing a lazy afternoon game of *bocci*.

The most popular destinations for *bodega* hoppers are the major, streamlined operations at **Giol** and **Trapiche Peña Flor**, in the suburb of **Maipú**, and **Arizú** in Godoy Cruz. One is taken on a standard tour (special arrangements must be made for tours in English) through the areas where the various stages of production take place. Huge oak casks are set on rollers as an antiseismic precaution. Tours end with an invitation to taste the company's wine. Bottles are also offered for sale, at reduced rates.

The most interesting time to be here is during the March harvest, when trucks spilling over with grapes congest the narrow roads.

Two of the less-visited but more interesting *bodegas* are **Gonzalez Videla** and **La Rural**. The first is located in the suburb of Las Heras, down a dirt road. It's a bit difficult to find, but one can stop to ask directions. Begun in 1840, this is the oldest surviving winery of the area. Visitors are not really expected, so you have to do your own looking around. Pieces of ancient equipment lie about, and the family house, filled with antiques, is next-door. Part of the complex is the old community church, where Sunday evening masses are held.

The **Bodega La Rural**, whose house brand is San Felipe, is located in Maipú. Started in 1889, this winery retains a lot of charm, with its original pink adobe architecture. It has the nicest wine museum of the area, small but filled with old presses and casks and basins made from single cow hides. Mornings are the best time for visits.

Other *bodegas* to visit include **Toso** and **Santa Ana**, in the suburb of Guaymallén, and **Norton**, in Luján.

Mountain pass: One of the most spectacular trips to be made from Mendoza is up the **Uspallata Pass** to the border with Chile. It is an all-day excursion which should be started early in the morning to allow enough time to see all the sights. One can sign on for a commercial tour, but hiring a car allows one to avoid being herded around. However, unless you're carrying on through Chile, going on your own is only recommended outside the winter months (July—Sept.) Road conditions in the upper reaches are often icily treacherous then, and snow and rock slides are common. At any time of year a set of warmer garments are needed for cooler altitudes. Also beware that altitude sickness can be a problem, as one goes from 2,500 feet to 8,200 feet (750 meters to 2,500 meters).

Those requiring visas for Chile should get them in Mendoza, as they will not be issued at the border.

One begins the trip by heading south from Mendoza on Route 7 to **Luján**. Turning right at the town square, you get onto Highway 7, which carries you up into the pass. This stretch of road, the "Camino de los Andes," is part of the vast complex known as the Pan-American Highway. Through the centuries, even back to before the Incas, the pass has been used to cross the mountains.

Immediately the landscape becomes more barren as one leaves behind the irrigated greenery of the lowlands to follow the Mendoza river up the valley. Trees give way to scrub and the occasional bright flower.

The first spot one will pass is the **Cachueta Hot Springs**, at a lovely bend in the river. Only those with a doctor's prescription can check in, however.

Next comes **Portrerrillos**, a scenic oasis where many Mendocinos have summer homes to escape the heat. The **Portrerrillos Hotel** has terraced gardens overlooking the valley, along with a swimming pool and facilities for tennis and horseback riding. There are campgrounds nearby.

Up from Portrerrillos, at the end of a side road, is the modest ski resort of **Vallecitos**. The resort is open from July to September.

Continuing up the valley, one reaches the town of **Uspallata**, set in a wide meadow. Further up, the valley widens again at **Punta de Vacas,** Cattle

Point, where long ago the herds were rounded up to be driven across to Chile. It is at Punta de Vacas that one submits documentation if wishing to continue across the border.

The ski resort of **Los Penitentes** is just beyond. Buses bring skiers up for day trips from July through September. Across the valley is the strange formation for which the resort is named; tall rock outcroppings look like hooded monks (the penitents) ascending toward the cathedral-like peak of the mountain. In winter, wind-swept ice on the rocks heightens the illusion.

The Redeemer: Off to the left of the road, a little further on, is a desolate, melancholy sight, a small graveyard for those who have died in the attempt to scale nearby Mount Aconcagua.

Just beyond this is the **Puente del Inca**, a natural stone bridge made colorful by the mineral deposits of the bubbling hot springs beneath it.

Just a few miles up the road lies the most impressive sight of the whole excursion. There is a break in the wall of rock, and looking up the valley to the right one can see the towering mass of **Aconcagua**, at 22,834 feet (6,960 meters) the highest peak in the Western Hemisphere, and the highest anywhere outside of Asia. The name means "stone watchtower" in an old Indian dialect. It is perpetually blanketed in snow, and its visible southern face presents a 10,000-foot (3,000- meter) wall of sheer ice and stone. Most expeditions tackle the northern face. The best time to climb is mid-January to mid-February. Information can be obtained in Mendoza at the Club Andinista (Pardo and Ruben Lemos Streets).

The clear mountain air creates the illusion that Aconcagua lies quite close to the road, but the peak is actually 28 miles (45 km) away. One can walk in as far as **Laguna de los Horcones**, a green lake at the mountain's base.

The last sight to see before heading back is the **Statue of Christ the Redeemer** that is situated on the border with Chile. On the way there, one will pass the beat town of **Las Cuevas**. From there the road branches: to the right is the new tunnel for road and rail traffic to Chile (passenger rail service from Mendoza to Santiago has been suspended in recent years for lack of customers). To the left is the old road to Chile, which climbs precipitously over rock and gravel to the **La Cumbre Pass**, at an altitude of 13,800 feet (4,200 meters). At the top is the Christ statue, which was erected in 1904 to signify the friendship between Argentina and Chile. It is most interesting for the little bits of colored rag tied onto it by visitors, in hopes of having prayers granted.

The best reward for having made it up this far is the view over the mountains. In every direction, the raw steep peaks of the Andes reach up, the tips still catching the late afternoon sun. If they don't take your breath away, the sharp icy winds of the pass surely will. The perfect cap for the journey is to catch sight of a condor soaring at this lonely altitude, so keep your eyes open.

Jet-set skiers: Another day trip from Mendoza is to the hot spring spa at **Villavicencio**, 28 miles (45 km) to the northwest along Alternate Route 7. The road continues on to reach the mountain pass at Uspallata, but this portion is not paved.

South of Mendoza, 150 miles (240 km) away, is the agricultural oasis of **San Raphael**. Nearby hydroelectric projects have created reservoirs which have become centers for vacationers. The river fishing is reported to be excellent.

To the southwest of San Raphael, in the **Valle Hermoso** (Beautiful Valley), is the ski resort of **Las Leñas**. This is becoming quite the place for the chic set of both hemispheres to meet between June and October. It has 28 miles (45 km) of dry powder slopes and beds for 2,000. Charter flights bring skiers from Mendoza to the nearby town of **Malargüe**, where buses take them the rest of the way.

Although **San Luis** does not really merit an extra trip, it lies on the road between Buenos Aires and Mendoza, so those going overland may want to rest here. The town sits at the northwest corner of the pampas, and was for many years a lonely frontier outpost; it retains a slightly colonial atmosphere. Several resorts in the area, clustered around reservoirs, are popular with fishermen and windsurfers. There is a spa at **Merlo**.

The area has several quarries for onyx, marble and rose quartz, and these stones can be purchased inexpensively. The town of **La Toma**, to the northeast of San Luis, specializes in green onyx.

River rafting: The town of **San Juan** is 106 miles (177 km) north of Mendoza along Route 40. An earthquake in 1944 leveled the town, and it has been completely rebuilt since then. It was his theatrical and highly successful efforts to raise funds for the devastated town that first brought Juan Perón to national prominence.

San Juan is another major center of wine production. However, it is most famous for being the birthplace of Domingo Faustino Sarmiento, the noted historian and educator who was president of the republic from 1868 to 1874. His home is now the site of the **Sarmiento Museum**. There is also a **Natural Sciences Museum** and an **Archaeological Museum**.

To the west there are mountains which have less strenuous climbs than those of the Mendoza peaks. One can inquire with the local tourism bureau about the possibility of white water rafting in the area's rivers.

In the north of San Juan Province lies the sculptured **Valle de la Luna** (Moon Valley), which is a paleontological treasure. (For a complete description, see the *Northwest* chapter.)

Wherever one travels in the Cuyo, at whatever time of year, one should look for local festivals. Small and grand scale celebrations are held for everything from wine and beer to nuts and apricots. Local gauchos put together rodeo competitions that are a treat to catch, and in January there is a *cueca* festival east of Mendoza. The *cueca* is a courtship dance inherited from Chile, and the perky strains of its music can be heard throughout the region.

World Cup Competition at Las Leñas.

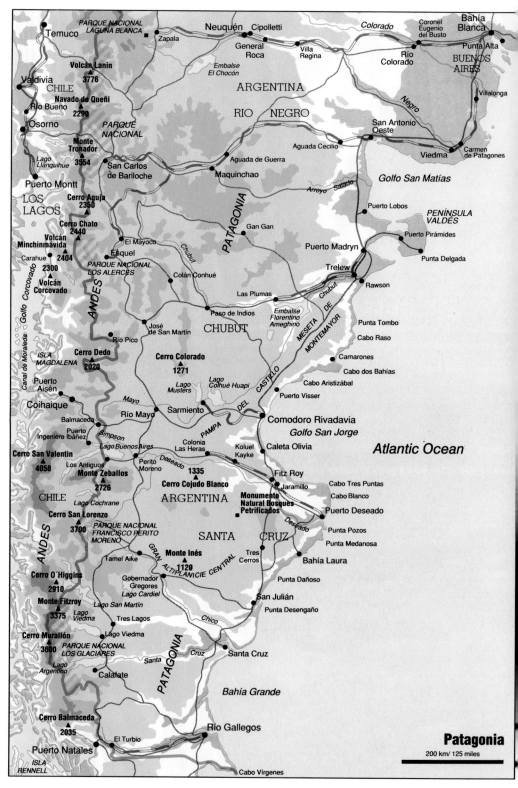

Patagonia

200 km/ 125 miles

ROMANTIC PATAGONIA

There is a temptation to say that Patagonia needs no introduction. This wild and isolated terrain has figured prominently in the exotic fantasies of many armchair adventurers through the ages, and to say one wished to head for Patagonia was akin to saying one yearned to go to Timbuktu. But perhaps some explanation is needed, as while the general idea is grasped, few are familiar with the specific enchantments of Patagonia. Even though the area is large, and comprises roughly a third of Argentina, one is still surprised by the wide range of spectacles that are contained here. It has some of the hemisphere's highest peaks, forests of strange primeval trees, fossil-rich coastal cliffs that were explored by Darwin, and several of the world's most noteworthy glaciers. The abundance of rare and entertaining wildlife is astounding, and for the athletic traveler, Patagonia has some of the most challenging skiing and mountain climbing to be found. So, whatever one's ambitions are for an adventurous getaway, Patagonia is worth the trip off the beaten track.

Preceding pages: the continental ice cap, high in the Andes; trekking above Nahuel Huapi Lake.

THE WINDY EXPANSE

Nobody has ever expressed more precisely than British naturalist Charles Darwin the feeling that remote Patagonia stirs in a visitor. Darwin, back in England after sailing five years on the Beagle, wrote, "In calling up images of the past, I find that the plains of Patagonia frequently cross before my eyes; yet these plains are pronounced by all wretched and useless. They can be described only by negative characteristics: without habitations, without water, without trees, without mountains, they support merely a few dwarf plants. Why then, and the case is not peculiar to myself, have these arid wastes taken so firm a hold on my memory?"

W.H. Hudson, in his book *Idle Days in Patagonia*, shares Darwin's impressions and adds, "It is not the imagination, it is that nature in these desolate scenes, for a reason to be guessed at by and by, moves us more deeply than in others."

At the very end of the South American continent lies the land that Magellan and his chronicler Pigafetta, while grounded on a desolate and cold coast during the winter of 1520, named Patagonia. The origin of this name, according to some historians, comes from the name given to the natives because of their large feet. Others think it might come from a famous character of chivalry stories, which were very popular at the time.

Bold explorers: Magellan, Sarmiento de Gamboa, Drake and Cavendish are only a few of the many explorers who set foot on this land. Here, on these dismal shores, European law and customs gave way to the most violent passions—revolts, mutinies, banishments and executions were common. In 1578, in the Port of San Julian (nowadays a town in Santa Cruz Province), Sir Francis Drake used the same scaffold Magellan had used to hang his mutineers half a century before.

In 1584, Sarmiento de Gamboa

founded the first settlements, naming them Jesus and Rey Felipe, on the Strait of Misfortunes. His first encounter with the native inhabitants should have sounded a warning: "Ten naked Indians approached us and pronounced words of welcome in an unknown language. The Chief, trying to prove their friendship, took a long arrow and swallowed it till it almost disappeared down his throat; when he slowly took it out, it was covered in blood." Two years later, Thomas Cavendish, the English privateer captain, found some survivors of this expedition wandering astray on the deserted coast, and after spending four days in the ruins of one of the settlements, gave it the shameful name of Port Famine.

Stretching from the white cliffs on the ocean shore, towards the west, lie the vast plains and mesas that remained unexplored for centuries. The Jesuits were among the few who, driven by the spell of the 'lost city of the Caesars,' dared to take a look at the endless plateau. They came from Chile, across the Andes, and never ventured far from the mountains. In 1670, they founded a mission in a remote place, on the shores of Lake Nahuel Huapi. It didn't last long. The Indians had a premonition: if the Spanish got to know the secret trails across the Andes, the Indians' fate would be sealed. Therefore, most of the missionaries were murdered.

The desert conquest: Only the Welsh settlers that arrived in the lower Chubut Valley in 1865 and the explorers of the late-19th century would unveil the inland secrets. The English explorer George Musters, one of the most famous adventurers of this time, rode with a group of Indians from Punta Arenas, Chile, on the Straits of Magellan, to Lake Nahuel Huapi, and from there to the Atlantic Ocean in nearly six months of uninterrupted traveling. His book of the journey has the most complete descriptions on the Patagonian inland and people of the 19th century.

The primitive inhabitants of this land were, from the start, part of the exotic spell that attracted the first settlers, but

Preceding pages: the marker for an *estancia* entrance. Below, Carmen de Patagones in the early-19th century.

soon became an obstacle to the settlers' purposes. They had been there long before the white man arrived and they stood their ground. The bravest were the Mapuche Indians, a nomadic tribe who lived on both sides of the border in the northern part of Patagonia. For 300 years they led a violent lifestyle on the northern plains by stealing and plundering the larger ranches of the rich pampas, herding the cattle over the Andes and selling them to the Spaniards on the Chilean side.

In 1879, the Argentine army, commanded by General Roca, set out to conquer the land from the native Americans. The campaign, which lasted through 1883, is known as the Conquest of the Desert. It put an end to years of Indian dominion in Patagonia and opened up a whole new territory to colonization.

The land and its beauty remained, but the native inhabitants vanished: some died in epic battles, others succumbed to agonizing diseases that had been unknown to them, and others simply be- came wcowhands on the large Patagonian *estancias*. Fragments of their world can still be found in this spacious land, in the features of some people, in some of the local habits and in religious ceremonies still performed on Indian reservations.

European settlement: When the Indian wars ended, colonization began. The large inland plateau, a dry expanse of shrubs and alkaline lagoons, was slowly occupied by people of very diverse origins: Spaniards, Italians, Scots and Englishmen in the far south, Welsh in the Chubut Valley, Italians in the Río Negro Valley, Swiss and Germans in the Northern Lake District and a few North Americans scattered throughout the country.

These people inherited the land and reproduced in the far south a setting similar to the American West. Ports and towns developed on the coast to ship the wool and import the goods needed by the settlers. Large wool-producing *estancias* were established on these plains. To the west, where the plains

meet the Andes, several National Parks were designated to protect the rich natural inheritance, to develop tourism, and to secure the national borders.

The Patagonian towns grew fast. Coal mining, oilfields, agriculture, industry, large hydroelectrical projects and tourism attracted people from all over the country and Chile, transforming Patagonia into a modern industrial frontier land. Some people came to start a quiet new life in the midst of mountains, forests and lakes. In the Patagonian interior, descendants of the first sheep-breeding settlers and their cowhands still ride over the enormous *estancias*, tending cattle and sheep.

A few geographical facts: With defined geographical and political boundaries, Patagonia extends from the Colorado River in the north, more than 1,200 miles (2,000 km) to Cape Horn at the southernmost tip of the continent. It covers more than 400,000 square miles (1,000,000 square km) and belongs to two neighboring countries, Chile and Argentina. The final agreement on this long irregular international border took a long time to come by and was not an easy matter to settle. Although the land was still unexplored, there were times when both countries were almost on the brink of war. Fortunately, it never reached that point, due to the common sense of both governments. An historical example of this attitude was the meeting of the Chilean and Argentine presidents in 1899 at the tip of the continent, in what is known as the Straits of Magellan Embrace. In 1978, a similar encounter was carried out in Puerto Montt, Chile, where both countries agreed on the last stretch of undefined boundary, which concerned some small islands in the Beagle Channel.

The Argentine part of Patagonia includes approximately 308,000 square miles (800,000 square km), and can easily be divided into three definite areas: the coast, the plateau and the Andes. Only 3.7 percent of the Argentine population lives in Patagonia. There are 0.5 inhabitants per square mile (1.3 inhabitants per square km), **Autumn comes to the plains.**

and in Santa Cruz Province, this density drops to 0.19 inhabitants per square mile (0.5 inhabitants per square km).

Seasons are well defined in Patagonia. Considering the latitude, the average temperature is mild; winters are never as cold and summers never as warm as in similar latitudes in the Northern Hemisphere. The average temperature in Ushuaia is 6°C and in Bariloche, 8°C. Even so, the climate can turn quite rough on the desert plateau. There, the weather is more continental than in the rest of the region. The ever-present companion to the Patagonian dweller and traveler is the wind, which blows all year round, from the mountains to the sea, making life here unbearable for many.

The change of seasons: In spring, the snow on the mountains begins to melt, flowers (lady-slippers, buttercups, mountain orchids, etc.) bloom almost everywhere, and ranchers prepare for the hard work of tending sheep and shearing. Although tourism starts in the late springtime, most of the people

Vinter
omes to
e moun-
ins.

come during the summer. All roads are fit for traffic, the airports are open, and normally, the hotels are booked solid. The summer season lasts through the month of February.

The fall brings changes on the plateau. The poplars around the lonesome *estancias* turn to beautiful shades of yellow. The mountains, covered by deciduous beech trees, offer a panorama of reds and yellows, and the air slowly gets colder. At this time of the year, tourism thins out, and the foot of the Andes, from San Martín to Bariloche turns into a hunter's paradise. Glacier National Park, in the far south, closes down for the winter. While the wide plains sleep, the winter resorts on the mountains thrive. San Martín de los Andes, Bariloche, Esquel and even Ushuaia attract thousands of skiers, including many from the Northern Hemisphere who take advantage of the reversal of seasons.

The two roads: Running from north to south, there are two main roads: Road #40 that runs along the Andes and Road

#3 that follows the coast. The first one, for the most part, is gravel. It starts at the Northwestern tip of the country and runs parallel to the Andes through places of unusual beauty. In the Northern Lake District, Road #40 is very busy, but south of Esquel it becomes one of the loneliest roads in the world, until it finally joins Road #3 and ends in Río Gallegos on the Atlantic coast.

Road #3, almost totally paved, starts in Buenos Aires and runs along the coast for more than 1,800 miles (3,000 km) until it reaches its end on the Beagle Channel in the Lapataia National Park. This road connects all the main cities and towns on the Patagonian coast like Bahia Blanca, Trelew, Comodoro Rivadavia, Río Gallegos and Ushuaia. In between these cities, the only inhabited places through miles and miles of desolation are the large Patagonian sheep-breeding *estancias*. The *estancieros* are known for the hospitality they offer the stray traveler.

Many roads link the mountains to the coast. There is also a main railroad line connecting Buenos Aires to Bariloche, which follows the trail Musters rode a hundred years ago. On the voyage, the traveler will see the scenery change from the rich pampa of Buenos Aires Province to the desert of Patagonia.

To some it might seem that time in Patagonia moves at a slower pace than elsewhere. The endless lonely roads, the long windy winters and the vastness of the sky have shaped a way of living that is simple and unpretentious. For the traveler, the kindness and hospitality of the local people will often make up for the occasional absence of some standard comforts. Those accustomed to European efficiency and fast pace will find things here a bit more relaxed.

Northern Patagonia: The northern boundary of Patagonia is the **Colorado River**. The steppe, or desert, as Argentines call it, comes from farther north and extends uninterrupted through inland Patagonia and the coast, down to the Straits of Magellan. The **Río Negro**, south of the Colorado, flows into an oasis of intensive agriculture, which stretches for more than 250 miles (400

km). The valley itself is a narrow strip of fertile land, in sharp contrast to the desert surroundings that threaten to swallow it. Those interested in visiting agricultural areas specializing in growing fruit (apples, pears, grapes), cannot miss this place. Fruit farms, juice factories and packing establishments give an intense economic life to this oasis. **Neuquen, Cipoletti** and **Roca** are the most important cities of this region.

Traveling along the Río Negro towards the Atlantic coast, along cultivated strips of land that alternate with sections of desert, one arrives at the twin towns of **Carmen de Patagones** and **Viedma**, having covered a distance of 330 miles (540 km) from Neuquen to very near the coast. Carmen de Patagones is one of the oldest settlements in Patagonia, founded in 1779 by the Spaniards. These settlers lived in constant fear of being invaded by foreign powers seeking to conquer Patagonia. Viedma, which lies on the opposite bank of the river, was slated in the mid-1980s by President Raul Alfonsín to become the new capital of the Argentine Republic—the Argentine Brasilia—on the southern end of the continent, a symbol of the gradual shifting of economic and political interest towards the less developed south. But as the cost of moving the capital from Buenos Aires became obvious, the plan was quietly forgotten.

Nearby, one can see the caves which were used for shelter by the first settlers. Where the river meets the sea, there is a sea lion colony similar to the many others along the coast. One hundred and ten miles (180 km) to the west lies the port of **San Antonio Este**, from where all the fruit production of the valley is shipped to foreign countries.

Dudes and swans: About 120 miles (200 km) southwest from Neuquen, on the road to Bariloche, is one of the few dude ranches in Patagonia. Near the small town of **Piedra del Aguila** is the enormous **Piedra del Aguila Hotel and Ranch**. It is open during the summer season and offers a variety of outdoor activities such as camping, horseback riding, sheep shearing and fishing.

Going west from Neuquen to the Andes, one reaches the top of the Northern Lake District. On the way there, close to the town of **Zapala** is a place no birdlife enthusiast should miss in spring: the **Laguna Blanca National Park** which includes a large closed-in lake. Although there are hundreds of interesting varieties of birds, the prime attractions in this park are the black-necked swans, which gather in flocks of up to 2,000 birds. Flamingos are also part of the scenery, and the surrounding hills give shelter to large groups of eagles, peregrine falcons, and other birds of prey.

Just one word of warning: this area has not been prepared as a tourist attraction. It is therefore not simple to reach. One might try the approach from Zapala.

The Northern Lake District: The Patagonia lake district covers a stretch of land extending from Lake Alumine in the north to Los Glaciares National Park in the south, over 900 miles (1,500 km) along the Andes. One can divide this region into two sections, the Northern and Southern Lake Districts. The zone that lies in between, where traveling is not easy and normal communications are scarce, is a challenge for only the most adventurous.

The Northern Lake District covers the area between Lake Alumine in the north and Lake Amutui Quimei in the south. It encompasses 300 miles (500 km) of lakes, forests and mountains divided into four national parks. From north to south we have the Lanín National Park and the town of San Martín de los Andes, Nahuel Huapi National Park and the city of Bariloche, Lago Pueblo National Park and the village of El Bolsón and, farthest south, Los Alerces National Park with the town of Esquel. This region is connected to the Chilean lake area.

The three main cities of this district have their own airports, with regular scheduled flights all year round, and offer a complete range of traveler services (hotels, restaurants, car rentals, travel agencies). The railroad journey

from Buenos Aires to Bariloche takes 32 hours. There are also daily buses to all parts of Argentina and to Chile, across the Tromen, Huahum and Puyehue passes.

If you want to reach Puerto Montt on the Pacific Ocean from Bariloche, try the old route the Jesuits and first German settlers used: across the lakes. The journey combines traveling by bus and boat across the beautiful Nahuel Huapi, Todos los Santos and Llanquihue lakes, through marvelous settings of forests, volcanoes and crystal waters. The route is open all year round; in summer the trek is made every day and the rest of the year, three times weekly. You can book this trip at any travel agency.

There are two well-defined tourist seasons in this district: summer and winter. During the summer there is plenty to do. One can go on the regular tours, or rent a car and do some individual sightseeing. There are also many sports to keep one busy, from mountain climbing and fishing, to sailing and horseback riding. In winter, the main activity is skiing. July is the busiest month because of the Argentine schools' winter holidays. For a quieter time, one might try August.

Monkey puzzles and trout: The northern part of the Lake District, around Lake Alumine, is well known for its Indian reservations where one can find handicrafts such as ponchos and carpets. This area is also home to one of the most peculiar looking trees in the world, the Araucaria Araucana or monkey puzzle. This tree, which grows at considerable altitudes, has a primeval look to it. The fruit of this tree, the piñon, was a treat for Indians on their way across the Andean trails.

Lanín National Park, near San Martín de los Andes, is 1,508 square miles (3,920 square km) and gets its name from the imposing Lanín Volcano, situated on the border with Chile. The volcano soars to 12,474 feet (3780 meters), far above the height of surrounding peaks.

The National Park is noted for its fine fishing. The fishing season is from mid-

An ethereal vision of the Lanín Volcano.

November through mid-April. The rivers and streams (Alumine, Malleo, Chimehuin and Caleufu) around the small town of **Junín de los Andes** are famed for their abundance and variety of trout. Fly-casters come from continents away to fish for the brook, brown, fontinalis and steelhead. The best catch on record was a 27 pound (12 kilogram) brown trout—the average weight is 9-11 pounds (4-5 kilos).

Although Junín has several restaurants and pleasant hotels like the **Chimehuin Inn**, most anglers prefer one of the several fishermen's lodges located in the park. Two of these are the **San Huberto Lodge**, on the Malleo River near the border with Chile, and the **Paimun Inn** on Loake Paimun at the foot of the Lanín Volcano. Lodging costs around US$50 per day, meals and taxes included.

The Lanín National Park is also well known for hunting. Wild boar and red and fallow deer are the main attractions in the fall, which is the rutting season. The National Park takes bids for com-

pounds over most of the hunting grounds. The same goes for the farm owners who make their own agreements with hunters and outfitters. For more information, contact Jorge Trucco in **San Martín de los Andes**.

There are many guided tours, by bus or boat, departing from San Martín de los Andes. There are car rentals, camping sites and fishing, and hunting and mountain climbing guides are readily available. Also recommended is a trip to lakes Huechulaufquen and Paimun and the majestic Lanín Volcano, with its unique monkey puzzle forest. In winter, **Mount Chapelco** (6,534 feet/ 1,980 meters), 20 minutes by car from San Martín, is a small, quiet resort for alpine and cross-country skiers.

All facilities are available in San Martín. For hotels, one can choose from **La Cheminee, Le Village** or **El Viejo Equiador**; for restaurants, **El Ciervo** or **El Munich de los Andes** are much frequented. Patagonian Outfitters can see to your travel needs.

There are three roads that link San

Above the clouds at Cerro Catedral.

Martín de los Andes with Bariloche: a paved one, running through the dry steppe, along the Collon Cura River, and two dirt roads. The middle road is the shortest one across the **Córdoba Pass**, running through narrow valleys with beautiful scenery, especially in the autumn when the slopes turn to rich shades of gold and deep red. This road reaches the paved highway at **Confluencia Traful**. From here, if you take a short turn and go back inland, you come to a trout farm that belongs to the **Estancia La Primavera**. On returning to the paved road that leads to Bariloche, you ride through the **Enchanted Valley**, with its bizarre rock formations.

The third road from San Martín is the famed **Road of the Seven Lakes**. This road takes you across a spectacular region of lakes and forests and approaches Bariloche from the northern shore of Lake Nahuel Huapi. In summer, all-day tours make the trip from Bariloche to San Martín, combining both the Córdoba Pass and the Road of the Seven Lakes.

Switzerland in Argentina: Situated in the middle of **Nahuel Haupi National Park, Bariloche** is the real center of the Northern Lake District.

Buses, trains and planes arrive daily from all over the country and from Chile, across the Puyehue Pass.

Bariloche has a very strong Central European influence; most of the first settlers were of Swiss, German or Northern Italian origin. These people gave the city its European style, with Swiss chalets, ceramics, chocolates and neat shop windows. However, something tells you that you are not in Europe; boats are seldom seen on the huge Nahuel Huapi lake, the roads are swallowed in the wilderness as soon as they leave the city and at night, there are no lights on the opposite shore of the lake.

The best way to begin your tour of Bariloche is by visiting the **Patagonia Museum** in the Civic Center. This building and the Llao Llao Hotel were designed by Bustillo, and give Bariloche a distinctive architectural personality. The museum offers displays

The Llao Llao Hotel, on Lake Nahuel Huapi.

on the geological origins of the region and of local wildlife. It also has a stunning collection of Indian artifacts.

There are many excursions to choose from in the Bariloche area: half-day tours of the **Small Circuit**, Catedral Ski Center and **Mt. Otto**, and whole-day tours by bus or boat to San Martín de los Andes, **Mt. Tronador, Victoria Island** and **Puerto Blest**. Two recommended trips are to Mt. Tronador, the highest peak in the Park (11,728 feet/ 3,554 meters) with its impressive vista of glaciers, and to Victoria Island and the Myrtle Forest on the Quetrihue Peninsula. The story goes that a visiting group of Walt Disney's advisors were so impressed by the amazing white and cinammon colored trees in this forest that they used them as the basis for the scenery in the film *Bambi*.

The range of activities in the Nahuel Huapi National Park includes windsurfing, rafting, mountain climbing, fishing, hunting, horseback riding and skiing. Major facilities are available for all these sports. The **Club Andino** will provide you with any information you need that is related to mountain climbing, from guides to trails and mountain lodges (where kitchens and food are available).

Those looking for a wild and wooly Patagonian experience should try a horseback trek with Carol Jones. Carol is the granddaughter of Texas pioneer Jared Jones, and her dude-ranching operation is run out of the **Estancia Nahuel Huapi**, which Jared founded on the shores of the lake in 1889. A ride can be arranged for a morning or an entire week and will take one through breathtaking terrain in the foothills of the Andes. For more informaiton, contact Polvani Tours or the Jones family at the ranch.

Regional buys: Chocolates, jams, ceramics and sweaters are among the most important local products. The large chocolate industry has remained in the hands of Italian families and a visit to some of the downtown factories is worthwhile. So is a visit to the ceramics factory, where you can watch the

counter-culture community t El Blosón.

artisans at work. Sweaters are for sale almost everywhere, a recommended shop is **Arbol**, on the main street. On the same street is **Tito Testone**, where you can buy jewelry and handicrafts.

The **Catedral Ski Center**, 11 miles (17 km) from Bariloche, is one of the biggest in the southern hemisphere. The base of the lifts is at 3,465 feet (1050 meters) above sea level, and a cable-car and chair-lifts take you up to a height of 6,633 feet (2010 meters). The view from the slopes is absolutely superb. The ski runs range in difficulty from novice to expert, and cover more than 15.5 miles (25 km). The ski season starts at the end of June and continues through September. Ski rentals, ski schools, restaurants, hotels and ski lodges are available.

Bariloche has a large variety of hotels, ranging from small cozy inns to first class luxury hotels. **La Pastorella, El Candil**, the **Edelweiss** and the exclusive **El Casco** are some of the choices.

Restaurants offer a variety of fare, from fondue and trout, to venison and wild boar. Try **Casita Suiza, Kandahar**, and **El Viejo Munich**, a meeting place for locals.

For an authentic taste of the regional barbeque, don't miss the **Viejo Boliche**, 11 miles (18 km) from Bariloche. The restaurant is located in an old shed which the Jones family used as a general store at the beginning of the century. If you need a travel agent, try Polvani Tours, where English and German are spoken.

Hippie refuge: **El Bolsón** is a small town 80 miles (130 km) south of Bariloche, situated in a narrow valley with its own microclimate. Beer hops and all sorts of berries are grown on small farms. The hippies of the 1960s chose El Bolsón as their sanctuary. Nowadays, there are just a few of these idealists left, leading peaceful lives on farms perched in the mountains.

The **Lago Pueblo National Park** (92 square miles/237 square km) is an angler's paradise and its mountains covered with ancient forests of deciduous

Below: left, graveyard, and right, a Welsh Bible. Opposite page: a Welsh farmer proud of his crop.

THE WELSH IN PATAGONIA

Patagonia has warm and intimate associations for the Welsh—a Welshman traveling in Patagonia's Chubut Valley enters a time warp framed in a culturally distorted mirror. On the streets of Trelew he will overhear Welsh spoken, in slightly archaic utterances, by elderly ladies, while in the Andean foothills around Trevelin he can converse in Welsh with a rancher who drinks *mate*, rides like a gaucho and whose other languages are Spanish and English.

Patagonia is partly pampas, largely desert and unrelentingly wind-blown, with only small areas of fertile soil and little discovered mineral wealth. Why would anyone leave the lush valleys and green hills of Wales to settle in such a place? The Welsh came, between 1865 and 1914, partly to escape conditions in Wales which they deemed culturally oppressive, partly because of the promise—later discovered to be exaggerated—of exciting economic opportunities, and largely to be able to pursue their religious traditions in their own language. The disruptions of the 19th century industrial revolution uprooted many Welsh peasant agriculturists; the cost of delivering produce to market became exorbitant because of turnpike fees, grazing land was enclosed and landless laborers were exploited. Increasing domination of Welsh public life by the arrogant English officials further upset the Welsh. Thus alienated in his own land, the Welshman left.

Equally powerful was the effect on the Welsh people of the religious revivals of the period, which precipitated a pietistic religiosity that lasted into the post-World War I period. For many, the worldliness of modern life made impossible the quiet spirituality of earlier times, and they saw their escape in distant, unpopulated areas of the world then opening up. Some had already tried Canada and the United States and were frustrated by the tides of other European nationalities which threatened the purity of their communities. They responded when Argentina offered cheap land to immigrants who would settle and develop its vast spaces before an aggressive Chile pre-empted them. From the United States and from Wales they came in small ships on hazardous voyages to Puerto Madryn, and settled in the Chubut Valley.

Although the hardships of those gritty pioneers are more than a century behind their descendants, the pioneer tradition is proudly remembered. Some remain in agriculture, many are in trade and commerce. Although it is mainly the older generation that still speaks Welsh, descendants will proudly show you their chapels and cemeteries (very much as in Wales), take you for Welsh Tea in one of the area's many tea houses, and reminisce about their forebears and the difficulties they overcame. They speak of the devastating floods of the Chubut which almost demolished the community at the turn of the century, the scouts who went on Indian trails to the Andean foothills to settle in the Cwm Hyfrwd (the Gorgeous Valley), the loneliness of the prairies in the long cold winters and the incessant winds, and the lack of capital which made all undertakings a matter of backbreaking labor.

Unfortunately, change comes rapidly; old ways mutate and are overtaken by technology. The Welsh language is losing its hold and will not long be spoken in Patagonia. But traditions remain, and the Patagonian Welsh hold Eisteddfods as of old to compete in song and verse, they revere the tradition of the chapel even when they do not attend, and they take enormous pride in their links with Wales.

beech trees and cypresses are a delight for wanderers and mountain climbers. The **Amancay Inn** and the **Don Diego Restaurant** offer food and lodging.

The gringo outlaws: Farther south, on the road to Esquel, you come across the beautiful **Cholila Valley**. According to some historians, this place was chosen by Butch Cassidy and the Sundance Kid as a temporary shelter while they were on the run from Pinkerton's agents. A letter sent by them to Matilda Davis in Utah, dated August 10th, 1902, was posted at Cholila. After their famous holdup of the Río Gallegos Bank, in 1905, they were again on the run, until they were finally killed by the Bolivian police. Other members of the gang who stayed on in this region were ambushed and shot to death, years later, by the Argentine constabulary.

Welsh tea: From Cholila, the road going south splits in two. Road #40 turns slightly to the east, through the large **Leleque Ranch**, along the narrow gauge railway, until it reaches Esquel. The other route to Esquel takes one right into **Los Alerces National Park**. This park covers 1,012 square miles (2,630 square km) and has a landscape similar to the others of the region, though it is less spoiled by towns and people. The tourists who visit the park during the summer stay at camping sites and fishermen's lodges around **Lake Futalaufquen**, such as the **Quimei Quipan Inn** and the **Futalaufquen Hotel**. One tour you should not miss is the all-day boat excursion to Lake Menendez, with the outstanding view of **Cerro Torrecillas** (7,260 feet/ 2,200 meters) and its glaciers. Be sure to see the huge Fitzroya's trees (related to the American redwood), which are over 2,000 years old.

As you get closer to Trevelin and Esquel you begin to leave behind the Northern Lake District. This area is strongly influenced by Welsh culture, as a sizeable community of Welshmen settled here in 1888 after a long trek from the Atlantic coast across the Chubut Valley.

Trevelin, 25 miles (40 km) east of the National Park, is a small village of Welsh origin. The name in Welsh means "town of the mill." The old mill has recently been converted into a museum which houses all sorts of implements that belonged to the first Welsh settlers, together with old photographs and a Welsh Bible. As in all the Welsh communities of Patagonia, you can enjoy a typical tea with Welsh cookies and cakes here. There is also a barbeque restaurant, El Quincho, which serves excellent food.

Narrow gauge adventure: Esquel, 14 miles (23 km) northeast of Trevelin, is also an offshoot of the Welsh Chubut colony. The town, with 25,000 inhabitants, lies to the east of the Andes, on the border of the Patagonian desert. The railway station here is the most southerly point of the Argentine railway network. The narrow gauge railway (2.48 feet/0.75 meters), connects Esquel with **Ingeniero Jacobacci** to the north. There is no better way to get acquainted with Patagonia and its people than by a trip on this quaint train pulled by an old-fashioned steam locomotive.

eft, tacking ay in hubut. ight, a aucho's omfort- ble ayered addle and he day's atch.

In its remote location, on the edge of the desert, Esquel has the feel of a town in the old American West. One is as likely to see a person riding along on horseback here as in a car. Sometimes the rider will be a gaucho dandy, all dressed up with broad-brimmed hat, kerchief, and *bombachas* (baggy pleated pants). Several times a year, a rural fair is held in Esquel. People come from miles around to trade livestock and supplies. January is your best bet for catching this colorful spectacle.

In town, several stores are well-stocked with riding tackle and ranch equipment. Ornate stirrups and hand-tooled saddles are displayed next to braided rawhide ropes and cast iron cookware. At **El Basco** you can outfit yourself with various items from a typical gaucho wardrobe.

From April 15th through December, the goose-hunting season is open, and Esquel and Trevelin become the centers of this sport.

In winter, Esquel turns into a ski resort, with **La Hoya Ski Center** 11 miles (17 km) away. Compared with Bariloche and Catedral, this ski area is considerably smaller and cozier. All rental facilities are available. For accommodations, try the **Tehuelche Hotel** or **Los Troncos Inn**. **Tour d'Argent** is one of the best restaurants in this part of Patagonia.

The beautiful valley: Between the Atlantic coast and Esquel lies the **Chubut Valley**. Only the lower valley, covering an area of 19 square miles (50 square km) is fertile, while the rest is parched.

The Welsh used this valley, which they called **Cwm hyfrwd** (Beautiful Valley), to reach the Esquel/Trevelin area. Eluned Morgan describes this route in her book *Dringo'r Andes* (Climbing the Andes) in a very romantic way.

Halfway down the valley, the river cuts through the plateau, forming an impressive canyon with red and white ravines named the **Altars** and **Martyrs Valleys**. The latter refers to an ambush set by the Indians in 1883, where a

Oil pumps in the Patagonian South.

group of young Welshmen was wiped out. The lone survivor, John Evans, managed to escape, thanks to his horse, Malacara, which leapt over the steep ravine. The graves of these unfortunate people, who are vividly described in Morgan's book, can still be seen alongside the road.

Before coming to the lower valley, you reach the **F. Ameghino Dam** and its artificial lake. These are nestled in a narrow rocky gorge and form an impressive sight.

The lower Chubut valley was the site of the first settlement established by the Welsh. The towns of Dolavon, Gaiman, Trelew and Rawson developed here, and today they are surrounded by intensively cultivated lands.

Gaiman has an interesting museum similar to the one in Trevelin. The *Eisteddfod*, the Welsh Arts Festival, which features singing and reciting, is held here every August. The river meets the sea close to **Rawson**, the provincial capital city. Coming back from an excursion to Punta Tombo, in the after-

noon, drive by the small fishermen's port at Rawson to watch the men as they unload their day's catch, and lazy sea lions grab whatever falls overboard.

Trelew is the most important city in the lower valley. Its Welsh ambience has faded, giving way to a modern industrial city. The airport of Trelew is the gateway to enter the Valdés Peninsula area.

Penguin highways: Puerto Madryn, on the Atlantic coast, 40 miles (65 km) north of Trelew, was founded by Parry Madryn in 1865 and has become a center for those visiting the Valdés Peninsula and Punta Tombo. In Madryn, one can stay at the **Tolosa Hotel** or the **Peninsula Valdés Hotel**, which has a wonderful view over the Atlantic. Good seafood can be found at **La Caleta**, and the **Club Nautica**. For information on excursions, car rentals and guides, ask at **Receptivo Puerto Madryn**, right beside the Peninsula Valdés Hotel.

There are two main areas to visit from Puerto Madryn: **Punta Tombo** and the

The José Ormachea Petrified Forest Reserve.

Valdés Peninsula. Punta Tombo, 102 miles (165 km) south of Madryn (67 miles/108 km of which is dirt road), is the largest rookery of Magellanic penguins in the world. The penguins arrive in September and stay until March. In this rookery you will have the opportunity to walk among thousands of these comic birds, to watch their regular comings and goings to the sea along well-defined "penguin highways," and to see them fish near the coast for their meals. On your way back to Madryn, don't forget to stop by Rawson's port and the Gaiman Museum.

More wildlife: The Valdés Peninsula is one of the most important wildlife reserves in Argentina. It is the breeding ground for southern right whales, elephant seals and sea lions. Guanacos, rheas and maras can be seen loping along the road. The peninsula itself is a large wasteland, with the lowest point on the South American continent, 132 feet (40 meters) below sea level. Years ago, the salt pits of the peninsula produced great quantities of salt which

were shipped out from Puerto Madryn.

The **Estancia La Adela** belongs to one family. It is spread over 100,000 hectares and has 60,000 sheep. The shearing sheds can be seen close to the elephant seal colony in **Caleta Valdés**.

The main elephant seal colony is in **Punta Norte**, and the elephant seal colony is close to **Puerto Piramides**. This little village, 59 miles (95 km) from Puerto Madryn, offers some camping sites, hotels and restaurants. Scuba diving is a popular sport in this area, along with water skiing and surfing. The real attraction of this area is the southern right whales. In the 19th century there were more than 700 whalers sailing in these waters. An international protection treaty was signed in 1935, and since then the recovery of the mammals has been very slow. Naturalists calculate the present population to be only 2,000 strong.

The whales come to breed near these shores in early spring and stay until the end of November. They are a delight to watch as they play in the water, diving and cavorting, spraying water all around. In Puerto Piramides you can hire boats that will take you near enough to enjoy this sight. At the same time, you can observe the sea lions and cormorant colonies at the foot of the pyramid-shaped cliff that gives this location its name.

On the small side road out of the peninsula stands a monument dedicated to the first Spanish settlement here, which only lasted from 1774 to 1810, when the settlers were forced to flee from the native warriors. In front of this monument there is a sea bird reserve, the **Isla de los Pajaros**. Farther on, as you leave the peninsula, you drive past the **Riacho San José**. Here, you may be treated to the sight of hundreds of flamingos standing by the sea.

Oil country: Two hundred and seventy miles (440 km) south of Trelew is the major city in Patagonia, **Comodoro Rivadavia**, with a population exceeding 100,000. The local airport has daily flights connecting the Patagonian cities. Accommodations can be found at the **Austral Hotel**.

Left, an itinerant sheep shearer plying his trade. Right, up close at the Perito Moreno Glacier.

In 1907, while a desperate search for drinking water was under way, oil was discovered. Since that time, this has become one of the most important oil-producing regions in the country. Today, Comodoro Rivadavia is a typical Patagonian city, with flat roofs, some tall buildings, fisheries, textile factories and the ever present Patagonian wind.

The town witnessed the immigration of Boers from Transvaal and Orange in southern Africa, who left their homeland in search of a new place to live after the Boer War. The first ones arrived in 1903, under the leadership of Conrad Visser and Martin Venter. Although many returned to South Africa after a while, there are still many of their descendants living in the region.

The fertile valley of **Colonia Sarmiento** lies 118 miles (190 km) west of Comodoro Rivadavia. Heading south of the valley for 19 miles (30 km), one reaches the **José Ormachea Petrified Forest** which has remains that are more than a million years old. This forest, like several others in Patagonia, tells us much of the geological past of this land, which a long time ago was covered by thick forests.

To the west is the town of **Perito Moreno**, near the enormous **Lago Buenos Aires**. This town is accessible by plane.

Thirty-seven miles (60 km) south on Road #40, turn left on a side road, and you'll arrive at the famous **Cuevas de las Manos**. The caves, set in a beautiful canyon, have walls that are covered by thousand-year-old paintings of hands and animals. This is one of the hidden secrets of Patagonia that only the most adventurous manage to enjoy.

Petrified wonder: Before one continues on to the southern end of the continent, special mention should be made of a pristine natural wonder, the **Monumento Natural Bosques Petrificados**, which is located in the northeastern part of Santa Cruz Province, 154 miles (248 km) south of Comodoro Rivadavia and 52 miles (84 km) west from the paved Road #3. This enormous petrified forest occupies over 10,000 hectares. At the edges of

the canyons and mesas, the stone-hard trunks of 150 million-year-old araucarias stick out of the ground. Some of the trunks are 100 feet long and three feet wide (30 meters by one meter), among the biggest in the world.

Southern Patagonia: Along the coast of Santa Cruz lie several ports which carry names well known in the history of world navigation. **Puerto Deseado** was named after Cavendish's flagship, Desire. From here one can visit nearby islands to see penguins and grey cormorants. **Puerto San Julian** is the harbor where Magellan spent the winter of 1520, and where Drake hanged the mutineer Thomas Doughty in 1578. Both towns have airports.

Farthur south is **Puerto Santa Cruz**, one of the most important harbors that can be found along this stretch of coast. Finally, at the far end of continental America, is **Río Gallegos**.

Myriads of sheep: The early settlers in the southern tip of Patagonia were Scottish and English sheep farmers. Many of them came over from the Falk-

Right, a climber contemplates Mt. Fitz Roy.

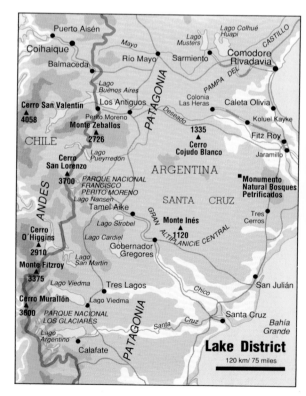

Lake District
120 km/ 75 miles

land/Malvinas islands at the end of the 19th century, encouraged by an offer, from the governor of Santa Cruz, of land on the new frontier. Others came over from Punta Arenas and Puerto Natales in Chile.

C. Siewart, a visitor to Río Gallegos at the turn of the century, wrote, "In this wonderful land there are no hotels and no one to carry the luggage. The normal language seems to be English, and one has the feeling of being in Old England, or at least in the Falklands. Except for the government officials, everything else is English: the money, the sheep, the language, the drinks, the ladies and the gentlemen."

Vast *estancias* were born around Río Gallegos, and thousands of tons of wool were shipped to England through the southern ports of San Julian, Puerto Deseado and Río Gallegos. No Argentine custom duties existed in the early days, and all sorts of goods entered this region for everyday life.

There was a time when Argentina had 80 million sheep and was one of the main wool suppliers in the world. Now there are only 30 million sheep left, almost all of them in Patagonia. In 1934, the area around Río Gallegos had 93 *estancias*, while the total number of people in charge of 180,000 sheep was only 800. The sizes of these *estancias* ranged from 2,000 to 200,000 hectares. Today the most common breeds of sheep raised are the Australian Merinos and Corriedales.

At least twice a year the sheep are herded for shearing and bathing. The farm work starts in October and lasts until January, and during this time, things get very lively. A *compara*, a group of men who travel with all the necessary gear, from one *estancia* to the next, are hired for the annual shearing. They lead a nomadic life, working hard and sleeping under the stars. The ox wagons that once carried the wool to the coast have been replaced by trucks.

A rugged life: After the shearing, quiet returns to these plains until the next season. The gauchos, or *paisanos* as they call themselves in the south, stay

after the shearing *compara* has gone. They work on the ranch all year round. Far away from the tourist areas they lead a hard life, riding long distances, looking after the sheep and the land. Their sunburnt, hard features speak for themselves. The paisano's only possessions are his horse, a saddle covered with a sheepskin (*recado*), a long knife (*facon*) and a poncho.

In Río Gallegos, the English influence of the early days has vanished with the arrival of the Argentines and Chileans looking for new opportunities, and the town's population has risen to approximately 80,000. In spite of its interesting history, Río Gallegos does not offer much to the visitor. It would, perhaps be more interesting to visit a nearby *estancia*.

Accommodations in Río Gallegos include the **Comercio Hotel and Restaurant** which serves seafood, and the **English Club**, with its nostalgic air. If you are in need of Argentine currency before leaving for the Calafate region, remember to change your money here, because it is not easy to do so elsewhere.

The Santa Cruz revolt: Between 1920 and 1921, Santa Cruz experienced an odd and bloody revolt. Strikes started, influenced by the Russian revolution and led by anarchists from various parts of the world, who worked in the port and cold storage plants in the main towns of the coast. Due to the miserable living conditions on the farms, the strikes spread to the countryside. Although the first strike ended peacefully in 1920, the second one turned into a violent encounter. There were several skirmishes throughout the area between strikers and the army. Many lonely graves reminds us of this tragic event, one of the saddest in Patagonia history.

The story does not end in Patagonia. In 1923, Colonel Varela, who had been in charge of the army troops during the strikes, was murdered by an anarchist, Kurt Wilkens, who threw a bomb at his feet on a street in Buenos Aires. Wilkens was subsequently murdered in prison.

The Southern Lake District: Calafate, the main town in the southern lake district, is 186 miles (300 km) to the west of Río Gallegos. LADE propeller flights connect Río Gallegos and Calafate daily, during the peak season (summer), and three times weekly the rest of the year. However, you must book in advance. By land, it is a six-hour drive on partly paved roads. On the drive across, if the day is clear, one can take in the view from Bajada de Miguens, of magnificent Mt. Fitz Roy (11,138 feet/3,375 meters).

Calafate is a small town that thrives in summer but is lonely and quiet during the long, cold winter months. The town lies at a latitude even farther south than New Zealand.

An excursion by foot or car in the environs of Calafate may reward the visitor with sightings of several rare species of birds, including black-necked swans and condors. Bring your binoculars.

West of Calafate, **Los Glaciares National Park** stretches parallel to the Andes for over 120 miles (200 km). There, on the boundary with Chile, lies the eastern side of the Continental Ice Cap. The whole Ice Cap covers an area of 8,400 square miles (22,000 square km), including both sectors north and south of the Bakar Sound. The southern sector is almost 248 miles (400 km) long. In this area of vast ice fields, those interested in geological phenomena can see numerous nunataks, ultra-hard rock outcroppings that have survived the onslaught of glaciers.

Glacial splendor: Fifty miles (80 km) to the west of Calafate lies the **Ventisquero Moreno**, a majestic glacier that descends from the ice cap into Lake Argentino, forming a barrier two miles wide by 165 feet high (three km by 50 meters).

The Moreno Glacier is one of the few in the world that is getting larger. Since 1937, the glacier has moved in cycles of approximately four years. In this cycle, the glacier front advances to meet a spit of land, thus cutting off a portion of the lake. The water level in the separated part begins to rise, and the pressure builds until, finally, the water breaks through the icy dam to rejoin the rest of the lake. The disintegration and eventual collapse of the glacial wall is one of the most breathtaking spectacles imaginable. Massive chunks of ice plunge into the lake, and there, become icebergs. The thunder caused can be heard as far away as Calafate.

Unfortunately, there is no way to know exactly when this breakup will take place, so catching it is pretty much a matter of luck. However, no matter what part of the cycle the glacier is in when you visit, you will almost certainly be treated to some degree of ice activity. Even a sliver breaking off the face of the glacier makes a deafening report and high splash as it hits the lake. Don't venture too far down the cliff face for a better look, as the waves caused by breaking ice have been known to wash away viewers.

The other major glacier in the area is **Upsala** (30 miles long and 6 wide, 50 km long and 10 wide), which faces the northwestern tip of Lake Argentino. This glacier can only be viewed from the lake, and daily boat excursions depart from **Puerto Bandera**, 25 miles (40 km) west of Calafate. It is an all-day trip, and the winds can get quite chilly, so be sure to bring appropriate clothing. One of the best parts of the trip is watching deep-blue icebergs floating on the milky glacial waters of the lake. On the return trip, a stop is sometimes made at the **Estancia La Anita**, with its enormous shearing shed.

Hotel space in Calafate is severely limited during the short summer season, so be sure to make reservations well in advance.

Soaring granite: One hundred and forty-three miles (230 km) north of Calafate, one reaches Lake Viedma and the rugged granite peaks of **Cerro Torre** and **Mt. Fitz Roy**, named Chalten (Blue Peak) by the natives. These peaks attract mountain climbers from all over the world. There is a small mountain lodge where one can have meals and hire guides and horses. These services should be requested in advance. Area hotels include the **Kaiken,**

Kau Yatun and the **Michelangelo**, which has an excellent restaurant (their speciality is mutton). The local travel agent is **Interlagos**.

From Calafate to the south, one can enter the **Paine National Park** in Chile. Although it is really quite close across the border, the best way to reach the park is by returning to Río Gallegos and going from there to **Puerto Natales** in Chile, via **Rio Turbo** on the border. Rio Turbo is the most important coal mining center in Argentina. The coal is transported by narrow gauge rail to Río Gallegos. Just to the south is the southern continental border of Argentina and the Strait of Magellan. Beyond that lies Tierra del Fuego.

Islas Malvinas/Falkland Islands: These islands cover a surface of 4,507 square miles (11,718 square km) and lie 340 miles (550 km) from the Patagonian coast. In 1690, Captain Strong, on landing on the islands, named them in honor of Lord Anthony Cary, Viscount of Falkland.

During the following centuries, most of the seafarers and whalers that navigated these waters came from the French port of St. Malo, and they gave the islands the French name of Isles Malouines. From this was derived Malvinas, the Spanish name for the islands.

The main activity on the islands has always been sheep farming. The surrounding area is a very rich fishing zone. The climate is rather oceanic, and the average temperature is 42.8F(6°C).

Before the 1982 conflict over these islands, there were about 1800 people of English descent living here. Since then, the British military presence has increased this number greatly.

King and Magellanic penguin colonies and large numbers of seals, wild geese and ducks offer endless interest to wildlife enthusiasts. Unfortunately, at the time of this printing, it is impossible to visit the islands from the Argentine mainland, due to on-going political tensions between Great Britain and Argentina.

Antarctica: Three hundred miles (500 km) south of Cape Horn rises the frozen continent of Antarctica. James Cook, while sailing round the South Georgia island in the 18th century wrote in his logbook:

"I find no words to describe its horrible and wild aspect. If thus is the land we discovered, what can we expect of the land that lies farther south? For it is reasonable to assume that we have seen the best, because it lies in the north. If someone has the resolution and perseverance to clear this matter, sailing farther south, I will not envy the honor of his discoveries, but I dare to say that the world will not take any advantage on it."

The Antarctica Treaty of 1959-61, signed by many interested countries, shows how wrong Cook's judgment was. This continent, which covers five million square miles (14 million square km), has an ice cap that at points is 10,000 feet (3,000 meters) thick. Incredible mineral resources are hidden beneath.

Many countries, among them Argentina, claim portions of Antarctica for themselves. Argentina has staked out the sector between longitudes 25°W and 74°W, which overlaps the Chilean and British claims. The Antarctica Treaty established that the region has to be used for peaceful purposes, for international cooperation in scientific research, and must not become the site or object of international hostilities. The treaty was declared valid for 30 years (1961-1991), and will automatically be extended, unless one of the signatories denounces it.

Under the conditions of the treaty, tourism has been developed over the last few years. Many agencies offer pleasure and scientific cruises, departing from **Ushuaia** and **Punta Arenas**. Among those specializing in such tours are Society Expeditions in the U.S.A. and Antartur in Argentina. Through rough seas and mountainous icebergs, the cruises visit penguin rookeries, seal colonies and research stations belonging to different countries. A visit to Antarctica promises to be a memorable experience.

arious
orms of
vildlife on
he Antarc-
c shore.

DISTANT LAND OF FIRE

Tierra del Fuego, the Land of Fire, lies at the very southern tip of the South American continent. Beyond it there is only the icy mass of Antarctica. The story goes that the area got its name from early European explorers, who when passing by on ships en route to riches further west, could see the landscape dotted with the camp-fires of the islands' original inhabitants. This eerie vision of glow-ing shorelines, combined with tales of early passages around the treacherous, stormy Cape Horn, provide a fitting psychological preparation for the modern day traveler; one truly does feel at the end of the earth down here, in a wild and mysterious land. But the feeling of isolation should be an invigorating one, allied with a spirit of adventure.

One does not just happen to pass through Tierra del Fuego; a concerted effort must be made to get here, and the manner of arrival can take several forms. Perhaps the most luxurious way to see the area is aboard one of the cruise ships that go from Punta Arenas, in Chile, to either Buenos Aires or Rio de Janeiro. Many of these tours specialize in exploring the exotic wildlife of the coast, and sail through the spectacular fjords of southern Chile and the islands of Tierra del Fuego. Certainly the most hair-raising way to arrive is by flying into the city of Ushuaia; diving down over the steep, curled tip of the Andes range, the plane comes to a screeching halt on the narrow coastal strip right at the edge of the Beagle Channel. Work is under way to lengthen the runway, which may just take some of the fun out of a visit. It is possible to drive to Tierra del Fuego, using a ferry to get across the Strait of Magellan, but it's a long way down. At the very tail end of the Pan-American Highway is a sign an-nouncing that there is no more. Buenos Aires is a rugged 2,010 miles (3,242 km) away.

Preceding pages: a testimony to the force of the wind in Tierra del Fuego; Fuegian King Crab rivals Alaska's in taste and size. Left, Isla de los Estados.

UTTERMOST SOUTH

The very name, Tierra del Fuego, evokes feelings of distance, fear of the elements, isolation, loneliness. Shrieking gales, towering waves, snow and ice, desolation—these are some of the images of what is considered the very end of the world.

In the days of sail, many people—the early explorers and scientists, merchants bound for Chile for nitrates, the East Indies for spices or Australia for wheat, the miners and settlers to the west coast of the Americas and Australia—were able to claim they had rounded Cape Horn; some were shipwrecked there, but few stayed to settle. With the opening of the Panama Canal in 1914, fewer ships went to the far south. By then Europeans had settled parts of Tierra del Fuego, but it was difficult for tourists to reach.

In the last 20 years this has changed; Tierra del Fuego is now a popular destination for discerning travelers and although all the above images can be true enough, most visitors are pleasantly surprised on reaching the uttermost south.

Geography and climate: Geologically, Tierra del Fuego (Land of Fire, Fireland, Fuegia) is a fascinating place. Eons ago, it rested under the sea. The land slowly rose and mountains were formed as the great tectonic plates which underlie the continents and sea floors pushed together; the Fuegian Archipelago is one of the places in the world where evidence of this phenomenon can be most readily seen. Ever so slowly, glacial ages came and went; at their height, most of what is now the Patagonian continental shelf was dry land. The waters of the Strait of Magellan broke through the tip of the continent some 10,000 years ago, at the end of the last ice age, isolating Tierra del Fuego from Patagonia.

Technically speaking, the Archipelago of Tierra del Fuego includes all the land south of the Strait of Magellan and north of the Drake Passage, although only one island, the Isla Grande, is actually called Tierra del Fuego. Locally, the Isla Grande de Tierra del Fuego is known simply as the Island. It is skirted to the south and west, by a maze of islands, islets, channels, fjords and caves, most of them uninhabited and many unexplored.

The Fuegian Archipelago, which lies between latitudes 52°25' and 56° S, with the southwestern South Atlantic meeting the southeastern South Pacific at Cape Horn, is well within the Subantarctic Zone. Its cool climate is dominated by the prevailing strong southwesterly winds which sweep in off the South Pacific waters further south. These often gale-force winds can occur throughout the year but are strongest from the end of August to March (spring and summer)—early sailors described this area as the "Roaring Forties, the Furious Fifties, the Screaming Sixties."

The Andes Mountains, curving from northwest to east across the archipel-

Left, a figurehead in the Territorial Museum. Right, headed for the barber's.

ago, insure high precipitation over the western and southern maze of islands, leaving less moisture for the northeastern plains. Temperatures along the Beagle Channel range from a record high of 86 F (30 C) in summer to a record low of about 7 F (-14 C) in winter. Temperatures in the plains region are more extreme, but all of Tierra del Fuego lives in a perpetual "cool spring" where the weather can "run through the four seasons on any day of the year."

The inhabitants: Plant and animal life in this subantarctic climate is extremely abundant but less varied in species than in warmer regions of the world. Only six kinds of trees are found; the dominant three are species of *Nothofagus* or southern beech. Only two of these trees, the *ñire* (*Nothofagus antarctica*) and the *lenga* (*N. pumilio*) are deciduous. The *coihue* (*N. betuloides*), the winter's bark (*Drimys winteri*), *leña dura* (*Maytenus magellanica*) and cypress (*Pilgerodendron uviferum*) are evergreen. The lat-

ter grows only in the western channels (Chile).

Several kinds of shrubs produce beautiful flowers or edible berries. The most famous is the *Calafate* (*Berberis buxifolia*); legend says you will come back again if you brave its long thorns to eat its delicious, seedy berries. The firebush (*Embothrium coccineum*) is covered with bright red blossoms in late spring. Most wildflowers are small but well worth searching for. Flowering plants and ferns total about 500 species, some 150 of which have been introduced or naturalized.

Native land animals are few: the guanaco, Fuegian fox (Andean wolf), bats, tucu-tucu, and mice. Introduced animals (Beaver, muskrats, rabbits, Patagonian foxes) are abundant. About 200 species of birds are resident or visit the archipelago. Even animals usually associated with warmer climates, such as parrots, flamingoes and hummingbirds, are found.

The sea is highly productive in algae, chief of which are two species of giant

Back from the barber's.

kelp. Twenty-seven species of cetaceans, six of seals and sea lions, two of otter and the nutria visit the archipelago. Fish, *centolla* (southern king crab), mussels, scallops, sea urchins and other invertebrates inhabit the waters.

Man arrived on the archipelago in two ways. The earliest record on Tierra del Fuego is a 10,400-year-old site at Bahía Inútil, occupied by a terrestrial people who, near the end of the last ice age, crossed the Magellanic land bridge before waters broke through it to form the strait. The oldest adaptation to a marine environment is a 6,000-year-old site at Tunel on the Beagle Channel, developed by indigenous canoe peoples who moved southward and then eastward through the channels.

On the arrival of the Europeans, four cultural groups peopled the area: the Ona (Shelknam) and Haush were the guanaco-hunting foot Indians of the plains, while the Yahgans (Yamana) and Alaculuf were the spear-hunting canoe natives of the islands and chan-

nels. Eliminated mainly by white man's diseases, fewer than five pure members remain of each tribe, although many persons of mixed blood have been incorporated into the general population.

Exploration and settlement: The European exploration of Tierra del Fuego—from Magellan in 1520, through pirates, explorers, collectors, scientists, sealers and whalers, missionaries, seekers of gold, merchants, and on up to the present population—is among the world's most fascinating. Many visit Tierra del Fuego because of childhood memories of stories of Drake, Cook, Darwin, the arduous, careful surveys of Fitzroy and King, and ships with names like the *Unity*, *Hoorn*, *Golden Hind*, *Resolution*, *Endeavour*, *Beagle*, *Pamir* and *Cutty Sark*. Others come because of books they read at some time—Darwin's *Journal of Researches*, Reisenberg's *Cape Horn*—but one book, *Uttermost Part of the Earth* by E. Lucas Bridges, towers above the others as one of the world's great adventure stories.

A sheep station near Río Grande.

Bridges, who was born in Tierra del Fuego, was a pioneer whose adventurous spirit led him all over the world. In *Uttermost Part,* Bridges writes of how his father, Thomas Bridges, began the Anglican Mission in Ushuaia (1870), explored unknown areas, worked with and taught the Yahgans and finally settled the first farm, now over 100 years old. The missionaries were followed by a prefecture (coast guard) station, gold miners, sheep farmers, small merchants, oil workers and all that makes up a modern town, the most recent being electronics factory workers. In one short century Tierra del Fuego has gone from being populated by near-naked natives to being visited by thousands of tourists arriving on jet planes and huge passenger liners.

Across the strait: Politically, Tierra del Fuego is divided between Chile (to the west and south) and Argentina (north and east). The Argentinian section is part of the *Territorio Nacional de Tierra del Fuego, Antártida e Islas del Atlántico Sur*, with its capital in the town of Ushuaia. The rough triangle that is Argentina's part of the Isla Grande covers some 8,300 square miles (21,340 square km), an area about the size of the state of Connecticut, USA, with 600 miles (970 km) of marine coastline and 150 miles (240 km) of land border with Chile to the west.

There are three towns: Ushuaia (begun in 1869, officially founded in 1884), on the Beagle Channel, Río Grande (begun in 1893, officially founded in 1921) on the northern plains, and Tólhuin (founded in 1972) on the eastern edge of Lago Fagnano in the center of the Territory. One main road, Ruta 3, joins the northern tip at Cabo Espiritu Santo at the eastern mouth of the Strait of Magellan to Ushuaia, and ends, as the end of the Pan-American Highway, at Lapataia, on the southwestern border with Chile.

Visitors arrive in Tierra del Fuego by several means. Aerolineas Argentinas and Austral airlines provide several 737 jets a day to Río Grande and Ushuaia, the latter being a four-hour flight from

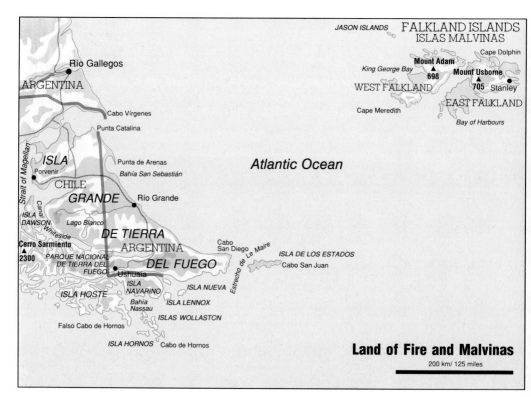

Land of Fire and Malvinas

200 km/ 125 miles

Argentina's capital, Buenos Aires.

Tourist ships (*Linea*, the *Jason*, the *Europa* and others) briefly visit Ushuaia as part of longer cruises between Rio de Janeiro, Buenos Aires and the west coast of South America. Ushuaia, like Punta Arenas in Chile, is a jumping off point for tourist ships going to the Antarctic.

Visitors coming by land must cross the **Strait of Magellan** by ferry, either at the **First Narrows** (a 20-30 minute barge crossing) or between **Punta Arenas** and **Porvenir**, a two-to-three-hour crossing. There are no regular bus lines between Río Gallegos and Río Grande and Ushuaia.

Hotel capacity has not kept up with the number of tourists reaching the island; it is best to make hotel and airline reservations well in advance. Campsites, mostly without sanitary facilities, are available at several localities. Prices are somewhat higher than in mainland Argentina; nearly all supplies, like the tourists, must come from far to the north. Tierra del Fuego is a "special customs area," (not a free port); there are many imported items but few local crafts.

Gold, fossils and sheep: Many visitors find the northern plains of Tierra del Fuego rather barren, but there is much to do and see if time and interest permit. Those arriving by road must enter from Chile at **Bahía San Sebastián**, where there is border control, a small *hosteria* (14 beds, make reservations at the Argentine Automobile Club, ACA, in Ushuaia), restaurant and fuel. Enormous mud flats, periodically covered by tides as high as 36 feet (11 meters), extend along the western side of the bay. This is sheep farming and oil country, where wells dot the grasslands and rolling hills back from the coast. Oil roads wander in all directions, while sheep, cattle, guanacos and wild geese graze among them.

The best way to see guanacos on Tierra del Fuego is to drive north along the bay from the San Sebastián border post. A 45-minute drive will take you to the base of the stony, super-barren

The ravages of a beaver dam.

Peninsula Páramo, but family groups of guanacos will be seen on the salt flats long before that. The base of the Páramo was once the main site of the gold rush (1887 - 1898). Julius Popper set up his mining operation here and became the dictator of the northern plains. Today, nothing remains of his buildings, dredges or cemetery.

Cliffs along the coast near **Cabo Espiritu Santo** and the roads near San Sebastián yield both marine and forest fossils, attesting to bygone eras. Sandstone hills farther south are littered with fossil shells and crabs.

The plains may look yellow or brown and appear to have little life, but this is Tierra del Fuego's best sheep land. A stop to look and listen will reveal many birds, and on a short walk one may find hidden wildflowers. Do not be dismayed by the ever-present wind: people, birds, animals and plants which live here find it natural. One must remember that coming to Tierra del Fuego is an adventure.

Going southeast toward Río Grande, **Estancia Sara**, Tierra del Fuego's largest sheep station, looks like a small town. In the old days, the *estancias* were essentially towns; each had its own bakery, workshops, gardens, club and library for the workmen (unskilled workmen are known here as *peones*, not a derogatory term in Argentina). After the gold rush and before the days of oil, sheep farming was the main industry of northern Fuegia and brought wealth to land owners. Thousands of sheep, mainly Corriedale, covered the plains. The *cabañas* of the larger farms produced (and still do) world-class, prize-winning pedigree sheep. *Estancias* such as Sara once had up to 75 employees; low wool prices, higher wages and difficulty in finding good workmen has reduced that number to 15-20. The sheep are raised mainly for wool, although there was once an extensive overseas market for meat.

Route 3 continues past Estancia Sara to follow the coastline southeastward. On a sunny day, the cold southwestern South Atlantic beaches may appear almost tropical. In the distance looms **Cabo Domingo**, a picnic and fossil hunting site.

Just south of it is the **Escuela Agrotécnica Salesiana**, which functions on the site of the Salesian Mission to the Ona Indians, established in 1897. The original church contains a small museum of artifacts and mounted birds.

Mealtime welcome: The town of **Río Grande** (population about 30,000) is the center of the sheep and oil region, as well as home of a number of companies producing television sets, radios, synthetics and other products brought from the north and assembled here, part of a special 1972 law designed to bring development and more residents to this far reach of the republic. The wide, windblown streets overlook the waters of the South Atlantic. The Río Grande river has silted up, allowing for little shipping. A wide bridge crosses it to the **Freezer**, a modern meat-packing plant on its southeast coast. Lambs from this freezer were once considered choice in Europe, but various difficulties have kept recent production low.

Río Grande sprawls over the flat northern coast of the river. Like Ushuaia, it has nearly tripled its population in the last 15 years. Building is going on at a furious rate everywhere, housing is difficult to find and so are hotel rooms. There is not much for the tourist to do in Río Grande; this is a working town.

Río Grande is Tierra del Fuego's trout fishing center. Trout (rainbow, brook, brown) and land-locked Atlantic salmon were introduced in the 1930s. The *Club de Pesca John Goodall* organizes fishing excursions, as do some of the *estancias* (see below). Fishing is along the banks of the many rivers running into the Río Grande, usually through *estancia* land, where permission is needed. For those prepared to brave the wind, record-sized trout can be caught.

Ruta 3 runs out the opposite side of town from the bridge, circling southwest to cross another bridge and head toward Ushuaia.

Near the airport, just west of town, Ruta C leads westward to **Estancia**

María Behety, a picturesque village with an enormous shearing shed (room for 40 shearers), reported to be the world's largest. This road then wanders northwest and west to near the Chilean border, passing two more *estancias*. Some sections of this road, reddish in color, are paved with fossils; the black sections can become a quagmire if it rains.

Back on Ruta 3, **Estancia José Menéndez** can be seen in the distance on the south side of the Río Grande as you cross the bridge southwest of the city. It is a lovely, old-style *estancia* set in grassy, rolling hills. Formerly called *la Primera Argentina*, it was the first farm in northern Tierra del Fuego. The original farm, like others that were once extremely large, has been divided into five smaller *estancias*. It should be noted that the word *estancia* in Spanish is translated in English as farm, not ranch (*rancho* means decrepit shack).

Traditionally, anyone who turned up at mealtime or in the evening was welcome on the *estancias* of Patagonia and Tierra del Fuego. The advent of passable roads, hundreds of cars and thousands of tourists soon put a stop to that, and some areas had to be patrolled to protect the sheep.

However, Estancia José Menéndez now offers a small guest house at the homestead (for 8-10 people), with live-in cook; visitors can ride, tour the area and take part in life on the *estancia*.

Forest and mountain: Near Estancia José Menéndez, Routes B, D, E and F branch off, each winding west or southwest into the mountains, each offering varied scenery of steep hills, plains, forest, *vegas* (damp meadows) and *estancias*. All are fascinating to explore, if you have time and a vehicle.

The gravel **Route B** leads westward, roughly paralleling the Río Grande, passing the farms Cauchicol, Despedida, Aurelia, San José and San Justo, near the Chilean border. The *vega* lands are full of sheep and cattle, the rivers with trout.

Kau-tapen ("fishing house" in Ona) **Lodge** on Estancia Despedida has re-

glacial alley in e island's terior.

cently opened for trout fishermen. Located on an ideal section of the Río Grande for sea-run brown trout, eight guests can be accommodated. Best fishing times are January to early April.

Routes D and **E** parallel each other going southwest from Route B and José Menéndez. Although these roads are scenically interesting, there are no particular tourist facilities at present. **Route F** winds almost south into the heart of Tierra del Fuego, up and down the steep glacial moraines to reach **Lagos Yéhuin** and **Chepelmesh**.

Lago Yéhuin, favored for camping, and the Río Claro to the west are also good fishing areas. There is a boat-launching ramp on the Yéhuin and a small hostel there is being readied for opening.

Route H runs eastward from the Yéhuin over the hills to meet Route 3 near Estancia Indiana. There are several sawmills in the area and among the hills to the south.

Driving from Río Grande to Ushuaia along **Ruta 3** is an education in ecol-ogy, for one goes from the flat sea coast through hilly grassy plains and *vegas*, from low bush land on to scrubby deciduous forest (*ñire* or low beech); then turning inland, the road climbs to healthier deciduous forest (*lenga* or high beech) up the mountain slopes to near the treeline, and then down on the south side of the mountains to thick forest interspersed with evergreen beech (*coihue* or *guindo*) and valleys filled with sphagnum swamps. The first part, on leaving Río Grande, is paved; the rest, like all other roads on Tierra del Fuego, is gravel.

Shortly after entering the northern forests, **Ruta A** runs eastward over high hills and grassy valleys to **Cabo San Pablo**, another favorite picnic spot. This road continues for some distance beyond San Pablo, but is not good for most vehicles. The eastern toe of Tierra del Fuego is a mostly unused wilderness of forest, swamp and mountain and can be reached only by foot, horseback or helicopter.

Meandering southward, Ruta 3 fol-

Cages and boats used to catch crabs, on the shores of the Beagle Channel.

lows the valley of the Río Ewan, gradually rising to a divide which separates the waters running into the South Atlantic from those of Lago Fagnano, which flow westward into Chile to empty via the Río Azopardo into Seno Almirantazgo (Admiralty Sound).

The new town of **Tólhuin** (population 460) lies just north of the 60-mile (100-km) -long **Lago Fagnano**. The word *Tólhuin* is the Ona name for a nearby heart-shaped hill, and the village is in the heart of the Island.

The **Hostería Kaiken** (Upland Goose Hostel) at the southeastern head of the lake is a stopping place for fuel, lunch or tea, and a magnificent view down the long lake toward mountains in Chile. Colors of the lake change greatly with the weather, being deep blue-green in sunlight, or cold grey under cloud. Winds can whip up towering waves in no time.

To the southeast of the *hostería* rises **Heuhupen**, a lone mountain reported to have a resident witch (see L. Bridges, 1948). Along this mountain pass is Lucas Bridges' trail leading from Estancia Harberton on the Beagle Channel to Viamonte on the South Atlantic. The area is now full of logging roads for the plywood factory just north of Tólhuin, but the trail is being restored and marked for adventure tourism.

The south coast of Lago Fagnano has several small bays, formed when the land dropped during a 1949 earthquake. One of these, **Lago Kosobo**, will be the launching station for boat trips to a new fishing lodge, **Los Reinos** (the reindeer), being built at the western end of Lago Fagnano, near the Chilean border, by Yaganes Turismo of Río Grande.

The highway turns inland past sawmills to wind up the mountains at **Paso Garibaldi**. Although sawmills here were once prosperous (Argentina has little forest), pine imported from Chile is now cheaper and generally used for construction. In the valley just north of the pass lies **Laguna Escondida**, with the **Hostería Petrel** almost hidden at its southern edge. This is a quiet and lovely place to stay, hike and relax.

Be sure to stop at the look-out on Paso Garibaldi to look north over Laguna Escondida and Lago Fagnano. Mountain climbers will find this a fascinating area.

The Beagle Channel: South of the pass, the road curves downward to **Rancho Hambre** (Hunger Shack) and the Tierra Mayor Valley. Ruta 3 winds along westward through this valley and then southward through that of the Río Olivia to the Beagle Channel and Ushuaia.

A branch road (**Ruta J**) turns sharply left at the bottom of the mountain to meander 30 miles (50 km) eastward through a valley along the Tierra Mayor or Lasifashaj River to reach the Beagle Channel at **Bahía Brown** and the small Prefectura station at **Almanza**. **Puerto Williams**, Chile, can be seen across the channel. The beach is lined with Yahgan shell middens, the circular mussel heaps that once surrounded their low round shelters.

Then wind over hills above the Beagle Channel to **Estancia Harberton**, the oldest farm in Argentinian Feugia (founded by the Rev. Thomas Bridges in 1886). Now open to tourists, the farm offers a guided (English or Spanish) walking tour of the establishment. On the hill behind the homestead, you can see the bay, channel, and the islands recently disputed with Chile, and almost feel what it was like to live here a century ago. Tierra del Fuego's oldest nature reserve (a small wood) has a trail to see all the native trees, Yahgan kitchen middens and a model wigwam. After visiting the shearing shed, carpenter's shop, Fuegia's oldest boat and the front garden, one can have tea in the original farmhouse, the oldest house in Tierra del Fuego, overlooking Harberton Bay.

Ruta J, the *Ruta del Atlántico*, winds eastward along the channel for another 19 miles (30 km) of spectacular views and hair-raising turns finally to reach **Estancia Moat** (no facilities at present). The whole of this area, Harberton and Moat, is ideal for birds: steamer ducks, cormorants, oyster catchers, perhaps an eagle or condor. Harberton's **Isla Yecapasela**, in the

Beagle Channel, has a small Magellan penguin rookery.

Back on Route 3, the **Valle Tierra Mayor** is a winter sports center, with two lodges for cross-country skiing and snowmobiles. **Las Cotorras**, built of local logs, offers Fuegian *asados* (roast lamb, beef or chicken) year round, as well as skiing and other sports in winter.

Further west, the **Tierra Mayor Lodge** serves fondue and hosts cross-country skiing competitions on the spaghnum swamps of the valley floor. It is admirably placed for views the length of the valley between the Sorondo and Alvear mountain ranges.

West of the Tierra Mayor valley lies the **Valle Carbajal**, between high mountains with excellent views westward toward Chile. To the north is the **Paso Beban**, a long disused hiking trail. The road follows the **Río Olivia** along the west side of the beautiful **Monte Olivia**, where peat is harvested from swamps in the valley. At last, the Beagle Channel appears in the distance.

At the mouth of the Río Olivia there are cabins for those who enjoy solitude. A hiking trail follows the coast eastward to **Estancia Túnel** (and eventually all the way to Harberton).

On the west shore of the river is the local government fish hatchery, which produces trout for release in the streams.

Ruta 3 turns westward on a new paved road above the city of Ushuaia, or you can follow the more scenic dirt road along the coast, with Ushuaia and the mountains to the west in the distance.

Gingerbread homes: Ushuaia (population about 23,000) sits in a picturesque bowl on the southern side of the mountains, overlooking **Ushuaia Bay**, the **Beagle Channel**, and **Navarino** and **Hoste Islands** (both in Chile) to the south. To the east rise the spectacular, pointed Monte Olivia and the **Cinco Hermanos** (Five Brothers). Ushuaia is the home of a large naval base, government offices, and stores for imported goods; it is a center for sawmills, crab fisheries and television and radio assembly plants.

Early morning over Ushuaia.

A single, simple triangular monument on the peninsula near the airfield marks the site of the **Anglican Mission** (1869-1907). Bishop W.H. Stirling was the first white man to live deliberately in Tierra del Fuego (for six months in 1869), but Thomas and Mary Bridges (1870) and John and Clara Lawrence (1873) became the archipelago's first non-indigenous permanent residents.

The official founding of the town came with establishment of a Sub-prefecture (coast guard) in 1884.

Ushuaia's famous **prison** (1906-1940) is now within the naval base, but houses with decorative cornices built by prisoners still exist throughout the town. The octopus-shaped prison can be visited on three afternoons a week.

A walk through the town's steep streets reveals a strange variety of architecture. The early wooden houses covered with corrugated iron (to help prevent fires), with their prisoner-produced gingerbread decorations, have a somewhat Russian flavor. They are intermingled hit or miss with modern concrete structures, imported Swedish prefabs, and hundreds of small, new, wooden shanties. As in Río Grande, the tax-protected factories have brought many more people than homes. Land is difficult to obtain in the small area hemmed in by mountain and sea; new houses climb the mountain sides and many people live in appalling conditions, considering the climate. Nevertheless, building and improvements are going on everywhere.

Ushuaia is much more geared to tourism than Río Grande, but still lacks sufficient hotels. The main hotels are the **Albatros**, **Canal Beagle**, **Las Lengas**, **Antartida**, **Cabo de Hornos**, **Mustapic**, and **Malvinas**; more are being built.

Tourist agencies (**Rumbo Sur**, **Tiempo Libre**, **Padín**, **Tolkeyen**, **Everest**, **Onas**) offer a variety of tours, a few bilingual guides and one or two specialist nature guides. The **government tourist bureau**, on Avenida San Martín behind the Hotel Albatros offers information and folders.

The restaurants of Ushuaia (**Tante Elvira**, **Canal Beagle**, **Mostacchio**, **Los Gringos**, **Los Canelos** and others) feature seafood, *róbalo* (mullet) and *centolla* (southern king crab) from the Beagle Channel. The *centolla* has been greatly overfished and rarely reaches the size it once did. Those who prefer *asado* (lamb, mutton or beef roasted over an open fire) can try the **Tolkeyen** or **Las Cotorras**, both outside of Ushuaia. For those in a hurry, there are several good *rotiserías* or carry-out places.

Be sure to visit the **Museo del Fin del Mundo**, the local museum which houses Indian relics, ships' figureheads, and an attractive collection of local birds. Active research, especially of the eastern tip of the Island, Península Mitre, is carried on.

The world's southernmost research center, **CADIC** (*Centro Austral de Investigaciones Científicas*), housed in modern buildings at the southwest corner of the inner bay, is usually not open to the general public, but visiting scientists are welcome. Investigators there study the vegetation, marine life, geology, hydrology, social history, anthropology and archaeology of Tierra del Fuego. There is a small center for upper-atmospheric studies and an associated astronomical center in Río Grande.

Chartered yachts: A winding road climbs behind the town (good for photos) to the slopes of the **Montes Martial**, where a chair lift goes up to the valley at the foot of the small, hanging **Martial Glacier**. In winter the lift takes you to ski slopes; in summer the glacial hollow at the top of the lift is an ideal place to hike and see andean flowers, such as the chocolate-scented *Nassauvia*, or even the rare mountain seed snipe. At the base of the lift, a small restaurant set among evergreen beech trees offers lunches, teas and party facilities.

Part way down the road, a cross-country ski track leads over the rise to Ushuaia's first ski slope, a steep cutting on the forested mountainside; most of Ushuaia's children learn to ski on its icy slopes.

There are daily boat trips (on a large catamaran) on the Beagle Channel, to islands offshore, to see sea lions and cormorants, as well as longer trips eastward on the channel as far as Harberton.

Two or three French yachts based in Ushuaia's harbor (Ksar Expeditions) offer charter service to the **Fuegian Channels**, **Cape Horn**, **Isla de los Estados** and **Antarctica** or wherever you like. Depending on the length of the trip, these can take four to six persons.

One of the most delightful spots in all of Tierra del Fuego is the National Park, which lies about 15 kms to the west of Ushudia, along the border with Chile. Here one finds the tail end of the Pan-American Highway. The park has two campsites, one with simple facilities and one very primitive. The park setting is magnificent, with the Andes to one side and the Beagle Channel on the other. Lakes, streams and marshes lie in between to be observed. Look for austral parakeets, upland geese, steamer ducks, buff-necked ibises, and perhaps even some torrent ducks.

Left, a firebrush blossom. Opposite page, the bright colors of Autumn.

If one stretched Argentina out over the better known parts of Europe, putting the northwest corner (Jujuy province) on London, Misiones (where the Iguazú Falls are) would lie over Budapest and Tierra del Fuego, the southern tip, would reach Timbuktu. Within this range of latitudes and between these longitudes one can expect to find a great variety of habitats, climates, plants, birds and mammals, to say nothing of the lesser forms of life. This variety is greatly augmented by the disparity in elevations between the Andes and the sea.

South America's isolation for vast eras of evolutionary time gave rise to species, even whole families, entirely unknown outside the confines of the neotropics, the name for this huge zoogeographical region.

In a country as large as Argentina, the relatively small and mainly urban population of about 30 million has as yet had little effect on huge tracts of natural habitats. Most of these can still be seen in near-pristine condition. Only recently, with modernization and the pressure of the foreign debt for increased production over the next decades, are certain habitats being hammered into less natural areas, thus harming wildlife.

Competition and survival: Argentina extends from the tropics to the subantarctic, from the highest point in the Americas to the lowest (Aconcagua at 22,800 feet /6,900 meters above sea level and the Salinas, on the Valdés Peninsula, at about 180 feet/55 meters below sea level). It has very dry areas and very wet ones, but lacks the extreme winter temperatures found in continental climates, due to the moderating effect of the sea at the lower latitudes. Birds and beasts are varied and abundant, mostly non-migratory and fairly visible because of the open nature of the terrain throughout the greater part of the country.

Some early arrivals to the Eden of the

neotropics were deer, foxes, cats and members of the otter and weasel families. These invaders from the north began to compete with and prey upon the balanced, isolated and vulnerable fauna already in the region. Later, man arrived on the continent, and in the 12,000 to 16,000 years of his presence, this super-predator, too, has had his effect.

Many large and primitive mammals have passed into extinction for a number of reasons. But their surviving cousins abound.

Many of these are small, shy, nocturnal creatures, in a variety of strange forms. Giant ground sloths have been replaced by slow, upside-down tree sloths. Small varieties of armadillos and anteaters are the only traces left of huge armor-plated mammals that used to roam here. The small and timid marsupials of today had large predatory ancestors similar to the saber-toothed tiger. The massive extinctions, some of not so long ago, have left behind an array of species no less peculiar or interesting than those that came before.

Argentina is today undoubtedly one of the major countries on the "must see" list of

Preceding pages: a female elephant seal; elephant seals and southern right whales. Left, a male elephant seal. Right, a greater rhea.

nature oriented travelers. The country offers an ideal combination of varied habitats, fascinating and rare wildlife and, in many cases, the amenities and facilities to see them in comfort.

The areas which are least known are those that are the least accessible and that contain species of esoteric value. Some areas require the mounting of a major expedition and are hardly to be considered by the average visitor. Distances are enormous and a many-thousand-mile car journey, unless carefully planned, will only give one a superficial view of wild Argentina.

Where to begin: Buenos Aires, the heart of the pampas, is the obvious stepping off

km) or so south of Buenos Aires on National Route 3, where the two main lakes of **Monte** and **Las Perdices** lap against the village itself. The lakeside promenade is along a wall, but away from the central visitor area, the shore holds a staggering variety of birds.

Another day excursion into the pampas from Buenos Aires is to the area of coastal woods south of **Magdalena**, some 40 miles (65 km) beyond La Plata. Here, *Tala* (celtis) woods provide a very different habitat, one not too representative of the pampas, but both natural and extremely beautiful all the same. There are two neighboring *estancias* which are concerned with preserving their wildlife and permit visitors to wander

point for a visit to Argentina. These huge, flat grasslands, where the soil is very fertile, have been almost completely fenced in, plowed in most places, and grazed all over, but they are still basically the habitat that W. H. Hudson describes in his *"Far Away and Long Ago"* of the mid-19th century. The birds mentioned by Hudson are still to be seen, though some of the mammals have adapted less well to the alterations produced by over a century of farming. Those areas which have been least modified are the marshes and coastal lowlands with woods and seashore or estuaries.

San Miguel del Monte is but 60 miles (97

around, providing they obey a few rules. **Estancia El Destino** is a private wildlife refuge. The nearby **Estancia San Isidro** is perhaps more interesting, being more natural and wild.

Night raiders: A longer two-day trip to **El Palmar National Park** in Entre Ríos is highly recommended. The Yatay palm is there in an isolated and protected area, and there are some pleasant walks and opportunities to watch mammals and other pampas fauna.

All around the campground one will see the Plains Vizcacha, a large gray and bewhiskered rodent of social burrowing habits. These creatures are extremely tame. Indeed, campers must be tidy, as anything that is left out at night is stolen and carted off to the dens. Vizcacha males weigh up to 20 pounds (9 kg), and their nocturnal vocalizations are loud, varied and unnerving.

Pampas Gray and Crab-eating Foxes and the capybara(a pig-sized aquatic grazing rodent, the largest in the world) are to be seen on the walks. There are European hares and wild boar (unfortunate introductions of the last century), and the Greater Rhea, the archaic ostrich of the area.

Pristine pampa: Perhaps the most representative pampas left, due to the absence of plowing, is the area surrounding General

wildlife sanctuary, managed by Fundación Vida Silvestre Argentina (the local wildlife group), where the last specimens of the once numerous Pampas Deer can be seen in the wild. The bird sanctuary and observatory at Punta Rosa is also run by Fundación. Along with the local species, many migrant shore birds from North America spend their "winters" here. A combination of dunes, sandy beaches, planted trees for shelter, mud flats, rivers of grass and sedges, salt marshes and brackish sloughs give this area a highly concentrated array of habitats and, consequently, of fauna.

All of this is within easy reach of San Clemente, but it is in a military zone, as the

Lavalle and south to Madariaga. Route 2 as far as Dolores, some 200 miles (320 km) southeast from B.A., has abundant wildlife all along it. Route 11, in places, offers views of the vast open plains as they were before the Europeans arrived with their fences, windpumps and shelter tree belts. **San Clemente del Tuyú** is the best town to lodge in, but only out of the summer season; Christmas to Carnival is booked solid.

Between Lavalle and San Clemente is a

Left, a puma picks up a scent. Above, a wildcat keeps a lookout.

local lighthouse is operated by the navy. Be friendly with any navy personnel you may encounter. A smile, a wave of the hand and the single word *aves* (birds) should be enough to open the gates.

Marsh drives: Two drives can be recommended as well worth your time. One is out and back along Canal 2, some 20 miles (32 km) east of San Clemente, where the road-crowned embankment gives an overview of the extensive marshes and all that they contain. The other drive is along the **Estancia El Palenque Camino Vecinal**, down the access road to the farms behind. The elevated road skips from one grassy island to another, and offers one a superb view of the marshes and water below. However, these roads are earth, and the drives are not to be attempted after rains. Given good conditions, all the earth roads in the area are well worth exploring as far south as Madariaga. The circuit can be completed by returning to B.A. by the coast road (Route 11), through Punta Indio and Magdalena, where the estancias El Destino and San Isidro are. Take an A.C.A.(Automobile Club of Argentina) map, a smattering of Spanish, an adventuresome spirit and a car, and drive around to see what you can see in two or three days. The best months for visiting the coastal pampas are September to December.

may be wise to consult the ranger, if you can find him at headquarters.

Endangered trees: The subtropical jungles or rain forest are best represented in Argentina at Iguazú , site of the internationally famous waterfalls. The falls have no equal and are a must on the itinerary of any visitor. The **Iguazú National Park** was established to preserve both the falls and the 135,000 acres (54,000 hectares) of varied jungle terrain that surround them.

It is a shame to see that, as elsewhere, these areas are coming under the ax. The trees are being replaced by crops of more immediate yield, cash crops on a yearly cycle or in some cases by grazing land. Some areas are being

Hill hikes: Only one outcrop of hills breaks the regularity of the pampas' sea of grass. Between Tandil and Tornquist a range of ancient granite and limestone hills rises gently in a southwesterly direction, and attains its highest points in the **Sierra de la Ventana** and **Tres Picos**, both around 4,000 feet (1,200 meters) high. For those who like hill walking, these small mountains offer opportunities to view guanaco and other animals in an unspoiled and beautiful setting. Be careful and sensible in the matters of clothing and orientation, as mists can descend unexpectedly. Part of the hills are a provincial reserve, Ernesto Tornquist, and it

planted with pines for the budding paper pulp industry.

Thunder and mist: Iguazú National Park's waterfalls offer one of the most breathtaking natural sights to be seen anywhere. In a wide swing above the drop, the river splits up into many channels of varying sizes, and each plunges into the ravine below in one or two steps, a total of some 250 feet (76 meters). The waters then join in the furious racing rapids of the boxed-in lower river, which still has some dozen miles to go before becoming an anonymous part of the ten times greater Paraná River.

A choice of walks at the falls offers a

variety of views and experiences. Especially attractive because of the sheer force of the spectacle is the **Garganta del Diablo** (Devil's Throat), reached by a catwalk of some 1,300 yards (1,200 meters) from Puerto Canoas. Standing at the railing on the edge of the drop, one is made to feel quite small.

The best time to see the falls is in the afternoon, for the angle of the light, and in the evening, for the spectacle of thousands of Great Dusky Swifts returning to roost on the bare basalt walls between the falling waters.

Toucans: Perhaps the best known birds of the South American jungles are the toucans. The biggest, the least shy and the classic

jungle: some 2,000 species of higher vascular plants, nearly the same number of butterflies and moths, 100 species of mammals from the jaguar on down, nearly 400 kinds of birds from the hummingbird up. All this, as well as thousands of varieties of insects, spiders, reptiles, frogs and fish can be seen.

Most wildlife activity in such hot places as Iguazú is limited to the early morning, from about an hour before sunrise to two or three hours after, and the evening, from just before to just after sunset. Avoid being out there between 11 a.m. and 4 p.m.

Hide and seek: Don't think, however, that all this abundance is to be found and observed on a brief visit. In this kind of habitat

toucan of advertisements and brochures, is the Toco Toucan. Its dry croak, which passes for a call or song, is as distinguishing as its enormous orange bill. From the top of the water tower, or from the lawn in front of the park's visitors' center, the toucans can be seen doing their rapid flap-then-glide flights from treetop to treetop.

Tracks and trails in the park encourage visitors to get to know the marvels of the

Left, flamingos along the Patagonian coast. Above, a group of alert vicuñas.

it is notoriously difficult to see anything other than that which is immediately at hand. The thick vegetation that surrounds one forms a curtain which effectively hides anything that may be behind it. Some creatures are only seen crossing gaps in the forest canopy at great speed.

The **Macuco trail** is for walkers only, and in its two and a half miles it varies as much in types of vegetation as in species of animals and birds seen. There are tapirs, jaguars, Capuchin Monkeys, small deer called brockets, pacas and agoutis, coati-mundis and even peccaries (two species) to be found, if one is quiet and lucky. Anyhow, look for their tracks. **Yacaratia Trail**, though suitable for vehicles, is little used by them, and one can return from the end of Macuco along it with hopes of seeing even more of the wonderful creatures of this habitat.

An observation blind over a marshy area is for those who enjoy waiting for the wildlife to pass by. Cayman, stealthy Tiger Herons, Muscovy Ducks (the original wild species), Coypu and many others are the reward for the patient.

There are plenty of other trails and roads to explore on foot or by car. Get all the information at the desk in the visitors' center. Here, too, you can obtain copies of the bird,

with marshes. West from Corrientes or Resistencia, Route 16 should be explored at least as far as the **Chaco National Park**. The wet season (summer) is to be avoided, for the heat is great and the roads become impassable. Between April and November, with a tent in preference to the available lodging, search the Chaco Park for Howler Monkeys, guans, and chachalacas (of the pheasant family, but with dull colors and loud voices). Or take a look at the many and varied forms of marsh life: Whistling Herons, Jabiru Storks, Jacanas, and ducks galore.

From Corrientes, both east and south, there are some very rich woodlands interspersed with wide open grasslands and

mammal and tree lists to help you. Don't hesitate to approach a ranger, even in sign language, to help you identify and enjoy the sights before you.

The Chaco: The Chaco covers areas of Bolivia, Paraguay and the north of Argentina. It is divided into two recognizable parts, of which only one will concern the traveler. The **Dry Chaco** is crossed by very few and dreadful roads, and there are no amenities for visitors.

The **Wet Chaco** has undergone some major clearing for agriculture in the last twenty years. There are still some very beautiful tracts of wet chaco woods interspersed

enormous marshes. Route 12 is paved in both directions, but the earth roads which run northeast-southwest between the paved stretches, through places like **Mburucuya** and **San Luis del Palmar** generally get into the better habitats. There is a nature reserve on **Isla Cerrito** in the Paraná River, where Howler Monkeys are abundant. Seeing this involves a boat ride from Resistencia or Corrientes.

The **Iberá Marshes** are hard to get to and, except for the edges, are virtually devoid of life. On the edges, however, water birds of many kinds provide a great spectacle. In Corrientes, in the region of the headwaters of the Iberá complex, where grass seas stretch from horizon to horizon, one may come across a Maned Wolf. This rare species is still fairly abundant here though shy. Here, too, the Marsh Deer survives in small numbers. On the larger *estancias* where there is a consciousness of the conservation ethic, one can even see the Pampa Deer in its last refuge. This region is also the best place to look for the Capybara. One has to be prepared for long hauls and rough nights in this area, but the adventure is certainly worth the trouble.

Northwest Argentina: The provinces of Jujuy, Salta and Tucumán have some extraordinarily scenic areas and good wild-

Going over the ridge to the west of **Abra Pampa** into the huge valley of **Pozuelos**, there are usually vicuña to be seen as one descends. Laguna Pozuelos is a national park monument. Thousands of flamingos of three species, mixed in with waterfowl and waders, are blanketed on the water. Walk slowly along the shore, binoculars in hand, or if feeling the height too much, take the car, but be careful of muddy spots. Look for Puna Teal, Avocets, and Giant, Horned and Andean Coots. At **Lagunillas**, on the western side of Pozuelos, there is a small lake some miles from the road that one can walk to, or perhaps drive to in order to get a better look at all these birds. The Puna Rhea is usually

life. Don't miss the Humahuaca Valley, which is on the way to the Puna zone. Take side roads to places like Purmamarca. As this area rises above the altitudes one may be used to, it should be covered in stages, over two or three days. This is the best way to avoid the Puna sickness of nausea and general discomfort from lack of oxygen. The last hotel in the region that offers any real comfort is in Humahuaca. From there, go up and beyond.

Left, the elusive Andean condor. Above, the noisy toco toucan.

somewhere to be seen in the Pozuelos area, so keep an eye open.

Varied vegetation: A visit to **Calilegua National Park**, on the eastern slopes of the Andes, between 2,000 and 15,000 feet (600 and 4,500 meters), is only to be attempted in the dry season—June to October/November, as the roads are washed out the rest of the year. The road through the park rises steeply, so a series of vegetation zones is traversed in short order. This starts with the Chaco vegetation at the foot, with the Palo Borracho (drunken or bottle trees, *Chorizia*), Jacarandas and Tabebuias, both yellow and pink. Then one passes up through a transition jungle dominated by Tipa (*Tipuaria*) and into the cloud forest of Podocarpus and Alder (*Alnus*).

As a consequence of the variation in vegetation, there is a change in the fauna. Jaguar, puma, ocelot and jaguaroundi are the larger cats to be seen. Their prey are brockets, tapir, peccaries, agoutis, even Capuchin Monkeys, squirrels and a large variety of birds. There is a campground at the foot of the park, in **Aguas Negras**, and there are many trails and river and stream beds to explore.

Córdoba: Córdoba is the starting point for exploring the hills to the north and west of the city itself. The Pampa de Achala, with its condors and mountain species, is not a long drive away. Nor is it far to the Sierras Chicas, where the spectacular Red-tailed Comet (a hummingbird) is common.

In the south of La Pampa province there is a very special national park, Lihue Calel. Here, guanacos, vizcachas, rheas and the introduced European Boar are easily seen on walks, and special birds such as the Yellow Cardinal and the Spot-winged Falconet (both endemic Argentine species) are also encountered. There is an Automobile Club motel at the entrance to the park.

Andean playground: The Patagonian Andes, which stretch from Neuquén, through Río Negro, to Chubut and Santa Cruz, are a scenic delight, and vary quite a lot with the latitude. Here lies one of the playgrounds of Argentina, with winter sports, fishing, hunting, boating, canoeing, camping and all that makes up a good outdoor holiday. Towns are spread along the foothills where the steppe meets the woodlands and mountains, and they offer all the commodities one could need.

From Zapala, a short distance west, is the Laguna Blanca National Monument. It lies at a considerable elevation on the open steppe, where thousands of water birds congregate. Chief among these is the majestic and beautiful Black-necked Swan.

Lanín National Park has communities of the primitive Araucaria tree, and the Southern Beeches of the genus *Nothophagus*, both *obliqua* and *nervosa*. Together with Nahuel Huapi National Park, just to the south, this park is the most developed in terms of roads, communications and lodging (San Martín de los Andes and San Carlos de Bariloche are the major towns in the region.)

There is a sharp increase in the precipitation as one moves westwards, so the richness and variety of the flora increases markedly in the 20 to 40 miles from the steppe to the Chilean border. There is no parallel increase in the types of birds and animals to be found, perhaps because the number of their species is not regulated by the availability of resources in the good months but rather by the severity of winter. Few of the local woodland species migrate.

Condors and parakeets: There is a much greater variety of birds in the steppe and transition zones. Here, it is definitely more clement in spring and summer into autumn. One can see huge flocks of Upland Geese in the grassy valleys, Ashy-headed Geese in the clearings in the woods near lake shores and rivers, and noisy Buff-necked Ibises nearly everywhere.

In the woods one meets flocks of Austral Parakeets and the Green-backed Firecrown (another hummingbird), vestiges of more temperate climates, now isolated and adapted to colder areas. The Andean Condor is fairly common, though the enormity of the landscape tends to reduce it to an unrecognizable size. Sighting one is a thrill, nevertheless. The most spectacular bird of the woods is certainly the Magellanic Woodpecker, the giant of his family. The male sports a scarlet head with a small crest, while his all-black mate has a very long and floppy crest that curls forward.

Here, too, one can find the Torrent Duck. As its names implies, the black and white striped drake with its fire-brigade red bill is only seen in white water rivers and streams. Torrent Ducks sport, dive and swim around in these furious and frightening rapids as if they were in a pond.

Mountain parks: South along the Andes chain are spread a series of parks, large, small, well-visited, or off-the-track, all similar but each with its own special attractions and character. From El Bolsón one can visit **Puelo National Park**. There is good fishing for the introduced trout, along with camping and boating. As for wildlife, the only sight of special interest is the rare Chilean Pigeon.

Esquel is the town from which Los Alerces National Park is most easily reached. *Alerces*, strictly translated, is "larch." This is the local misnomer of *Fitzroya Cupressoides*, the giant evergreen equivalent of the redwood of the western United States. Though it is present in several other parks, it is here that it reaches its greatest size. A boat trip takes one to the more beautiful stands of these giants. Above the treeline is the rare and unafraid Andean Huemul, a type of deer, waiting for the intrepid hill-walker.

Francisco P. Moreno National Park is very far from any amenities. Camping equipment and extra gasoline are a must. The eastern steppe section of the park, some 160 miles (260 km) west of **Gregores**, lies at about 3,000 feet (900 meters). Here, two species of the peculiar seed-snipe are to be seen in abundance, along with many Upland Geese, Huemuls and some Mountain Cara-

Tempest." It is some 150 miles (240 km) long and, at times, 45 miles (70 km) wide.

The Moreno Glacier, the one accessible by car, is about 50 miles (80 km) west of the town of **Calafate**, on the shores of Lago Argentino. From just in front of the glacier, one has a grandstand view of the ice tumbling into the milky waters of the lake and creating just such an ice dam as was formed in Alaska in 1986. This damming and flooding cycle has happened with increasing regularity since 1937, when it first occurred. The cycle now runs for three to four years, with the pressure building until it is sufficient to tear away the front. Few people have the opportunity to witness the rupture, as it is

caras. One can see guanacos on the peninsula of **Lago Belgrano**.

Glaciers at their best: The next park southward is **Los Glaciares**. Both by land and on lake excursions one can see glaciers at their best in this region. They all originate as over-spillage from the South Patagonian Icecap, which is out of view on the crest of the Andes, in virtually permanent cloud. This icecap area is what Eric Shipton, the famous mountaineer, called "the Land of

Above, sea lions at the Valdés Peninsula.

unpredictable, and even folks from town are often late for the show because it goes so fast. Add the 40 percent likelihood that it will break during the hours of darkness and you can see it's not worth waiting around for.

The lake trip to the **Upsala Glacier** starts from **Puerto Bandera**. The shores leading to Bandera are always good for sighting waterfowl, maybe even some Black-necked Swans. The trip on the boat starts early and takes most of the day. Look for Black-chested Buzzard-eagle nests on the *elefantes* rock formations and condor nests on the low cliffs over the water. Upsala is a classic, with icebergs all around the front, in incredible tones of blue. The medial moraines stand out just like in the textbooks.

Tierra del Fuego: The wildlife of Tierra del Fuego and the national park there (12 miles/ 19 km west of Ushuaia) comprise just about everything one has encountered all the way south from Lanín, with species dropping out as conditions get more severe. However, there is a marine coastal environment here along the north shore of the Beagle Channel. One can see the Kelp Goose, the stunning white male against the black coastal rock, and the Flightless Steamer Duck, a local special, whose name derives from the paddlewheel-like spray it generates as it chases or escapes from a rival.

One may also get a chance to see Austral Parakeets, Buff-necked Ibises and condors. A sighting, this far south of the Torrent Duck is a rare treat indeed.

Beavers and muskrat were introduced in the 1940s and are creating havoc with the woodlands by felling, damming, and flooding. Early sailors introduced rabbits, which now thrive here. There is a very good boat trip available on the Beagle Channel, where one can see cormorants, sea lions, fur seals and some penguins.

In Tierra del Fuego, the scars left by road construction, gas line digging, petroleum exploration, uncontrolled forest fires, con-

vict clear-cutting of the native woods and the filth and litter of both Río Grande and Ushuaia, especially, are shocking, and it is a relief to get away from such disrespect for nature into the less disturbed National Park. Here, the autumn foliage (from March on) is a real sight.

The Valdés Peninsula: Once back on the mainland, the dominant scene all the way up to Buenos Aires and its surrounding pampas is the Patagonian steppe and coastline. These are best represented in Chubut, a pioneer province in the conservation of nature in Argentina. Throughout the year there is some spectacle of sea life frolicking on land or in the sheltered gulfs north and south of the Valdés Peninsula.

The wildlife calendar looks something like this:

Jan-Mar: Southern sea lions breed in rookeries (Punta Norte, Pirámides)

Mar-May: Killer whales visit these rookeries to prey on sea lion youngsters.

June: Arrival of southern right whales starts in both gulfs.

Sept: Elephant seals start breeding and are finished by mid-October; magellanic penguins arrive to start nesting at Tombo and stay until March, when they start leaving on migration.

Dec: Last whales leave for feeding grounds south.

One can see that it is a busy year, and that spring and summer offer the promise of greater activity.

In the Valdés region there are also many steppe animals: Guanacos at their best, Darwin's Rhea, maras (Patagonian Cavy) and the Elegant Crested Tinamou, a game bird that looks like a squat guinea fowl and the Hairy Armadillo or its smaller relative, the Patagonian Pichi Armadillo.

Heading north, one arrives back in Buenos Aires, and the circuit has been completed. Some things may have been missed but others encountered unexpectedly, as if by consolation. By this time, certainly, the dedicated nature lover should have a full appreciation of Argentina, with its geographical uniqueness and its stunning array of flora and fauna.

Left, a fox sits for a portrait. Right, Magellanic penguins at Punta Tombo.

FROM THE KINGS OF SPORT
TO THE SPORT OF KINGS

It is an average enough day in Buenos Aires, but the streets are deserted. The banks are empty, the restaurants are quiet and an eerie silence has settled over the city. The only people in sight are huddled around portable radios or television sets, their attention focused on the latest news.

The outbreak of war? Some national disaster? Election returns, perhaps? Quite the contrary. This scenario occurs every time Argentina's national soccer team takes to the field, ample evidence of that sport's hold on the country. Every match commands the nation's rapt attention, and victories are cause for unrivaled celebration.

When Argentina won the 1986 World Cup tournament in Mexico, the sport's highest honor, hundreds of thousands of people flooded the streets of Buenos Aires, Córdoba, Rosario, La Plata and beyond. Make-shift parades materialized out of nowhere, thousands of cars jammed the avenues and sidestreets, and the nation found itself swathed in blue and white.

The world championship was actually the second for Argentina, which also captured the cup in 1978. But that tournament, hastily staged in Argentina by the ruling military government that had come to power not long before, fostered little of the pride and enthusiasm seen in 1986. The 1978 World Cup was perceived by many as a simple exercise in public relations designed to avert the world's eyes from Argentina's soaring inflation, mounting national debt and human rights violations.

That Argentines flocked to the match, still cheered their players, and still celebrated wildly when it was all over shows their affinity for the sport.

Soccer was introduced to Argentina in the 1860s by British sailors who passed the time in port playing pick-up games before curious onlookers. Buenos Aires' large British community finally organized the game in 1891, and the balls, goalposts and nets imported from Europe were checked through

customs as "some silly things for the mad English."

By the turn of the century, Argentina had established its own soccer league. The Quilmes Athletic Club was formed in 1897, making it the oldest soccer team in Argentina. Rosario Central (1899), River Plate (1901), Independiente (1904) and Boca Juniors (1905) quickly followed suit.

Argentina's national team also progressed rapidly, as proven by its performance in the

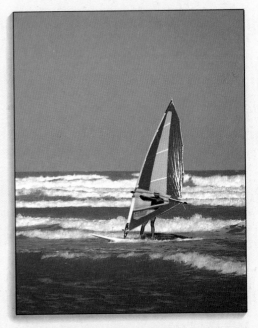

inaugural World Cup held in Uruguay in 1930. Although still amateur and lightly regarded, Argentina defeated such established soccer powers as France and Chile en route to a place in the finals, before narrowly losing to Uruguay, 4-2.

Soccer became a professional sport in Argentina in 1931, and the league games began to draw large, vociferous crowds. River Plate and Boca Juniors, two teams that emerged from the Italian Boca district in Buenos Aires, quickly became the two most popular teams in Argentina. Even today, 75 percent of the nation's fans support one of the two clubs.

Preceding pages: a polo match. Left, sailing. Right, windsurfing.

Such unbridled support is not necessarily a good thing—Argentine soccer has been increasingly troubled in recent years by crowd violence at its league matches, especially when rivals like River Plate and Boca Juniors meet. As a result, many of the country's stadiums—including La Bombanera, Cordero, Cordiviola and Monumental—have been turned into virtual armed camps, complete with moats, fences and barbed wire designed to keep fans off the field and rival factions apart.

Nineteen teams compete annually in the Argentina First Division, playing a total of 36 matches between September and June. In addition, many of the top clubs compete exodus abroad. Unable to match the lucrative contracts offered in Europe, Argentine clubs are accustomed to losing their stars to the larger, richer, more powerful teams in England, Spain and Italy. Even neighbors such as Brazil and Mexico regularly raid Argentine soccer, a situation that is not likely to change until the economic situation in Argentina improves.

But soccer is not the only sport in Argentina. Blessed with a climate that allows for a wide variety of sports year round, Argentina is also known for its polo, rugby, auto racing and tennis.

Polo: The first thing many visitors ask upon arrival in this country is where they can

concurrently in international tournaments such as the World Club Cup and the Libertadores Cup.

Argentines, like most South Americans, seem to have a special skill for soccer. The name of Diego Maradona readily comes to mind, but he was a national hero long before he gained international prominence at the 1986 World Cup. When Maradona threatened to leave his club, Boca Juniors, for Europe in 1982, the government attempted to intervene by declaring him part of the "national patrimony."

But that attempt failed and Maradona, like many of Argentina's top players, joined the see polo being played. Although it did not originate in Argentina, polo has evolved into an integral part of the national sporting heritage. Many of the world's best players and teams have come from this country. In addition, Argentina has top-flight breeding programs for ponies.

As with soccer, Englishmen introduced polo to Argentina in the mid-19th century. The inherent riding skill of the Argentines and the abundance of space helped the sport to flourish. At present, there are more than 6,000 polo players registered in Argentina.

Polo tournaments are held all over the country throughout the year, but the bulk are played in spring and autumn. The top teams compete each November in the Argentine Open championship in Buenos Aires, which was begun in 1893.

There is no distinction between amateur and professional polo in Argentina. But many of the top players are regularly hired by foreign teams for huge sums. In fact, the favorite team in an international tournament is often the one that can sign up the most Argentine players.

Polo ponies are also regularly exported from Argentina. Specially trained by *petiseros* (laborers) at an *estancia* where polo is played, the short, stocky ponies are prized for their speed, strength and ability to work

by two teams of horsemen—often farm workers or Indian tribes—who attempted to grab the basket and return to their *estancia*. Any number could play, and anything from lassoing an opponent to cutting free his saddle was permissible.

The only rule was that the rider in possession of the *pato* had to keep it extended in his right hand, thus offering it to any opponent who caught up to him. Such skirmishes inevitably resulted in a fierce tug-of-war, and riders pulled from their saddles were often trampled to death.

The government banned *pato* in 1822, but a group of ardent supporters revived the game in 1937. They drew up a set of rules,

with their riders.

Pato: *Pato*, described by some as basketball on horseback, is one of the few sports indigenous to Argentina. Earliest references to the game date as far back as 1610, and it was probably played long before that.

Pato is Spanish for "duck," and the duck certainly got the worst of it in the game's formative stages. Placed inside a leather basket with handles, the duck was contested

Left, the national soccer hero, Diego Maradona. Above, the Pumas face off against France in rugby.

refined the sport, and established a federation in 1938.

Today, *pato* is played by teams of four horsemen with a basket (similar to the type used in basketball) at each end of a regulation field. The hapless duck has been replaced by a leather ball with handles, and points are scored by passing the ball through the basket.

Although still a working class game, *pato* has steadily grown in popularity. The annual national open championship is held each November in Buenos Aires.

Other equestrian sports: In a country where horses are plentiful and breeding is a big business, horse racing and show jumping are also quite popular.

There are racetracks in most towns and plenty of off-track betting, although the government oversees the official odds. The big races are held in Buenos Aires, often at the Jockey Club in the suburb of San Isidro.

Horse shows are staged at numerous clubs in Buenos Aires and other major cities almost weekly from March to December. There is a fine tradition in this sport—as there is for dressage—and only the regular exportation of top horses has kept Argentina from gaining international stature.

As the concept of private sports clubs—where one must either be a member or the

guest of a member to use the facilities—is very popular in Argentina, it is difficult to rent horses. The stables in Buenos Aires and Belgrano that used to have such services have closed down, and most horses are now privately owned. Only sea-side resorts along the Atlantic Coast still offer this option, and they include both instruction and organized outings.

For those who want to have a real adventure on horseback, there is a rather unique dude ranching operation run out of Bariloche, which offers expeditions to the spectacular Andean foothills. The contact point in Bariloche is Polvani Tours.

Tennis: Tennis has been played in Argentina since the last century, but it remained a game largely for the middle and upper classes—until now. Fueled by the meteoric rise of Guillermo Vilas, an energetic and talented player who gained international prominence in the 1970s, tennis has experienced an unprecedented boom ever since.

The driven, dashing Vilas won the Masters in 1974 and the U.S. Open in 1977, and became an international playboy. Linked romatically with such women as Princess Caroline of Monaco and countless Hollywood starlets, Vilas emerged as a hero at a time when Argentina had none.

Virtually overnight, every youngster wanted to be a tennis player. The number of players skyrocketed, as did the sales of racquets, balls and shoes. Courts sprang up all over the suburbs of Buenos Aires—both municipal and privately owned—and Argentine players flooded the pro circuit.

One of the products of that boom is Gabriela Sabatini, the teenage sensation who emerged as one of the top women's players of the mid-1980s. Dubbed "Gorgeous Gabby" by the international press, Sabatini cracked the top 10 rankings in 1986. That same year, she reached the semi-finals of the prestigious Wimbledon tournament.

Although few players have yet equaled Vilas' and Sabatini's accomplishments, the sport remains very popular in Argentina. Countless courts are available for rent, and the Buenos Aires Lawn Tennis Club regularly sells out its 6,500-seat stadium for top matches.

Rugby: As with soccer and polo, rugby was introduced to Argentina by the British. But the sport inexplicably failed to catch on until the mid-1960s. That was when the Pumas, Argentina's national rugby team, rose to prominence with a string of international successes. Like tennis, the sport experienced rapid growth and a massive infusion of young talent.

Today, Argentine rugby ranks among the best in the world, and Hugo Porta is regarded as one of the greatest players ever. Virtually every province has its own federation, and attendance continues to grow impressively. Fifty-five thousand fans turned out for a recent game between Argentina and France, as compared to only 15,000 who showed up for international matches in the 1960s.'

In the future, most international matches will be played at the 76,000-seat Monumental Stadium in Buenos Aires.

Cricket: It may come as a surprise to many that cricket is played in Argentina. Yet another British import, it remained the property of that close-knit community for much of this century. It is only quite recently that other Argentines have taken an interest in the game and produced a number of top-notch players.

Golf: Golf is another sport that has benefited from the wide-open spaces and even climate of Argentina. There are numerous golf clubs all over the country, including the prestigious Jockey Club course in Buenos

Cup downhill events in Argentina in the 1985-86 season.

The two main resorts are at Bariloche (1,050 miles/1,700 km from Buenos Aires in the southern province of Río Negro) and the newer Las Leñas (750 miles/1,200 km away in the western province of Mendoza). Although the Argentine snowfall is notoriously unpredictable (including a shortage during the aforementioned World Cup competition), the best season for snow is generally from June to October.

The price of equipment and remoteness of the two main resorts has kept skiing an elitist sport in Argentina. But Bariloche—which has been called the Switzerland of South

Aires and the picturesque Mar del Plata course on the Atlantic Coast.

Yachting: Argentina has some of the most ideal sailing conditions in the world: gentle climate, strong winds and an abundance of lakes, rivers and reservoirs.

There are yacht clubs all along the banks of the fabled River Plate where the public can rent sailboats, sailboards and yachts.

Skiing: Skiing has grown steadily in popularity, especially since the staging of World

Left, dressage has its followers. Above, snow pato at Las Leñas.

America—is a holiday resort worthy of its European counterparts, offering tourists a wide range of diversions, including saunas, restaurants and nightclubs. Las Leñas is not yet as developed, but many prefer its slopes.

Neither resort is inexpensive, although package tours can keep the cost down.

Fishing: Argentina is criss-crossed by rivers and lakes (both natural and artificial) and includes more than 2,500 miles (4,000 km) of coastline along the Atlantic Ocean. Those features make it a fisherman's paradise, and such species as eel, catfish, trout, salmon, corvina, shark, swordfish, sole, shad and piranha are plentiful.

Year-round fishing is available at Argentina's coastal resorts, many of which are between 180 and 300 miles (300 and 500 km) from Buenos Aires. Mar del Plata is a prime fishing spot, as are the nearby resorts at Laguna de los Padres and Laguna Brava, where authorities regularly stock the waters and boats can be rented.

Quequen Grande, situated on the banks of the Necochea River, is noted for its excellent trout fishing.

Salmon and trout are also plentiful in the inland rivers and lakes to the south of Buenos Aires, in the provinces of Neuquen and Río Negro. These regions are under the jurisdiction of the National Parks Commission,

however, and a fishing license is required. This can be obtained at the respective provincial offices in Buenos Aires.

The picturesque town of San Carlos de Bariloche, previously mentioned as a ski resort, is situated on the shores of Nahuel Huapi Lake. This is one of the best locations for trout fishing in Argentina; a record trout specimen weighing 36 pounds (16 kg) was recently caught there.

In San Martín de los Andes, north of Bariloche, there is at least one flyfishing outfit that provides comprehensive service, including lodging and equipment as well as skilled guides.

Mountain climbing: The Andes Mountains, which run the length of Argentina's western border with Chile, have long attracted climbers from around the world. The main center for climbing is in the province of Mendoza, approximately 800 miles (1,300 km) west of Buenos Aires, where the highest peak in the Western Hemisphere—Aconcagua 21,000 feet/7,000 mts)—is found.

Scores of expeditions scale the Aconcagua peak each year, including teams from as far away as West Germany, Italy, Switzerland and the United States. There are 10 recognized routes up the mountain, with the northern route being the most popular—most climbers use this route.

But not every climb has been successful. Since Matias Zurbriggen of Switzerland first scaled the mountain in 1897, several climbers have lost their lives in the attempt, and are buried in a small cemetery at the foot of Aconcagua in Puente del Inca.

The Tupungato peak (22,000 feet/6,650 meters) in Mendoza is also difficult, and can only be reached by riding mules part of the way. Less demanding peaks in the Andes include Catedral (17,500 feet/5,300 meters), Cuerno (18,000 feet/5,500 meters), Tolosa (18,000 feet/5,400 meters), Cupula (19,000 feet/5,700 meters), Almacenes (18,500 feet/5,600 meters) and Pan de Azucar (17,600 feet/5,300 meters).

One popular range is the Cordon del Plata, just 50 miles (80 km) from the city of Mendoza. Here one can find fairly easy climbing. Such peaks as El Plata (21,000 feet/6,300 meters), Negro (19,100 feet/5,800 meters), Pico Bonito (16,500 feet/5,000 meters), Nevado Exelcior (19,800 feet/6,000 meters), Rincon (18,400 feet/5,600 meters) and Vallecitos (19,000 feet/5,800 meters) regularly attract large numbers of hikers, local as well as foreign.

There are other popular peaks in the provinces of San Juan, Río Negro, Neuquen and Santa Cruz. The Fitz Roy peak (11,000 feet/3,400 meters), which is located in Santa Cruz province, was not successfully scaled until 1953, when the Europeans Lionel Terray and Guido Magnone reached the top.

Left, man with a catch of the feisty dorado. Right, granite climbers.

The gaucho stands as one of the best-known cultural symbols of Argentina. This rough, tough, free-riding horseman of the pampa, proud cousin of the North American cowboy, is maintained in Argentine culture as the perfect embodiment of *argentinidad*, the very essence of the national character. He has been elevated to the level of myth, celebrated in song and prose, endowed with the virtues of strength, bravery and honor.

However, as with all elements of the national history, the gaucho and his culture continue to be hotly debated topics among the Argentines. Some say the gaucho disappeared as an identifiable social character in the late-19th century. Others will argue that, although his world has undergone radical changes in the last several centuries, the gaucho still survives here. However, while there are still people scattered throughout the country who call themselves gauchos, their lives bear limited resemblance to those of their forebears.

Pampean orphans: Gaucho life had its beginnings on the pampa, the vast grasslands of the east-central Southern Cone some time in the 18th century. There is some dispute as to the exact location, but a favored theory gives the gauchos their origin on the so-called East Bank, in the territory that is today called Uruguay.

As to the origin of the name gaucho, there are again many theories which trace the word to everything from Arabic and Basque, to French and Portuguese. The most likely answer, however, is that the word has joint roots in the native Indian dialects of Quechua and Araucanian, a derivation of their word for orphan. It is not hard to imagine how the word for orphan evolved into a term for these solitary figures, as they were neither loved nor ruled by anyone.

The first gauchos were mostly mestizos, of mixed Spanish and native American stock. As with the North American cowboy, some also had varied amounts of African blood, a legacy of the slave trade.

Hides and tallow: Cattle and horses that had escaped from early Spanish settlements in the 16th century had, over time, proliferated into enormous free-roaming herds, and it was this wild, unclaimed abundance that was the basis for the development of the gaucho subculture. The horses were caught and tamed, and then used to capture the cattle.

Beef at that time did not have any great commercial value; there was more meat than the tiny population of Argentina could consume, and methods to export it had not yet been developed. This surplus led to waste on a grand scale; excess meat was simply thrown away.

The primary value of the cattle was in the hides and tallow they provided, which were nonperishable exportable items. The first gauchos made their living by selling these in exchange for tobacco, rum and *mate*; gauchos were said to be so addicted to this stimulating tea that they would rather have gone without their beef. Their existence was fairly humble, with few needs. Most did not possess much beyond a horse, a saddle, a poncho and a knife. The work was not terribly rigorous, and early travelers' accounts of the gauchos portray them as savage and uncouth vagabonds. They were left with plenty of extra time on their hands, and much of this was spent drinking and gambling. This unwise combination of activities often led to a third favorite pastime: the knife fight. Their violent lifestyle was looked upon with horror and disdain by the city folk, but the animosity was mutual. The gauchos had nothing but scorn for the fettered and refined ways of the *porteños*.

Skilled horsemanship: The primary reputation of the gaucho, however was that of a horseman, and this was well deserved. It was said that when a gaucho was without his horse he was without legs. Almost all his daily chores, from bathing to hunting were conducted from atop his steed.

The first gauchos hunted with lassoes and boleadoras, both borrowed from Indian cul-

Preceding pages: a gentleman gaucho displays his wealth. Left, gauchos of Salta with their stiff leather guardamontes.

ture. The boleadoras consisted of three stones or metal balls attached to the ends of connected thongs. Thrown with phenomenal accuracy by the gauchos, this flying weapon would trip the legs of the fleeing prey.

Charles Darwin, in his descriptions of Argentine life in the 1830s, has an amusing account of his own attempt to throw the bolas. He ended up catching nothing more than himself, as one thong caught on a bush, and the other wound around his horse's legs. As one might imagine, this ineptitude was the source of much chiding and laughter from the attendant gauchos.

The great emphasis placed on equestrian tions were born of the necessity to develop skills in everyday survival is the practice of *pialar*. In this challenge, a man would ride through a gauntlet of his lasso-wielding comrades, who would try to trip up the feet of his mount. The object was for the unseated man to land on his feet with reins firmly in hand. This kind of control was quite practical on the open plain, where hidden animal burrows presented a constant danger underfoot.

As outsiders bent on enforcing order in the countryside sought to control the lives and acitivites of the gauchos, these competitions came under increasing restrictions. Organized and contained rodeos became the forum

skills inevitably led to competition. Strength, speed and courage were highly prized, and the chance to demonstrate these came often.

In one event, the *sortija*, a horseman would ride full tilt with a lance in his hand to catch a tiny ring dangling from a crossbar. Another test of both timing and daring, the *maroma*, would call for a man to drop from a corral gate as a herd of wild horses was driven out beneath him. Tremendous strength was needed to land on a horse's bare back, bring it under control and return with it to the gate.

A good illustration of how these competi-

for the showing off of skills.

Ranch hands: Profound change came to the gauchos' way of life as increasing portions of the pampa came under private ownership. Beginning in the late-18th century, large land grants were made to powerful men from Buenos Aires, often as a form of political patronage. The gauchos, with their anarchistic ways, were seen as a hindrance to the development of the land. Increasing restrictions were put on their lives, in order to bring them to heel and to put them at the service of the new landowners.

Not only the land came under private ownership, but the cattle and horses that were found on them as well, making them at once inaccessible to the free riders.

The gauchos were suddenly put in the position of being trespassers and cattle thieves. This made their situation similar to that of the remaining tribes of plains Indians. The gauchos' shaky reputations grew worse. When they got into trouble in one area, they simply rode on to another, and little by little they were found further from the settled areas.

New order: With such an obvious conflict of interests, there had to be a resolution, and it was, predictably, in favor of the landowners. The open prairie lands were fenced off, and the disenfranchised gauchos were put to

Europe. As the opportunities for exports to the European market opened up, more of the land was turned over to agriculture, and the business of planting and harvesting was all done by the immigrants.

When barbed wire fencing was put up, fewer hands were needed to maintain the herds. Combined with the increase in agriculture, this led to even harder times for the gauchos and animosity grew between them and the employable newcomers. Many of the gauchos could only find temporary work on the *estancias*, and they moved from one place to another, branding cattle or shearing sheep. These itinerant laborers were paid by the day or task.

work at the service of the *estancieros*. Their skills were employed to round up, brand and maintain the herds. Wages were pitifully low. However, the gauchos maintained their pride. They refused to do any unmounted labor, which was seen as the ultimate degradation. Chores such as the digging of ditches, mending of fences and planting of trees were reserved for the immigrants who were arriving in increasing numbers from

Left, early gaucho, with toe-held stirrups. Above, roundup in Corrientes.

Through the 19th century a whole new order came to rest on the pampa; the gaucho had ceased to be his own man. His new status as a hired ranch hand did not sit well with the gaucho's rebellious spirit. But the forces working against him were strong. The landowners had powerful friends in the capital, and the politicians saw the ordering of the countryside as a major priority. Argentina was finally beginning to take its place among the developing nations, and the traditional life of the gaucho could only be seen as a hindrance to that course.

Informal armies: However, while the gaucho ceased to present an independent threat, he still had a role to play in the new social structure of the rural areas. As the domestication of the gaucho increased, new bonds of loyalty were formed between the worker and his master. Powerful *caudillos* were gaining control over large parts of the interior, backed up by their gauchos, who served as irregular troops in private armies. This formation of regional powers was in direct contradiction to the goals of centralized government.

Years of civil warfare followed Argentina's independence from Spain, and it was only when the Unitarians gained the upper hand, late in the 19th century, that the

powerful Federalist bands were brought under control.

Gauchos were also, at various times, put to work in defense of the central government. These skilled horsemen were first used in the armies that routed the British invasion forces in 1806 and 1807, and by all accounts, their services were invaluable. Although they were forcibly inducted; they fought bravely and did not have the high desertion rates of other groups.

Gaucho squadrons were next used in the war of independence from Spain, and again they displayed great valor. The last time that the gauchos fought as an organized force in

the nation's army was during the Desert Campaigns of the 1880s. Ironically, the gauchos, many of whom were of mixed Indian blood, were being used this time to exterminate the Indian tribes who were seen as an obstacle to territorial expansion. The campaigns opened up vast new areas for settlement, but gaucho songs from the period lament their compromise of honor in the endeavor.

Las Chinas: The family life of the gaucho was never a very settled one. Supposedly, the women of their early camps were captives from raids on nearby settlements. This primitive theft was perhaps one of the practices that made the gauchos so unpopular with the forces of civilization. But even as women moved voluntarily out onto the pampa, the domestic arrangements were rather informal. Church weddings were seen as inconvenient and expensive, and common law marriages were the norm.

The *chinas*, as these women were called, were rarely welcome on the *estancias* where the gauchos worked. The few that were allowed were employed as maids, wet nurses, laundresses, and cooks. They also participated in the sheep shearing. Home life for the *china* reflected the primitive conditions on the *estancias*. Shelter was usually a simple adobe hut, thatched with grass. Crude furniture was fashioned from the bones and skulls of cows. Some women managed to find independent employment as midwives and faith healers.

Snappy dressers: Although gaucho clothing was designed for comfort and practicality, the men were born dandies, and their outfits were always worn with a certain amount of flair.

The *chiripá*, a loose diaper-like cloth draped between the legs, was very suitable for riding. It was often worn with long, fringed leggings. These were later replaced by *bombachas*, pleated pants with buttoned ankles that fit inside their boots.

Although store-bought boots with soles became popular in later years, the first boots were homemade, fashioned from a single piece of hide, slipped from the leg of a horse. The skin was moulded to the gaucho's foot while still moist. Often the toe was left open. This had a practical function, as the early stirrups were nothing more than a knot in a hanging leather thong. The rider would grasp the knot between his first and second toes. Over time this caused the toes to be permanently curled under, and gave the gaucho an awkward gait in addition to the permanent bowleggedness of the professional rider.

Around his waist the gaucho wore a *faja*, a woolen sash, and a *rastra*, a stiff leather belt adorned with coins according to the man's wealth. This last provided back support for the long hours in the saddle. At the back, between these two belts was tucked the *facón*, a gaucho's most prized possession after his horse. This knife was used throughout the day for skinning, castrating, eating and self defense.

guards called *guardamontes* were used. The *rebenque*, a heavy braided leather crop, was always carried in hand.

Martín Fierro: As the traditional gaucho way of life was fading in reality it was being preserved in art. Poetry and music had always been popular with the gauchos, and the poet was a very revered figure within the community.

The songs, tales and poems of the *gauchesco* tradition, many of them composed in colorful dialect, often deal with the themes of love and nostalgia, but many of them are highly political in nature.

One of the masterpieces of Argentine literature is a two part epic poem, *El Gaucho*

The outfit was completed with a kerchief, a hat, a set of spurs and a vest, for dress occasions. Over all this, a gaucho wore his poncho, which served as a blanket at night and a shield in a knife fight.

The saddle was a layered set of pads, braces and molded leather, on top of which sat a sheepskin that made the ride more comfortable. In the region where high thistles grew, a set of stiff, flaired leather

Left, a sortija competition. Above, a gaucho sorely tested.

Martín Fierro. Written by José Hernandez, and published in the 1870s, the work is a strong defense of the proud and independent ways of the gaucho, and a diatribe against the forces that conspired to bring him down, from greedy landowners to corrupt policemen and conscription officials.

A second work, *Don Segundo Sombra*, by Ricardo Güiraldes, was published in 1926 and is heavily nostalgic for the lost part of the national heritage that the romantic gaucho represented.

Ironically, these poems and stories served to elevate the stature of the gaucho in the minds of the public, but not enough and not in time to save him. The free-riding gaucho passed into the realm of myth, a folk hero who was the object of sentimentality and patriotic pride in a nation searching for cultural emblems.

Gauchos, paisanos and peónes: Although the traditional historical line places the demise of the gaucho in the late-19th century, there is much that remains of the culture in Argentina today. While the reduction of labor needs in the countryside forced many gauchos into the cities to work as policemen, firemen, plumbers and carpenters, many remained on the *estancias* to work under the new established order.

Wherever cattle and sheep ranching is

done in Argentina, one will find ranch hands working at the rough chores of herding, and branding. Most are settled with a regular wage, but there are still itinerants who provide services of fence mending and sheep shearing.

While many of these men call themselves gauchos, the job of ranch hand has taken on different names in different regions of the country. Some are called *paisanos*, others *peónes*. These cowboys are still found on the *estancias* of the pampas but in reaches further and further from Buenos Aires. A number are employed in huge cattle operations covering thousands of acres,

while others work on small family farms, from the rugged brush country of the northwest to the plains of Patagonia.

As with the original gauchos, many of these men are mestizos. Generally those in the northeast are of Guaraní stock, and Araucanians work on the ranches of Patagonia. However, over the years there has been a mixing of blood with everything from Basque to Italian to North American cowboys who came down to work in the 19th century.

Despite the regional differences in nomenclature, dress and blood, these men share the one tradition that makes them all gauchos in spirit, that of excellent horsemanship. A gaucho's pride is still his horse, and as before, he usually does not own much beyond this besides his saddle, his poncho and his knife.

Low wages and poor living conditions have continued to drive these workers into other pursuits. In recent years, many have left to work on hydroelectric projects, and then have drifted to the cities rather than return to the hard life of the *estancias*.

The rodeo: The visitor can be rewarded for a little exploration along the back roads of Argentina, for that is where one can still find the gauchos at work. On a visit to an *estancia*, one might see a *domador* breaking horses, or men riding at breakneck speed with lassoes flying. In small towns it is possible to stop for a drink in the local *boliche* or *pulpería*, where men gather for cards and a little gambling after a hard day.

One of the biggest treats is to see a rodeo. Some of these are large organized events, with an accompanying fiesta of eating, dancing and the singing of traditional songs. Bowlegged men dressed up in their finest hats, *bombachas*, and kerchiefs, with their chinas by their sides, gather at these celebrations. With some luck and investigation, it is possible to find more informal rodeos in the villages of the outback, where gauchos have come from miles around to compete in rough tests of skill and bravery. Amid flying dust and spirited whooping one will see gauchos barrel racing and lassoing cattle with as much panache and pride as their ancestors had.

Left and right, gauchitos and gauchos in the distinctive ponchos of the Northwest.

TRAVEL TIPS

Getting There
294   By Air
294   By Sea
294   Overland

Travel Essentials
294   Visas & Passports
294   Money Matters
294   What to Wear

Getting Acquainted
295   Geography &
       Government
295   Climate
295   Business Hours
295   Public Holidays
295   Weights & Measures
296   Electricity

Communications
296   Media
296   Postal Services
296   Telegram & Fax
297   Telephone

Emergencies
297   Medical Services
298   Security & Crime

Getting Around
298   From the Airport
298   Domestic Air Travel
299   Ferries
299   Public Transport
299   Private Transport

Where to Stay
301   Hotels

Food Digest
303   Where to Eat

Culture Plus
304   Art Museums
305   Theaters
305   Movies
305   Festivals

Nightlife
306   Tango Shows

Shopping
307   Shopping Areas

308 Sports

Further Reading
310   General Travel
310   History
310   Patagonia &
       Tierra Del Fuego
       Travel
310   Culture

Useful Addresses
311   Tourist Information
312   Travel Agencies
312   Foreign Representa-
       tives in Buenos Aires
313   Airlines Companies
314   Bus Companies

315 Art/Photo Credits

316 Index

GETTING THERE

BY AIR

Ezeiza International Airport (EZE) is the arrival point for all foreign travel. It is located about 30 minutes from downtown Buenos Aires, the capital city. However, there is another airport, **Jorge Newberry**, located within the city and used mostly for local travel as well as for travel to and from bordering countries. The following are airlines most commonly used: Aereolineas Argentinas, Pan American, Eastern, Canadian Pacific, Air France, Aeroflot, Avianca, Iberia, Swissair, Lufthansa, Lan Chile, Varig, V.I.A.S.A. Local travel can be on Austral Airlines, Aereolineas Argentinas, Lapa, and Pluna.

BY SEA

There are only a few cruise ships that come to Buenos Aires. Most of these originate in Brazil or in Europe. The better known cruises are with the Linea C Company, on their *Eugenio* and *Enrico* ships. These operate from December to March.

Another cruise ship, the *Pegasus*, from the Epirotiki Line, also operates from December to April. Antartur Lines has cruises from Ushuaia to the Antarctic and Tierra del Fuego. These only operate in January.

OVERLAND

Most tourists would not be arriving by land. However, for the adventurous type, this can be accomplished by bus, train or automobile. Bus service is available from Chile, Bolivia, Paraguay, Uruguay and Brazil. Large air-conditioned buses are available for long distance overland travel. But the traveler must remember the part of the world he/she is in. Caution must be always exercised. The trains available are only to Bolivia. Local

travel can be done on trains very effectively and cheaply. Service is good. Traveling by automobile is also possible. Most of the roads are paved but cautious driving is a MUST. There are speed limits posted. The **Automobile Club of Argentina**, located in Buenos Aires on Avenida Libertador 1850 (tel: 802-6061/7061), is very helpful and can provide the traveler with maps and useful information.

TRAVEL ESSENTIALS

VISAS & PASSPORTS

All tourists coming to Argentina must have valid passports from their country and a visa to enter the country. In some cases a tourist card is all that is required, but this must be verified with a travel agent. Citizens from the bordering countries of Brazil, Chile, Paraguay, and Uruguay only need their I.D. cards.

MONEY MATTERS

The currency for Argentina is the **peso**. Travelers checks are usually cashed anywhere. In the exchange houses or **Cambios** they are usually exchanged a few points below the cash rate. Should a black market for dollars develop, the "unofficial rate" will be clearly published in all newspapers and can usually be obtained by asking around at hotels and travel agencies. Exchange houses are forced to exchange at the official rate.

WHAT TO WEAR

In general, the atmosphere is somewhat formal, especially in the winter months. As Buenos Aires is a very cosmopolitan city, fashion is very important, and the people are always up-to-date with the latest styles from Europe. Dressing in Buenos Aires for dinner is customary. The Argentine man will always wear a suit or at least a sports coat with a tie. Women are always very well dressed.

GETTING ACQUAINTED

GEOGRAPHY & GOVERNMENT

Official name: The Republic of Argentina.
Capital: Buenos Aires.
Population: 31,000,000.
Language: Spanish.
Religion: Roman Catholic.
Government: Federal Republic with the Senate and Chamber of Deputies and President as the head of state.

CLIMATE

Most of Argentina lies within the temperate zone of the Southern Hemisphere. The northeastern part is very humid and subtropical. The northwest is tropical but has a mild winter. The Pampas are temperate. The southern part of the country has colder temperatures and rain most of the year. The rainfall varies in the Humid Pampa (which comprises the province of Buenos Aires, and some of the Córdoba and La Pampa provinces) from 39 inches in the eastern parts to about 20 inches in the areas near the Andes. Summer months in Buenos Aires are indeed very hot and the majority of the people leave soon after Christmas to the beaches and mountain resorts. The city is almost empty during the months of January and February, when the heat and humidity can be overpowering. Wintertime is pleasant, although rather damp – the thermometer doesn't drop drastically, but it still gives the ladies a chance to wear their beautiful furs.

BUSINESS HOURS

Monday through Friday, the business hours are from 9 a.m. to 6 p.m., and the banking hours are from 10 a.m. to 3 p.m. The stores open at 9 a.m. and are generally open until 7 p.m. In some parts of the country, the stores open from 9 a.m. to 1 p.m. and from 4 p.m. to 7 p.m.

PUBLIC HOLIDAYS

All government agencies as well as the banks close on the public holidays. These are listed below.

New Year's Day: January 1
Holy Friday: April 17
Labor Day: May 1
Comm. of First Government: May 25
Malvinas Day: June 10
Flag Day: June 20
Declaration of Independence: July 9
Anniversary of the death of Gral. San Martín: August 17
Columbus Day: October 12
Christmas Day: December 25

WEIGHTS & MEASURES

The metric system is used in Argentina. This is a useful conversion table:

LENGTH

Inches	Centimeters
1	2.54
2	5.08
3	7.62
4	10.16
5	12.70
6	15.24
7	17.78
8	20.32
9	22.86
10	25.40
20	50.80
50	127.00
100	254.00

WEIGHT

Pounds	Kilograms
1	0.45
2	0.90
3	1.36
4	1.81
5	2.27
6	2.72
7	3.18
8	3.63
9	4.08

10	4.53
20	9.07
50	22.68
100	45.36

VOLUME

Gallons	Liters
1	3.78
2	7.57
3	11.36
4	15.14
5	18.93
6	22.71
7	26.50
8	30.28
9	34.07
10	37.85
20	75.71
50	189.27
100	378.54

Temperature is in Centigrade degrees.

CLOTHING

Clothing is sized the European way. Below are a few sizes that might be helpful when shopping.

Women's dresses:

American	10
Canadian	12
European	40
British	34

Women's shoes:

American	5
European	36
British	4

Men's shirts:

Canadian	15
European	38

Men's shoes:

American	9½
British	9
European	43

ELECTRICITY

The electric current for Argentina is 220 volts (50 cycles). Be certain to bring proper transformers and adapters. Some hotels provide adapters, but not transformers.

COMMUNICATIONS

MEDIA

Several newspapers are available. The local papers are *La Nación*, *Clarín*, *Ambito Financiero* and *Página 12*. The English paper is the *Herald*. There are newspaper and magazine stands throughout the city, where these and some foreign papers, as well as many international magazines, may be found.

Television is a favorite pastime here, as it is in most of the world. There are five stations, and cable TV is also available. Most of the programs are brought in from the U.S. and some from Europe. Many dramatic series are locally made. Soap operas are also very popular and a favorite with the afternoon viewers.

The radio stations carry a variety of programs. The BBC is on from 5 p.m. to about 12.30 a.m. A number of stations carry international top hits, local tango music and talk programs.

POSTAL SERVICES

The main Post Office is located on Sarmiento 189, and operates Mon. to Fri. from 9 a.m. to 7.30 p.m. Other small post offices are located throughout the city. The hotel is the best source for stamps and any other needed information.

TELEGRAM & FAX

Telegrams can be sent from any Post Office in town or they can be dictated to the ENCOTEL telephonogram system. The phones to use are 33-9221/35 for domestic telegrams and 33-9251/60 for international telegrams. Fax facilities are usually available at most of the larger hotels in town. If, however, this is not available, the following ENTEL offices have these facilities:

San Martín
San Martín 332, Mon. to Fri. from 8 a.m. to 8 p.m.
Ezeiza Airport
Daily from 9 a.m. to 10 p.m.
Once
Located at the train station, Mon. to Fri. from 9 a.m. to 7.30 p.m.
Republica
Corrientes 707, 24-hour service.
Catedral
Peru 1, Mon. to Fri. from 7 a.m. to 10 p.m. and Sat. from 7 a.m. to 1 p,m.

TELEPHONE

Using the telephone in Buenos Aires is an unforgettable experience. The user must indeed be armed with courage, but most of all LOTS OF PATIENCE! The system here is by no means up to par. However, the calls do go through, after a considerable number of odd beeps, buzzes, etc. Most of the tourists will probably be using the phones in their hotel rooms. For those who venture out and want to try a Pay Phone, please make sure you follow this advice: some of the public phones here are yellow-greenish pear-shaped domes located on the streets, in public buildings, bus terminals, and in some bars and restaurants, and the others are orange boxes and located in most *confiterias* and restaurants. Before using the apparatus, a token or *ficha* must be purchased from any *KIOSCO* (cigarette and candy stand visible throughout the city) or from the cashiers at restaurants or bars. These *cospeles* are good, generally, for a two minute phone call. This, however, depends on the time of day the call is made. Good Luck! Long distance calls can be placed through the international operator from the hotel room or at any of the offices of ENTEL.

EMERGENCIES

MEDICAL SERVICES

The health care in this country is good. Hospitals have trained personnel who have studied here and abroad. There are excellent specialists in most of the medical fields, who make it a point to attend international medical congresses, to inform themselves on the recent advances in medical science and to bring these to Argentina.

Medical equipment is very costly, but all efforts are coordinated in order to maximize benefits.

In some sections of the country, the hospitals may not have up-to-date equipment, but what is available is adequate for an emergency situation.

Costs of medical care are difficult to establish because of the fluctuating economy. A medical consultation runs from $20 to as high as $150.

For emergencies in the Buenos Aires area:

Burn Wounds Hospital	923-3022
City Medical Attention	34-4001
Coronary Mobile Unit	107
Poison Unit	87-6666
Fire Department	23-2222
Police	101

HOSPITALS

British Hospital
74 Perdriel St., tel: 23-1081/1089
Children's Hospital Pedro Elizalde
40 M. Oca St., tel: 28-5898
French Hospital
951 Rioja St., tel: 97-1031/1081/3412
German Hospital
1640 Pueyrredon Ave., tel: 821-4083/7661
Guemes Hospital
3933 Córboda Ave., tel: 89-1675 to 79/5081 to 86

Italian Hospital
450 Gascon St., tel: 981-5010/5160/5990/7670
Municipal Hospital
Juan A. Fernandez, 3356 Cervino St., tel: 801-5555/0028/2233
Odonthological Hospital
940 Pueyrredon Ave., tel: 941-5555
Ophthalmological Hospital Santa Lucia
2021 San Juan Ave., tel: 941-7077

In the Provinces, for medical attention or in case of an emergency, all hospitals are well known and the hotel clerk or any taxi driver should be able to take you there.

PHARMACIES

Most drugs can be purchased over the counter without a prescription. There are, however, restrictions on some. There is always a pharmacist on duty. If you are prescribed any form of injections, the pharmacist offers this service. All over the country, pharmacies rotate being open 24 hours. A listing of the ones on duty and nearest to you appear in the local newspaper as "Farmacias de Turno."

The pharmacist can also recommend remedies for common ailments, flu, stomach disorders, headaches etc.

SECURITY & CRIME

Like in any other part of the world, the traveler must always be cautious and use a little common sense. When registering at the hotel, don't leave luggage unattended. Always keep your belongings close to you. If carrying valuables, ask to have them locked in a safe. Carry money in different parts of your clothing rather than all in a wallet or purse. Don't display large amounts of cash when making purchases. Beware of pickpockets on the crowded pedestrian mall Florida, although there are also plenty of police here.

Buenos Aires and most of the bigger cities are very much alive till the late hours of the night. You can go out to dine, dance to the wee hours and still go at 4 or 5 in the morning to get a *bife* (steak). But, a little caution can prevent a bad experience. Don't walk on desolate streets and try not to walk alone. If driving, lock the car and don't leave any valuables in it. It is common for thieves to break the windows of cars to steal the radio/cassette players.

Crime is on the rise, mainly in the large cities. Fortunately, the crime rate doesn't compare with other cities of the same population. Just exercise a little caution.

GETTING AROUND

FROM THE AIRPORT

Eeiza International Airport lies some 20 km out of downtown Buenos Aires. Depending on the exchange rate, a taxi into the center can cost from US$50 down to around US$10. It's more reliable, however, to take a *remise* or organized car service directly to your hotel – buy a ticket from the *remise* desk in the airport foyer. The cheapest option is to go by the airport bus that runs regularly to the center for a few dollars, then take a short taxi ride.

DOMESTIC AIR TRAVEL

Traveling by air in Argentina is done on the local airlines, which are Austral, Aereolineas Argentinas and Lade. **Jorge Newberry Airport**, also known as **El Aereoparque**, is used for national traffic.

For tourists who wish to visit several cities, there is a special package offered by Aerolineas Argentinas called **Visit Argentina**. This is a booklet of 4, 6 or 8 coupons, each of which allows a segment of travel within Argentina. For example, one segment might be Buenos Aires to Rio Gallegos one way, another might be Buenos Aires to Mendoza; each city (apart from the hub Buenos Aires) can only be visited once.

The Visit Argentina booklets can only be bought in conjunction with an international air ticket, and is fully refundable if not used. There is no set time limit on using the coupons, although they are only valid for as long as the international ticket on which they are bought.

The price is US$359 for 4 coupons, US$409 for 6 and US$459 for 8 – which works out rather economically, since distances in Argentina are huge and flying is expensive. A return ticket to Ushuaia, for example, costs US$456.

FERRIES

Going to Uruguay on the Ferry is a pleasant trip, inexpensive and entertaining. The well known companies are Ferrytur located on Florida 780, tel: 394-2103/5336/5431; Aliscafos located on Av. Córdoba 787, tel: 392-4691/2473/0969/2672; Tamul located on Lavalle 388, tel: 393-2306/1533, 362-8237. Other companies can be contacted through a travel agent.

PUBLIC TRANSPORT

BUSES

The buses are a very good way to get around Buenos Aires, a very large city. They are one of the means of mass transportation, being usually prompt and very inexpensive. However, try not to get one during the rush hour, as the queues are very long. Any part of the city can be reached. Bus stops are located throughout the city. The number and destination is clearly marked. Long distance travel on buses is also available. A very large and modern bus terminal is located in **Retiro**. Information on their destinations can be obtained at the terminal from the different companies.

TRAINS

Another means of public transportation is the train system. There are two main train stations located in the Buenos Aires area. One is **Retiro** and the other is **Constitución**.

The trains go to the different suburbs of Buenos Aires as well as to the interior of the country. Information on national travel can be obtained either through a travel agent or at the offices of **Ferrocarriles Argentinos** (Argentine Railways) located at 735 Florida St., tel: 311-6411.

UNDERGROUND

The subway system, better known as the **SUBTE**, is the fastest and definitely the cheapest way to get around town. The rides are quick, taking no more than 25 minutes, and the waiting is about three to five minutes. The art work that can be observed at some of the stations is quite unique and has an interesting background. Many of these painted tiles were baked by artisans in Spain and France at the beginning of the century and around the 1930s.

TAXIS

These can be easily recognized: black with a yellow roof, and are readily available 24 hours a day. The meter registers a number that will correspond to the amount of the fare appearing on a list. These must be shown to the passenger by law. A bit of advice: be careful when paying and make sure the correct bill is given; quick exchanges of bills have been known to take place, especially with the tourist who doesn't know the language or the currency. A small tip is usually given.

PRIVATE TRANSPORT

Remises are private automobiles, with a driver, that can be rented by the hour, excursion, day or any other time period. They are more expensive than taxis, and a list of these can be located in the telephone directory or at the information desks of the hotels.

CAR RENTAL

Rental of automobiles may be done at the airport upon arrival. The following are some of the better-known car rental agencies:

Avis
Suipacha 268, 7th floor, tel: 45-1943.
Belgrando Sar
Ciudad de la Paz 2508, Belgrano, tel: 781-5802.
Fast Rent
Uruguay 328, 1st floor, tel: 40-0220.
Hertz
Esmeralda 985, tel: 312-6832.
Liprandi
Esmeralda 1065, tel: 311-6832.

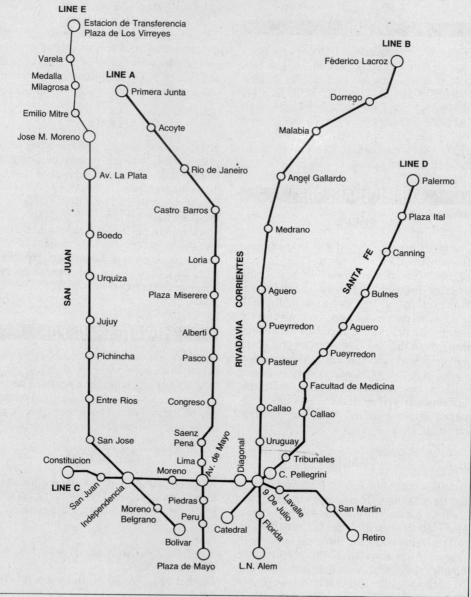

BUENOS AIRES — THE SUBWAY

National Car Rental
Esmeralda 1084, tel: 312-4318/311-3583.
Rent A Car
M.T. de Alvear 678, tel: 311-0247.
Serra Lima
Córdoba 3100, tel: 821-6611/84.

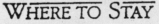

WHERE TO STAY

HOTELS

BUENOS AIRES

*** Deluxe
 ** First class
  * Moderate

Buenos Aires Sheraton (***)
San Martin 1225/75, tel: 311-6310/19. High-rise commanding magnificent view of the River Plate, port area, in front of the historical Torre de los Ingleses and the Retiro train terminal. Uncrowded, it stands atop a tiny rise in one of the very few "hilly" areas of the city. 24 stories, 800 rooms, heated pool, tennis courts, sauna, roof-top bar, a sprinkling of top-notch international restaurants, High-level entertainment. A favorite of traveling business people.
Plaza (***)
Florida 1005, tel: 311-5011 or 312-6001. A favorite of visiting royalty and heads of state. Very French, very formal, host to high-fashion shows etc. Superb service. Known for its well-stocked wine cellar. Jewelers, furriers, banks and travel agencies have shops on the ground floor.
Bauen (***)
tel: 804-1600. 250 rooms, 32 suites and two penthouses, Callao and Corrientes. View from 19th-floor restaurant is breath-taking.
Hotel Libertador (***)
tel: 392-2095. Modern, glass-plated. Maipú and Córdoba. Convention halls. Two excellent restaurants, El Portal and the Pérgola.

Claridge (**)
Tucuman 555, a few steps from the glittering Florida shopping strip, tel: 393-4301/7448. 180 rooms. Well-known for its excellent restaurant.
República (**)
On 9 de Julio avenue. 250 rooms. Fairly new.
Continental (**)
Diagonal Roque Saenz Peña 725. A few streets away from the main maddening crowd, on an avenue adorned twice a year by blooming jacaranda trees. Steer away from it if you are allergic, it could send you into sneezing fits by mere approach. Otherwise very stately hotel. Good eating.
Salles (*)
On Cerrito and Presidente Perón. Modern and efficient. Pleasant setting, with a view of the 9 de Julio greenery and in fall, and spring, the "palo borracho" pink, yellow and cream flowers on the trees and carpeting the minuscule park areas separating the main central avenue from two lateral streets, Cerrito to the West and Carlos Pellegrini to the East. A few blocks' walk from the banking and shopping area.
Dos Chinos (*)
Close to the Constitución train station. 14 floors, 120 rooms. "E" subway line takes less than 10 minutes to downtown BA.
Nogaró (*)
Reasonable. Famous Bob's Bar Avenida Julio A. Roca (Diagonal Sur) 562. Good cooking at the Chez Louis restaurant.
Tres Sargentos (*)
Reconquista 730. A favorite with smart shoppers.

For names of hotels in the Provinces, you may go to the addresses already listed for the Province Houses. Here, the representatives can give you a complete listing of hotels, motels, campsites and student quarters. They'll be able to quote prices and availability. Some will make a reservation, but usually you'll have to do this yourself or contact a travel agency. Prices vary from season to season, so it's best to check upon arrival, unless you come at peak season, when reservations are recommended. Vacations here begin the week of December 15th and end as late as March 15th for summer. Winter vacations begin around the 5th of July and end around the middle of August. The schools have two weeks' winter break, but the Provinces have different schedules in order to prevent overcrowding in the ski resorts. A few of the hotels in the provincial cities are listed below, to give the traveler at least a name. Complete listings can be obtained from the Province centers.

IGUAZÚ

Hotel International de Iguazú
Reservations in Bs. Aires, tel: 311-4259. In the National Park where the falls are located, offering a magnificent view of the falls. Very modern and with all the facilities.

Hotel Esturion Iguazú
Reservations in Bs. Aires, tel: 30-4919. Located in Puerto Iguazú, moderately priced and not as ideally located, but a good hotel.

SALTA

Hotel Plaza
Reservations Bs. Aires, tel: 962-5547. Located in the center of Salta.

Hotel Salta
Reservations in Bs. Aires can be done through Cosmopolitan Travel, tel: 311-6684. Located in the center of town.

JUJUY

Hotel Termas de Reyes
tel: 0382; telex: 66130 NASAT. Located about 12 miles (19 km) from the city, offers thermal baths in all rooms, good facilities and heated pool.

MENDOZA

Hotel Aconcagua
San Lorenzo St. A few blocks from the main shopping area, very modern architecture, pool and air-conditioned rooms. Also has a good restaurant.

Hotel Huentala
Primitivo de la Reta 1007, Mendoza, tel: 24-0766/0802. Very well located, in the center of town, modern and very well equipped.

Plaza Hotel
Chile 1124, tel: 23-3000. A more traditional hotel, located in front of a beautiful plaza, with lovely antique furnishings.

BARILOCHE

El Casco Hotel
Casilla de Correo 436. An established and very well-known hotel. Situated on the shores of the lake, with magnificent surroundings. The rooms are furnished with antiques. The restaurant is internationally famous. Expensive, but worthwhile if you can afford it.

Edelweiss Hotel
Tel: 26142; telex: 80711 EDEL AR. A large hotel, with up to 90 rooms plus several suites. A ***** rating, located in town and close to everything.

Hotel Tronador
Reservations in Bs. Aires, tel: 311-6684/2081-2478. A unique small lodge-type hotel with excellent food, offering fishing, horseback riding, hiking and beautiful surroundings for relaxation. Located in front of the Mascardi Lake, southwest of Bariloche. Open from November to April.

CARLOS PAZ (CÓRDOBA)

Hotel Avenida
Gral Paz. 549, Carlos Paz, Córdoba. A small hotel with 50 rooms, pool and other facilities.

Hotel Ciervo del Oro
Carlos Paz, Córdoba. A lovely small lodge-type hotel right on the lake, with pool, excellent food and very cozy.

VILLA GENERAL BELGRANO (IN THE SIERRAS)

Hotel Edelweiss
Villa Gral. Belgrano, Córdoba, tel: 6317/6284. A very well-run hotel, with swimming pool, tennis courts and recreational activities for children. Set in the scenic sierras of Córdoba, the temperature is very good. Excellent place to stay if attending the Oktoberfest or just relaxing a few days in the summer. Nearby tours available to La Cumbrecita and the many lakes surrounding the area for fishing.

USHUAIA

Hotel Albatros
tel: 92504/6; telex: 88639 ALBAT AR.

Malvinas Hotel
Deloqui 615, tel: 92626.

Cabo Hornos Hotel
Ave. Sn Martin y Triunvirato, tel: 92137.

CALAFATE (LAGO ARGENTINO)

Hotel La Loma
tel: 16-El Calafate. Located in the Glacier National Park, has 27 rooms, centrally located with lovely views. Open from October to April. Several languages spoken.
Posada
Los Alamos, Gobernador Moyano y Bustillo 94, tel: 74 Calafate. A new small hotel, with recreation for children, restaurants and interesting movies about the area.

MAR DEL PLATA

Mar Del Plata
Gran Hotel Provincial, tel: 24-4081 Mar del Plata. The oldest and most traditional of hotels, still considered a grand hotel. Large number of rooms are available and a very good restaurant.

FOOD DIGEST

A person could eat out every day of year and still not savor the cuisine of all the restaurants of Buenos Aires. Dining out here is a delightful experience. Food, wine and service are excellent, for the most part. Argentina is well known for its beef, and most tourists will prefer this to other types of food. The typical meal will be *empanadas* (meat pastries, although the filling will vary according to the region), *chorizos* or *morcillas* (pork, blood sausages), an assortment of *achuras* (sweetbreads) of course, this is only the appetizer. For the main course, a good *bife de chorizo*, or *tira de asado*, or *lomo* are the most popular choices, accompanied by various types of salads. To finish off, one might choose a nice flan (custard), topped with *dulce de leche* and some whipped cream. Don't think of calories, just enjoy.

WHERE TO EAT

A complete listing of all restaurants in the city would be impossible. Many short-term visitors just choose a place from the dozens along Florida and Lavalle walkways. The most popular are the ones listed here:

PARILLA (BEEF)

La Cabana
Entre Rios 436
Los Años Locos
Ave. Costanera Norte
Las Nazarenas
Reconquista 1132
La Estancia
Lavalle 941

INTERNATIONAL CUISINE

Harper's
Junin 1763
Gato Dumas
Roberto M. Ortiz 1809
Lola
Roberto M. Ortiz 1805
El Repecho de San Telmo
Carlos Calvo 242
Hotel Claridge
Tucuman 535

FRENCH CUISINE

Catalinas
Reconquista 875
Tomo I
Las Heras 3766
Au Bec Fin
Vicente Lopez 1827
Chez Moi
San Juan, 1200 block
La Crevette
San Juan 639
El Gato Que Pesca
Rodriguez Pena 159, Martinez
Refugio del Viejo Conde
Cervino 4453, Palermo
Oso Charlie
Segui 4676

SWISS/FONDUE

La Cave Du Valais
Zapiola 1779, Belgrano R

Charlie's Fondue
Pelliza 4399, Olivos

ITALIAN CUISINE

A Mamma Liberate
Medrano 974
Subito
Paraguay 640, lst floor
Robertino
Vicente Lopez 2158
Cosa Nostra
Cabrera 4300
La Fabbrica
Potosi 4465
A'Nonna Immacolata
Costanera Norte

Spanish, German, Chinese and other cuisines are also available. Check with the hotel. Prices at most of these restaurants are moderate. The more expensive ones will average about $50 per person, with drinks, wine/champagne and dessert included.

CULTURE PLUS

The Argentine people are extremely culture orientated. Thus, a wide range of activities are available. Museums, galleries, theaters, bookstores and several libraries are among the places to be visited. Be sure not to miss any of the ones listed below while in Buenos Aires.

ART MUSEUMS

Ornamental Art Museum
Displays art of the period between the XV and XIX centuries, housed in a beautiful baroque-style home. Located on Ave. Libertador 1902, tel: 802-0912. Open: Wed. to Mon. from 3 p.m. to 7 p.m.

National Museum of Fine Arts
34 halls displaying more than 300 pieces on permanent exhibition. Many Argentine painters as well as famous works by Van Gogh, Picasso, Manet, Rodin, Renoir, etc. Located on Ave. Libertador 1437, tel: 803-4062. Open: Tue. to Sun. from 9 a.m. to 12.45 p.m. and 3 p.m. to 7 p.m.

The José Hernández Museum of Argentine Motifs
This houses the most complete collection of folkloric art in the country. Many gaucho artifacts, earthenware, silverware, musical instruments, etc. Located on Ave. Libertador 2373, tel: 802-9967. Open: Mon. to Fri. from 10 a.m. to 8 p.m.

Museum of Modern Art
Wonderful collection of works by Matisse, Utrillo, Dali, Picasso, etc. Located on Corrientes 1530, 9th floor. Open: Tue. to Sun. from 4 p.m. to 8 p.m.

Historical and Scientific Museums
National Historical Museum of the Cabildo and May Revolution. Located Bolivar 65. Open: Thurs. to Sun. from 2 p.m. to 6 p.m.

Historical Museum of the City of Buenos Aires
Located on Republiquetes 6309, Saavedra. Open: Tue. to Sun. from 2 p.m. to 6 p.m.

Argentine Museum of Natural Sciences
Located on Angel Gallardo, tel: 89-6595. Open: Tues., Thurs. to Sun. from 2 p.m. to 6 p.m.

Throughout the provinces, there are also many museums. Information on these can be obtained from the tourist information centers for each of the provinces.

Art is very appreciated in this country. Many lovely art galleries can be found as you walk around the city. These three are very well known:

Galeria Ruth Benzacar
Florida 1000
Galeria Praxis
Arenales 1311
Galeria Palatina
Arroyo 821

But, if you have the time to browse, take the side streets and you might run into some exquisite old houses containing interesting exhibits.

THEATERS

Teatro Colón: Most of the renowned performers of the world are well acquainted with this magnificent theater. The building is in the Italian Renaissance style with some French and Greek influence. It has a capacity for 3,500 people, with about 1,000 standing. The acoustics are considered to be nearly perfect. Opera is one of the favorite programs for the season. In 1987, Luciano Pavarotti performed *La Boheme* here and tickets were sold out well in advance. Ballets are another favorite, performed by greats such as Nureyev, Godunov and the Bolshoi Ballet. The local company is very good and many of its members go on to become international figures. The Colon also has a magnificent museum, where all of the theater's history and its mementos are stored. It is an enlightening experience to have a guided visit of the theater and the museum. This can be arranged by calling 35-5114 or 35-5116 and setting up an appointment. Tickets can be purchased at the box office located on Libertad Street.

San Martín Theatre: Offers a variety of plays and musicals. Check the local paper for performances.

The theater season in Buenos Aires usually opens in March, with a large number of varied plays to please everyone. The Argentines like to go to see a good play and are highly critical. There is always something worthwhile seeing. Check the local paper or with the hotel for the current and best ones available. Recitals and concerts are promoted by the Secretary of Culture in an effort to bring culture to the people. The public responds enthusiastically by attending all events. Open-air concerts are very popular on hot summer evenings and are held in any one of the numerous parks in the city.

MOVIES

Going to the movies is another popular form of entertainment. Recent national and international films are shown, and the price of a ticket is less than in most countries. Listings appear in any of the local papers.

FESTIVALS

A number of colorful annual festivals take place around Argentina. A few of these are:

MENDOZA

Festival de la Vendimia. The grape harvest festival is held here, in the center of Argentina's wine country, every March. Three days of festivities culminate with an extravaganza of lights, music and dancing, held in an amphitheater set in the Andean foothills.

CÓRDOBA

This central town has several festivals throughout the year. The most important of these is the Cosquin, a celebration of international folkloric music and dancing. Check with a travel agent for the dates.

VILLA GENERAL BELGRANO

This small village near Córdoba hosts at least two festivals a year: the Alpine Chocolate Festival in winter, and an Oktoberfest (Fiesta de la Cerveza) in October.

SAN ANTONIO DE ARECO

In November this town, 70 miles (115 km) from Buenos Aires, celebrates Tradition Week, when gauchos show off their skills in rodeo events. The town also has a gaucho museum (R. Guiraldes) and, on weekends, the local artisans sell their wares around the town plaza.

NIGHTLIFE

The nightlife in Buenos Aires is quite a bit more active than in most major cities of the world. People walk carefree in the late hours of the night. Crime, although on the rise, is still not a major concern. The center part of town, on Calle Florida and Lavalle, at midnight might appear to most as midday.

Movies are open past 11 p.m. and there are some restaurants in the city that never close.

Discos, nightclubs, cabarets and bars can be found in most of the city. Hear the latest hits from around the world and dance into the morning at, for example, "Cemento," located on Estados Unidos 1238, or for a more formal crowd, dance at "Le Club," on Quintana 111, or at "Hippopotamus," Junin 1787. Other possibilities are:

Africa
AV. Alvear 1885
Contramano
Rodriguez Pena 1082
Mau Mau
Arroyo 866
New York City
Av. Alvarez Thomas 1391
Puerto Pirata
Liberated 1163
Snob
Ayachcho 2038
Club 100
Florida 165

For the very young crowd, there are new discos opening up every day. Ice skating has become the latest form of entertainment for young and old alike. You'll be able to find ice skating rinks all over Buenos Aires and in most of the major cities of the provinces.

The Argentines, as a whole, enjoy staying up late. Restaurants in Buenos Aires open up as early as 8 p.m., but in the provinces many don't open until 9 p.m. The big cities of the interior, like Cordoba, Mendoza, Bariloche,

Salta, etc., that attract many tourists, have a considerable nightlife. The theater shows are not as varied as in Buenos Aires, but a little bit of everything is available. A good tango show will be found almost everywhere, but the best shows are in Buenos Aires.

TANGO SHOWS

Taconeando
Balcarce 725, tel: 362-9596/9599
Casa Rosada
Chile 318, tel: 361-8222
El Viejo Almacén
Av. Independencia corner Balcarce, tel: 362-3602
Cano 14
Talcahuano 975, tel: 393-4626
II Castello
Pedro de Mendoza 1455, tel: 28-5270
Michelangelo
Balcarce 4332, tel: 30-6542

* Reservations are suggested at all the above.

Throughout Argentina, there are bars, cafés and confiterias, or tea rooms, serving a wonderful cup of expresso, tea, soft drinks, alcoholic beverages and an array of fast foods. As a point of interest, one of the most famous cafés in the city is **La Biela**, in the exclusive area of Recoleta – a must see for every tourist.

Others include the **Tortoni** on Avenida de Mayo around number 800, the **Ideal** on Suipacha (near Corrientes) and the **Molino** on the corner of the Plaza Congresso (just look for the giant windmill). All these are classic meeting places from Argentina's golden age. For a taste of modern Bohemia, and a younger crowd, head for the **Cafe La Paz** on the corner of Corrientes and Montevideo.

SHOPPING

SHOPPING AREAS

A few words of advice before mentioning some fine places to go shopping; there are two main streets for good shopping. The most known and the most "touristy" is Florida. Anything the average tourist might want to buy can be found here. The next main street is Avenida Santa Fe. Many shopping galleries are located on either side of the avenue, and once again nice things are available. The exclusive part of town, with the most expensive boutiques, is located in the Recoleta area, along Ave. Alvear, Quintana, Ayacucho and some little side streets. The antique stores in this area are exquisite – and so are the prices! But, more on antiques a little later on.

The fine jewelry stores are located at the beginning Florida and on Ave. Alvear. Also, Sterns is located in the lobby of the Sheraton Hotel.

The garment district is known as Once, and is accessible by taxi.

Buenos Aires also has quite a number of factory outlets, where good quality is available, there is a larger selection and best of all – the price is right! People who live here are well acquainted with these and will shop here rather than in stores. The only inconvenience is that they're usually located far from downtown.

LEATHER GOODS

Coalpe (handbags)
Mexico 3325, tel: 97-4620 b
Colicuer (handbags)
Tte. Gral. Peron 1615, lst floor, tel: 35-7463
Maximilian Klein (handbags)
Humberto Primo 3435, tel: 93-0511
Viel (handbags and shoes)
Viel 1550, tel: 922-2359

La Mia Scarpa (custom made shoes)
Thames 1617, tel: 72-6702
Belt Factory
Fco. Acuna de Figueroa 454, tel: 87-3172
Kerquelen (custom made and quick service)
Santander 747, tel: 922-2801
Le Fauve (latest leather fashions [jackets, skirts, dress pants] & competitive prices with personalized attention)
Sarandi 1226, tel: 27-7326
Arenales 1315, tel: 44-8844.
Casa Vuriloche
Uruquay 318, tel: 40-9673

SWEATERS

YSL
Catilan, Obligado 4422 (at the 4400 block of Cabildo), tel: 70-3991

FURRIERS

Pieles Chic
(5th generation furrier, excellent furs and very competitive prices)
Hipolito Yrigoyen
1428-Vicente Lopez, tel: 795-3836/8836
Pieles Wendall (Ted Lapidus Representative)
Av. Córdoba 2762, tel: 86-7220
Dennis Furs (YSL Representative)
M.T. de Alvear 628, tel: 312-7411

JEWELERS

Koltai Joyeria (Antique quality jewelry)
Esmeralda 616, tel: 392-4052/5716
Ricciardi
Florida 1001, tel: 312-3082
Antoniazzi-Chiappe
Av. Alvear 1895, tel: 41-6137
Sterns Jewellers
Sheraton Hotel
Lovasi Joyeria
Rodriguez Pena 419, tel: 46-5131

REGIONAL HANDICRAFTS

Tuyunti
Florida 971, tel: 542-8651

ANTIQUES

The best known area of Buenos Aires for antiques is San Telmo. It's one of the most historic barrios (neighborhoods) of Buenos Aires. Every Sunday the San Telmo Fair takes place. The plaza is surrounded by stalls which sell quite an array of objects, from new to old, ordinary to odd, and that can be very cheap or outrageously expensive. Only the trained eye can find the bargains. The rest just think they have found a unique piece, when, in fact, they have only purchased a copy. So, beware! Around the plaza, there are many reputable antique stores. The prices are high, but some beautiful pieces can still be found.

Auction houses are very popular and good buys can be obtained. Some of these are:

Roldan y Cia, Rodriguez Peña 1673, tel: 30-3733
Naon y Cia, Guido 1785, tel: 41-1685
Banco de la Ciudad, Esmeralda 660, tel: 392-6684

Small antique shops can be found throughout the city. The prices are negotiable. Along Rivadavia avenue, around the 4000 block, quite a number of these shops are located. As these stores are not known to many, the prices and the attention are good. Also, along Libertador Avenue, towards Martinez and the San Isidro area, there are a number of shops with some very worthwhile pieces. It just takes time and a little knowledge on the subject.

La Baulera, located on Av. Monroe 2753, has quite a different assortment of collectibles, and the owners will try to help find that unique piece. Other listings of shops can be obtained either from your hotel or from your copy of the *Buenos Aires Times*.

Artisan Fairs take place on the weekends in different parts of the city. Some of these are:

Plaza Francia – near the Recoleta area on Sun.
Plaza Manuel Belgrano – Juramento 2200 every Sun.
Plaza Mitre – San Isidro on Sun.
Tigre – Puerto de Los Frutos every Sat. and Sun.

SPORTS

A complete description of sports activities, both for spectators and participants, can be found in the Sports Chapter of this book. A few bits of useful information are listed in the following coloumns:

HORSEBACK TREKKING

Spend from half a day to a week riding under the open skies of the Andean foothills, near the town of Bariloche. Similar to dude ranching operations in the U.S., but more rugged, with camping beneath the stars. Contact: Carol Jones, Estancia Nahuel Huapi, (8401) Nahuel Huapi, Neuquen, Argentina, or Hans Schulz, Polvani Tours, Quaglia 268, (8400) Bariloche, Argentina, tel: (0944) 23286, telex: 80772 POLVA AR.

FLY FISHING

Spend a secluded vacation fishing for trout in the clear lakes and streams of the Andes. Accommodations, equipment and guides provided. Contact: Caleufu River SRL, M. Moreno 1185, (8370) San Martín de Los Andes, Neuquen, Argentina, tel: (0944) 7199, telex: COSMA CALEUFU or for similar facilities: Cosmopolitan Travel, L. Alem 986, 7th floor, Buneos Aires 100l, Argentina, tel: 311-7880/6695/2478/6684, telex: 9199 CASSA AR.

OTHER FISHING: Chascomus is a small city beside a lake, about 78 miles (125 km) south of Buenos Aires. It is accessible by car or train. The lake has brackish water fishing, and the main catches are pejerrey (a type of catfish) and a very aggressive fish called the tararira. Equipment is available for rent at the local fishing club.

Argentina is famous for its fishing, and the trout fishing here is considered to be among the best in the world. One can fish along the coast, in the streams up in the Andes, or in the countless lakes and rivers in between.

Ask a travel agent for more details, and reservations.

TREKKING

Trekking in the Andes, including an eight day trip, through spectacular scenery, to the foot of Aconcaqua. Contact: Fernanado Grajales, Optar Tours, Mendoza, Prov. Mendoza, Argentina.

SKIING

The main ski resorts in Argentina are: The Cerro Catedral Complex, located near Bariloche. Valle de las Leñas, in the south of Mendoza Province. Los Penitentes, a small resort near the town of Mendoza.

There are also a number of small facilities located throughout the southern provinces, including one in Tierra del Fuego, and another near Esquel. Contact a travel agent for details and reservations. Package tours are available, and tend to keep down the costs of a ski vacation.

PATO

This uniquely Argentine sport is sometimes played for public audiences on the *estancias* around Buenos Aires. Contact a travel agent for information.

HORSE RACING

The two main tracks in Buenos Aires are the Jockey Club Track, in San Isidro, and the Palermo Track, in Palermo. Races are run about four times a week. Smaller tracks are located in most of the major Argentine cities.

POLO

The best place to see polo in Buenos Aires is at the centrally located Palermo field. The most important championship is usually held here in November. Tickets can be purchased at the box office.

DUCK HUNTING

Duck and partridge hunting, on a very large *estancia* nestled in the marshlands of Santo Fe Province, about 800 km from Buenos Aires. Very comfortable accommodations

for groups of up to 6. Contact: Condor Special Safaris, Adriana Maguirre, Ave, Las Heras 3790, 5th floor, Buenos Aires, 1425 Argentina, tel: (54) (1) 801-4742, telex: FIRPO AR 23924 or Salty Salztman, P.O. Box 648, Manchester, Vermont 05254, U.S.A., tel: (802) 362-1876, telex: 495-0637.

Tren a las Nubes: The "Train to the Clouds" is an all-day excursion from the N.W. town of Salta. It gets its name from the dizzying heights reached at the top stretch of the journey. The scenery is spectacular. Information can be obtained in Salta, or from the central Ferrocarriles office in Buenos Aires.

ESTANCIA GETAWAY

Visitors to Buenos Aires have the chance to get away from the buzz of the city, in the small town of San Antonio de Areco, just 71 miles (115 km) away. In this peaceful location, with beautiful scenery, the Aldao family has converted the Estancia La Bamba into a country inn, with all the facilities to make a stay both comfortable and memorable. For more information, contact 392-0394/9707.

FALABELLA HORSES

A visit to the Estancia El Peludo will provide an interesting side trip from Buenos Aires. Located 120 miles (65 km) from town, this ranch raises the unique and famous miniature Falabella Horses (named for their breeder). Some of these horses are owned by such international figures as the Kennedys, the Carters, and Juan Carlos of Spain. Those interested in visiting the estancia, and perhaps buying a horse, can contact Mrs. Falabella at 44-5050/1404.

FURTHER READING

GENERAL TRAVEL

Durrell, Gerald. *The Whispering Land.*
Durrell, Gerald. *The Drunken Forest.*
Erize, F. *Los Parques Nacionales de la Argentina.* Buenos Aires: Incafo, 1981.

HISTORY

Andrews, George Reid. *The Afro-Argentines of Buenos Aires: 1800-1900.* Madison: Univ. of Wisconsin Press, 1980.
Darwin, Charles. *The Voyage of the Beagle.* USA: Bantam Books, 1972.
Hastings, Max and Jenkins, Simon. *The Battle for the Falklands.* New York: W.W. Norton and Co., 1983.
King, Anthony. *Twenty-Four Years in the Argentine Republic.* Reprint of 1846 edition.
Mac Cann, William. *Two Thousand Miles' Ride Through the Argentine Provinces.* Reprint of 1853 edition.
Musters, George. *Life Among the Patagonian Indians.*
Page, Joseph. *Perón: A Biography.* New York: Random House, 1983.
Partnoy, Alicia. *The Little School: Tales of Disapperance and Survival in Argentina.* New York: Cleis Press, 1986.
Perón, Juan. *The Speeches of Juan Domingo Perón.* Gordon Press.
Scobie, James R. *Argentina: A City and a Nation.* New York: Oxford Univ. Press, 1964. The best general introduction to the country's history and geography.
Shipton, Eric. *Land of Tempest.*
Slatta, Richard W. *Gauchos and the Vanishing Frontier.* Lincoln: Univ. of Nebraska Press, 1983.
Tschiffely, A.A. *Tschiffely's Ride.* New York: Simon and Schuster, 1933.

PATAGONIA & TIERRA DEL FUEGO TRAVEL

Bridges, E. Lucas. *The Uttermost Part of the Earth.* New York: Dutton, 1949.
Chatwin, Bruce. *In Patagonia.* New York: Summit Books, 1977
Falkner, P.T. *A Description of Patagonia and the Adjoining Parts of South America.* Reprint of 1935 edition.
Goodall, R. Natalie P. *Tierra del Fuego.* Buenos Aires: Ediciones Shanamaiim, 1979.
Hudson, W.H. *Far Away and Long Ago.*
Hudson, W.H. *Birds of La Plata.*
Hudson, W.H. *Idle Days in Patagonia.* London: Everyman's Library, 1984.
Hudson, W.H. *Tales of the Pampas.* Berkeley: Creative Arts Book Co., 1979.
Ruiz, B.M. *La Colonización Galesa en el Valle del Chubut.* Buenos Aires: Ed. Galerna, 1977.
Shipton, Eric. *Tierra del Fuego, the fatal Lodestone.*

CULTURE

Foster, David. *Currents in the Contemporary Argentine Novel.* Univ. of Missouri Press, 1975.

The fictional writings of Jorge Luis Borges, Ernesto Sábato and Julio Córtazan all give an insight into Argentina's cosmopolitan culture.

Note: The Suggested Reading list was compiled by Philip Benson.

USEFUL ADDRESSES

TOURIST INFORMATION

Local and national tourist information can be obtained from the various tourist offices in the city. The following is a list of the most important ones:

Argentine Chamber of Tourism
Tucumán 1610, 3rd and 6th floor
Buenos Aires – tel: 40-5108 ext. 13

National Direction of Tourism
(for information)
Santa Fe 883, P.B.
Buenos Aires – tel: 312-2232/5550

Direction of Tourism for Buenos Aires
Sarmiento 1551, 4th floor
Buenos Aires – tel: 46-1251

Perhaps easiest to find are the several tourist information centers along **Florida**, a pedestrian boulevard. Here in these booths, the traveler can obtain maps of the city and a bilingual (Spanish and English) tourist information newspaper called *The Buenos Aires Times*. It offers complete listings of what is happening in the city, as well as other pertinent and useful information. *Where*, a booklet giving a complete list of shopping, dining and entertainment, can be obtained in most hotels.

The provinces of Argentina have offices in Buenos Aires where the tourist can obtain valuable information of a particular province. Pamphlets about special events, attractions, lists of hotels, restaurants, etc., are readily available. The following is a list of these offices with their telephone numbers. All are located in the center part of town and can be easily found.

PROVINCIAL TOURIST OFFICES IN BUENOS AIRES

Santa Cruz
Ave. Córdoba 1345, 14th floor, tel: 42-0381/0916-42-1169/1116
San Juan
Maipu 331, tel: 45-1698/3797 45-638
Santiago Del Estero
Florida 274, tel: 46-9398/9417
San Luis
Azcuenaga 1083, tel: 83-3641
Entre Ríos
Pte Perón 451, 4th floor
Formosa
H. Yrigoyen 1429, tel: 37-1479/3699
Buenos Aires
Ave. Callao 237, tel: 40-7045
Tucumán
Bme. Mitre 836, 1st floor, tel: 40-2214
Corrientes
San Martín 333, 4th floor, tel: 394-7432/7418/0859/7390
Santa Fe
25 de Mayo 358, P.B., tel: 312-4620/0394/5160
Neuquen
Pte. Perón 687, tel: 49-6385; 46-9265
Tierra Del Fuego
Sarmiento 747, 5th floor, tel: 40-1995/1881/1791
Chubut
Paraguay 876, tel: 312-2262/2340/4333
La Pampa
Suipacha 346, tel: 35-0511/6797/1145
Salta
Maipu 663, tel: 392-5773/6019
Chaco
Ave. Callao 322, 1st floor, tel: 45-0961/3045
Córdoba
Ave. Callao 332, tel: 45-6566, 49-4277
Mendoza
Ave. Callao 445, tel: 40-6683, 46-1105
La Rioja
Ave. Callao 745, tel: 44-1662/1339, 41-4524
Río Negro
Tucuman 1920, tel: 45-9931/7920/2128
Catamarca
Cordoba 2080, tel: 46-6891/94
Misiones
Ave. Santa Fe 989, tel: 393-1615/1812/1343/1714
Jujuy
Ave. Santa Fe 967, tel: 393-1295/3174/6096

Cosmopolitan Travel
L. Alem 986, 7th floor, Buenos Aires, Argentina, tel: 311-6684/6695/2081/2474, telex: 9199 CASSA AR. 24-hour service available and many languages spoken.

Flyer Travel
Reconquista 621, 8th floor, Buenos Aires, Argentina, tel: 313-8165/8201/8224

STO Travel
Hipolito Yrigoyen 850, Buenos Aires, Argentina, tel: 34-0789/5913/7336, telex: 22784 SHABA

Sol Jet Travel
Florida 118, Buenos Aires, Argentina, tel: 40-8361/3939/7030, telex: 17188 SOLIT AR

FOREIGN REPRESENTATIVES IN BUENOS AIRES

Albania
Olazabal 2060, tel: 781-7740

Algiers
Montevideo 1889, tel: 22-5969

Australia
Santa Fe 846, 8th floor, tel: 312-6841

Austria-French
367, tel: 802-7195

Belgium-Oefensaaa
113, 8th floor, tel: 33-0066

Bolivia
25 de Mayo 611, 2nd floor, tel: 311-7365

Brazil
C. Pellegrini 1363, 5th floor

Bulgaria
Manuel Obarrio 2967, tel: 802-9251

Canada
Suipacha 1111, 25th floor, tel: 312-9081

Chile
Sn. Martin 439, 9th floor, tel: 394-6582

China
Republiquetes 5349, tel: 541-5085

Colombia
Florida 939, 4th floor, tel: 311-7399

Costa Rica
Esmeralda 135, 6th floor, tel: 45-8427

Cuba
V. del Pino 1810, tel: 783-2213

Czechoslovakia
F. Alcorta 3240, tel: 801-3904

Denmark
L. Alem 1074, 9th floor, tel: 312-6901

Dom.Republic
Sta. Fe 1206, 2nd floor, tel: 41-4669

East Germany
Olazabal 2201, tel: 781-2002

Ecuador
Quintana 585,10th floor, tel: 804-6408

Egypt
Rodriquez Pena 1474, tel: 42-8542

El Salvador
Sta. Fe 882, 12th floor, tel: 394-7628

Finland
Sta. Fe 846, 5th floor, tel: 312-0600

France
Sta. Fe 846, 4th floor, tel: 312-2425

Gabon
F. Alcorta 3221, tel: 802-4631

Greece
R.S. Pena 547, 4th floor, tel: 34-4958

Guatemala
Sta. Fe 830, 5th floor, tel: 313-9160

Haiti
F. Alcorta 3297, tel: 802-0211

Holland
Maipu 66, 2nd floor, tel: 33-6066

Holy See
Alvear Ave. 1605, tel: 42-9697

Honduras
Sta. Fe 1385, 4th floor, tel: 42-1643

Hungary
Col. Diaz 1874, tel: 83-0767

India
Córdoba 950, 4th floor, tel: 393-4001

Indonesia
Ramon Castilla 2901, tel: 801-6622

Iraq
Villanueve 1400, tel: 771-8369

Iran
F. Alcorta 3229, tel: 802-1470

Ireland
Sta. Fe 1391, 4th floor, tel: 44-9987

Israel
Arroyo 916, tel: 392-4481

Italy
M.T. Alvear 1149, tel: 393-9329

Jamaica
Corrientes 127, 4th floor, tel: 311-4872

Japan
Paseo Colon 275, 9-11th floor, tel: 30-2561

Korea (South)
Libertador 2257, tel: 802-8865

Lebanon
Libertador 2354, tel: 802-2909

Libya
A. Aquador 2885, tel: 801-2872

Mexico
Larea 1230, tel: 824-7061

Morocco
Ramon Castilla 2952, tel: 802-0136
Nicaragua
Esmeralda 1319, 3rd floor, tel: 22-6292
Nigeria
3 de Febrero 1365, tel: 782-6614
Norway
Esmeralda 909 3rd floor, tel: 312-1904
Pakistan
Tel: 393-0355
Panama
Esmeralda 1066, tel: 311-7661
Paraguay
Maipu 464, 3rd floor, tel: 392-6536
Peru
Tucumán 637, 9th floor, tel: 392-1344
Philippines
Juramento 1945, tel: 781-4170
Poland
A.M. Aquado 2870, tel: 802-9681
Portugal
Córdoba 315, 3rd floor, tel: 312-3524
Romania
Arroyo 962, tel: 392-2630
Saudi Arabia
A.M. Aquado 2881, tel: 802-3375
Syria
Callao 956, tel: 42-2113
South Africa
M.T.Alvear 590, 7th floor, tel: 311-8991
Spain
Guido 1760, tel: 41-0078
Sweden
Corrientes 330, 3rd floor, tel: 311-3080
Switzerland
Sta. Fe 846, 12th floor, tel: 311-6491
Switzerland (British interests)
Luis Agote 2412, tel: 803-7070
Thailand
V. del Pino 2458, 6th floor, tel: 785-6505
Turkey
R.S. Pena 852, 8th floor, tel: 46-8779
U.S.S.R.
Guido 1677, tel: 42-1552
United States
Colombia 4300, tel: 774-7611
Uruguay
Las Heras 1907, tel: 803-6032
Venezuela
Esmeralda 909, 4th floor, tel: 311-8337
West Germany
Villanueva 1055, tel: 771-5054
Yugoslavia
Rodriguez Pena 1012, tel: 41-1309

Zaire
Villanueva 1356, 2nd floor, tel: 771-0075

AIRLINE COMPANIES

Aeroflot
Tel: 312-5573
Aereolineas Argentinas
Tel: 393-1562
Aero Mexico
Tel: 392-4821
Aeroperu
Tel: 311-4115
Air France
Tel: 313-9091
Alitalia
Tel: 312-8421
Austral
Tel: 49-9011
Avianca
Tel: 312-3693
British Airways
Tel: 392-6037
British Caledonian
Tel: 392-3489
Canadian Airlines
Tel: 392-3765
China Airlines
Tel: 312-0664
Cruzeiro-Varig
Tel: 35-3014
Eastern Airlines
Tel: 312-5031
Ecuatoriana
Tel: 311-1117
El Al
Tel: 392-8840
Flying Tigers
Tel: 311-9252
Iberia
Tel: 35-5081
Japan Airlines
Tel: 392-2005
KLM
Tel: 311-9522
Korean Air
Tel: 311-9237
Lade
Tel: 361-0853
Lan Chile
Tel: 311-5336
LAPA
Tel: 311-2492
Lloyd Aereo Boliviano
Tel: 35-3505

Lufthansa
Tel: 313-4431
Pan Am
Tel: 45-0111
Pluna
Tel: 394-5356
Qantas Airway
Tel: 312-9701
SABENA
Tel: 394-7400
Singapore Airlines
Tel: 33-3402
South African Airways
Tel: 311-5825
SAS
Tel: 312-8161
Swissair
Tel: 312-0669
Thai International
Tel: 312-8161
United Airlines
Tel: 312-0664
Viasa
Tel: 311-5298

BUS COMPANIES

Ablo
Tel: 313-2835
travels to Prov. Córdoba
Anton
Tel: 313-3078
travels to the coastal cities
Costera Criolla
Tel: 313-2503
travels to the coastal cities
Chevalier
Tel: 312-3297
travels throughout the entire Province of
Buenos Aires

Chevalier Paraguaya
Tel: 313-2349
travels to Paraguay
Expreso Singer
Tel: 313-2355
travels to the northern provinces
Fenix
Tel: 313-0134
travels west to Chile
Gral Urguiza y Sierras de Córdoba
Tel: 313-2771
travels to Córdoba
La Internacional
Tel: 313-3164
travels to Paraguay and Brazil
Micro Mar
Tel: 313-3128
travels to the seaside cities
Onda
Tel: 313-3192
travels to Uruguay
Plum
Tel: 313-3901
travels to Brazil
Tata
Tel: 313-3836
travels to the northern provinces of the
country and the border with Bolivia.

ART/PHOTO CREDITS

Photography by

INDEX

A

Aberdeen Angus, 149
aborigine Indians, 92
Abra Pampa, 186, 267
Acheral, 179
Aconcagua, 20, 193, 199
  see highest peak
Aconquija range, 178
adobe, 162, 173
Aerolineas Argentinas, 137, 246
  see airlines
Aeroparque Jorge Newbery
Airport, 137
  see airports
Africans, 38
Afro-Argentine, 32, 38
agoutis, 265, 268
agriculture, 25-27
Aguas Negras, 268
Aguas Verdes, 138
airlines
  Aerolineas Argentinas, 137, 246
  Austral, 246
  LADE, 233
  LAPA, 137
airports
  Aeroparque Jorge Newberry, 137
  Camet, 137
Air Force Plaza, 122
Alaculuf, 245
Alamito culture, 27
Alaska, 24
Albatros, 253
Alberdi, Juan Bautista, 37
alfajores marplatenses, 140
Alfonsín, Raúl, President, 50, 51, 53
algarrobo forests, 148, 177
Alianza Argentina Anticomunista, 47
Almirante Brown Avenue, 121
alpaca, 25, 28
Alumine, 218
Alvear Avenues, 123
Alvear, General, 125
Amaicha del Valle, 179
Amancay Inn, 225
Anchorena family's residence, 122
ancient settlements, 175
Andes Mountains, 18, 19, 20, 243
Anglican Mission, 246, 253
Anglo-Argentine, 61
Anizacate River, 153
Antarctica, 17, 234, 235
Antarctica Treaty, 235, 241

Apipe Islands, 163
Apostoles, 166
Araucanians, 290
Araucano-Mapuches, 61
Araucaria Araucana, 218
Araucaria trees, 268
Archaeological Museum, 183, 198, 203
archaeological record, 27
archaeological sites, 26
archipelago, 245
architecture, 28, 94, 114
argentinidad, 285
argentum, 17
Arizu, 201
armadillo(s), 145, 146, 261
Armadillo, Hairy, 270
Armadillo, Patagonian Pichi, 270
art(s), 25, 67, 94, 289
artifacts, 28
Artisans' Market, 199
asado(s) (barbeque), 63, 106, 153, 252, 254
Atamarca Desert, 176
Ateneo Bookstore, 112
Atlantic coast, 20, 24, 145, 216, 225
Atlantic Ocean, 212
Atlantida, 137
Atlantida Argentina, 136 137, 140
Aurelia, 249
Austral, 53 137
Austral Airlines, 246
  see airlines
Austral Hotel, 230
Austral parakeets, 268, 270
Australian Merinos, 232
Avenida 9 de Julio, 103, 105, 107, 111, 123
  see widest street
Avenida de Mayo, 98, 103, 104, 107
Avenida Florida, 111
aves, 263
Avocets, 267
Aztecs, 175
A.C.A.(Automobile Club of Argentina), 264

B

Bahia Blanca, 54 140, 216
Bahia Brown, 251
Bahia Inutil, 245
Bahia Samborombon, 137
Bahia San Sebastian, 247
Bajada de Miguens, 233
Baker Sound, 233
Balcarce, 116
Balcarce Street, 115
Bambi, 221
Banco de la Nacion Argentina (National Bank of
  the Argentine Nation, 104)
Bariloche, 215, 216, 219
Baron Bisa, 153
barrio(s), 95, 97, 113, 114, 117
Barrio Norte, 115, 123
Bascilica, Pilar, 123
Basilica de Lujan, 129
Basilica of our Lady of Pilar, 124
Basque, 290
Beagle Channel, 20, 26, 51
Beagle (Darwin's vessel), 140, 245

beef, 103, 106
Beerbohm, Julius, 76
Belen, 176
Belgrano Avenue, 115
Belgrano, Manuel (General), 33, 49
Bering Strait, 24
Bern, painter, 112
Bethlemite priests, 114, 116
bife de chorizo, 106
bife de costilla, 106
Bigone, Reynaldo, 49
birds
  Andean Coots, 186
  Andean Flamingo, 269
  Blackchested Bluebeard, 126, 268, 270
  Green-backed Firecrown, 268
  Jaibaru Storks, 266
  Magellanic Woodpecker, 268
  Spot-winged Falconet, 268
  Torrent Duck, 268, 270
  Yellow Cardinal, 268
Blacks, 32
Boca Juniors, 121, 275
  see football clubs
bocci, 201
Bodega La Rural, 201
bodega, 201, 180, 193, 195
Boers, 230
bolas, 286
boleadoras, 35, 285, 286
boliche, 290
Bolivar Street, 113
Bolivar, Simon, 34
bombachas, 226, 288, 290
bombos, 102
Bonete Volcano, 176
books
  Far Away and Long Ago, 262
  Idle Days in Patagonia, 210
  Journal of Researchers, 245
  Letters from Paraguay, 78
  Mi Buenos Aires Querido, 119
  Mi Noche Triste, 119
  Uttermost Part of the Earth, 245, 251
bookstores, 108, 109
Bordeaux, 196
  see wines
Borges, Jorge Luis, 51, 92
Brandson Street, 121
Brazilian Embassy, 123
Bridges, E. Lucas, 245, 251
Bridges, Mary, 253
Bridges, Rev. Thomas, 251, 253
Bridge, Avellaneda, 120
British Men's Hospital, 115,
British Tower, 122
Buenos Aires, 13, 17, 18, 93, 94, 97, 102, 122
Buenos Aires Lawn Tennis Club, 278
Buffed-necked Ibises, 268
Bustillo, 220
Butch Cassidy and the Sundance Kid, 225

C

cabana, 135, 248
Cabernet Sauvingnon grape, 196
  see wines
Cabildo (the Town Council), 93, 98, 103, 152-153
Cabo Corrientes, 139
Cabo Domingo, 248
Cabo Espiritu Santo, 246, 248
Cabo San Antonio, 137, 138
Cabo San Pablo, 250
Cabot, Sebastian, 31
Cabral, Sargeant, 161
Cabrera, Jeronimo Luis, de, 146, 152
Cacheuta, 177
Cachi, 182, 183
Cachueta Hot Springs, 201
caciques, 146
CADIC (*Centro Austral de Investigationes Cientificas*), 254
Cafayate, 180, 181, 182
café(s), 95, 108, 109
Calafate, 233, 234, 269
Calchaqui, 179, 181, 182
Caleta Valdes, 228
Caleufu, 219
Callao, 107, 108, 111
Calle San Martín, 140
calle **Casanovas**, 68
camelids, 25
Camet Airport, 137
  see airport
Camino de Comechingones, 154
Camino de La Punilla, 153
Camino de los Andes, 20, 201
Camino de los grandes lagos, 154
Campero, de, Marques, 186
Campo del Cielo, 177
Campora, Hector, 46, 47
campsites, 24, 247
Canal Beagle (hotel), 253, 254
canasta, 135
candelabra, 182
caninas, 120
canyons, 20
Cape Horn, 234, 241, 243
Capilla del Monte, 153
capital city, 37
  see Buenos Aires
captain of the Argentine army, 116
  see Cespedes
Capuchin monkeys, 265, 268
Caputo, Dante, 51
Capybara, 263, 267
Caraffa, Emilio, 151
Cardenosa, Manuel, 151
cardon, 182
Carilo, 139
Carlos Calvo, 115, 116
Carlos Pellegrini Plaza, 123
Carmen de Patagones, 216
Carnival, 163
Cary, Anthony, Lord, Viscount of Falkland, 234
Casa de la Independencia, 178
Casa Rosada (Pink House), 46, 47, 50, 98, 99, 103
Casabindo, 186
Caseros, 37

Caseros Street, 151
casino, 136, 140
Casita Suiza, 222
Castagnino, painter, 112, 116
Castillo, Pedro de, 194
Castillo, Ramon, 42
Catalinas, 122
Catamarca, 20, 28, 32, 175, 176
Catedral Ski Center, 222
Cathedral of La Plata, 130
Cathedral, the, 150
Catholic Church, 103, 114
Catholicism, 66
cattle, 18, 149
Cauchico, 249
caudillo(s), 31, 35, 36, 37, 39, 288
cave and rock paintings, 28
Cave of the Painted Hands in Santa Cruz, 28
Cavendish, Thomas, captain, 210, 212
Cayasta, 162
Cayman, 266
Centinela del Mar, 140
centolla (southern king crab), 245, 254
Central Market, 119
Central Mountains, 25
Central Sierras, 145
Ceramic Period, 27, 28
ceramics, 25, 26
ceremonial buildings, 25
Cerro de la Gloria, 199
Cerro de los Siete Colores, 185
Cerro Torre, 234
Cerro Torreicillas, 225
Cespedes, Martina, 116
  see Captain
cetaceans, 245
Chacabuco, 34
Chaco, 19, 37, 61, 176, 177, 266
Chaco National Park, 266
  see national parks
Chalten (Blue Peak), 234
Champaqui, 147
Chandon, 196
Chapel of Yavi, 186
chaquena savanna, 19
Chardonnay, 196
  see wines
Charly Garcia Band, 68
Charrua tribesmen, 31
Chenin, 196
  see wines
Chepelmesh, 250
Chile Street, 115
Chilean Araucanian migrations, 25
Chilean Embassy, 125
Chilean Pigeon, 268
Chilecito, 176
Chimehuin, 219
Chimehuin Inn, 219
chinas, 288
chinchulin (the lower intestine), 106
Chiriguan, 61
chiripa, 288
Cholila Valley, 225
choripan, 127
chorizo (a spicy sausage), 106, 115, 116
Choroti, 61
Christianity, 48

Chubut, 223, 268, 270
Chubut Valley, 212, 213, 223, 225, 226
churches, 50, 66, 99, 150
Cinco Hermantos, 252
Cipoletti, 216
circuito, 150
Cisplatine War, 35
citrus fruits, 20
City Council, 98, 107
city dwellers, 62
City Museum, 113
City Tourism Bureau, 109
City Zoo, 127, 199
Ciudad de los Ninos, 130
civil warfare, 288
Clarin, 68
Claromeco, 140
clerico, 199
climate, 17, 19, 20, 148, 200, 261
Club Andinista, (Pardo and Ruben Lemos
  Streets), 202
Club Andino, 221
Club English, 233
Club de Pesca John Goodall, 248
Club Hurlingham, 248
Club Jockey, 23
Club Nautica, 227
Club Quilmes, 275
coati-mundis, 265
Cochinoca, 186
Coctaca, 186
Colegio Maximo, 151
Colmeiro, painter, 112
Colon, 166
Colon Theater, 104, 110
Colonia Sarmiento, 230
colonial cities, 13
Colorado River, 214, 216
Columbus, 31
Comechingones, 146
Comercio Hotel and Restaurant, 233
commercial districts, 98
Comodoro Rivadavia, 216, 228, 230
compara 232, 233
Complejo Museo Grafico Enrique Udaondo, 129
Concordia, 166
Condorhuasi, 27
condor(s), 267, 268, 270
Confederacion del Trabajo, 44
Congresco, 115
Congress, 108
Congress Building, 107
Conquest, 196
Conquest of the Desert, 39, 213
Conquistadors, 194
Consejo Municipal (City Council), 103
Constitution, 129
Constitution Train Station, 130
Continental Ice Cap, 17, 233
conventillo(s), 115, 116
Cook, James, 235, 245
Copahue-Caviahue, 177
cordilleras (ranges) 20
Córdoba, 18, 25, 32, 111, 112, 145, 147, 149, 150,
  151, 153, 268, 275,
Córdoba Pass, 220
Cordobazo(Córdoba coup), 46
Corriedales, 232, 248

Corrientes, 35, 105, 108, 109, 111, 163, 266
Corrientes Avenue, 108
Corrientes Street, 98
corvina negra, 138
corvina rubia, 138
cosmopolitian center, 62
Cosquin, 153
Costa Azul, 138
Costa Bonita, 140
Costa del Este, 138
Costanera, 163
country folk, 62
country life, 76
coup d'etat, 42
Coya People, 185
Coypu, 266
Coyte, Manuel, de, 104
Crab-eating Foxes, 263
creatures of habit, 63, 64
cricket, 279
  see sport
criollos (Argentine-born colonists), 32, 33, 118
Cruz del Eje, 153
cueca, 203
Cuesta de Miranda, 176
Cuesta del Obispo Pass, 183
Cuevas de las Manos, 230
cultural development, 24
culture, 13, 285, 290
customs, 78
Cuyo, 193, 194, 195, 200, 201, 203
Cwm hyfrwd, 223, 226
cypress (Pilgerodendron uviferum), 244

D

Darwin, Charles, 35, 73, 74, 75, 76,77, 209, 210,
  245, 286
  Rhea, 270
  Journal of Researchers, 245
day of independence, 33
Defensa, 113
Defensa Street, 115
Delta, 128, 161
Democracy, 48
demographic factors, 60
Depression, 60
descamisados, 43, 44, 45
Description of Patagonia, 75
desert, 20, 194
Desert Campaigns, 35, 288
Despedida, 249
desaparecidos, 48
Diagonal Norte, 105
Diaguita natives, 179
dirty war, 48, 53
disappeared, 102
Dixie, Florence, Lady, 76
Dolavon, 227
dolmens, 179
Domestic Chapel, 151
Don Diego Restaurant, 225
Dona Encarnacion, 36
dorado, 280
  see fishes
Doughty, Thomas, 230
Drake, Sir Francis, 210, 230, 245

Drake Passage, 243
Drier, Katherine S., 75
Duarte, Juan, 44
Dulce de leche, 106
Dulce River, 146

E

eagle, Black-chested Buzzard, 269
  see birds
early Americans, 24
Early Ceramic Period, 27
early traveler, 73
earthquakes, 195
East Bank, 285
Eberhardt, 26
economic development, 93
Edelweiss, 222
Eiffel, 162
Eisteddfod, 227, 223
El Angosto, 185
El Basco, 226
El Bolsón, 217, 222, 268
El Cadillal, 178
El Candil, 222
El Casco, 222
El Chaco, 177
El Destino, 264
El Enterriano, tango, 118
El Gato Que Pesca, 106
El Gaucho, 289
El Globo, 105
El Infiernillo, 179
El Munich de los Andes, 219
El Palmar National Park, 262
  see national parks
El Quincho, 225
El Respecho, 115
El Viejo Equiador, 219
El Viejo Munich, 222
election, 65
Elegant Crested Tinamou, 270
El que no salta es un militar, 102
empanadas, 106
employment, 55
en famille, 78
Encarnacion, 163
Encarnacion Escurra, Maria, de la, 35
Enchanted Valley, 220
English Club, 233
  see club
entertainment, 97, 98
Entre Ríos, 262, 35, 162
Epecuen, 177
equestrian sports, 277, 286
Ernesto Tornquist, provincial preserve, 264
Escuela Agrotecnica, 248
Esquel, 215, 216, 217, 225, 226, 228
estancia, 130
Estancia Despedida, 249
Estancia El Destino, 262
Estancia El Palenque Camino Vecinal, 263
Estancia Harberton, 251
Estancia Indiana, 250
Estancia Jose Menendez, 249
Estancia La Adela, 228
Estancia La Anita, 234
Estancia La Candelaria, 152

Estancia La Primavera, 220
Estancia la Primera Argentina, 249
Estancia Maria Behty, 249
Estancia Moat, 251
Estancia Nahuel Huapi, 221
Estancia San Isidro, 262
Estancia Sara, 248
Estancia Tunel, 252
estancia(s), 18, 35, 54, 62, 213-216, 232-233, 248-249, 267, 277, 287-288, 290
estancieros (large landowners), 33, 54, 216, 287
Estero, 177
Estrella Pharmacy, 113
ethnic make-up, 59
etiquette of introductions, 63
European explorers, 17, 136
European immigrants, 38
European settlements, 27
Europeans, 26
Evans, John, 227
Everest (tour agency), 253
Executive Branch, 104
explorers, 78

F

F. Ameghino Dam, 227
facon, 233, 289
faja, 289
Falkland/Malvina Islands, 99, 232
Falkner, Thomas, 75
fania, 121
Faro Punta Mogotes, 138
Faro Querandi, 138
Faro San Antonio, 138
faros, 138
fascist, 43
fauna, 148, 261, 263, 268, 270
Federal District, 95
Federal Justice Tribunals, 110
Federal Pact, 35
Federalists, The 33, 36, 93, 288
Federalist cause, 35
Felipe, Ray, 212
Fells cave, 24, 26
Ferrocarriles Argentinos, 184
Ferrocarriles Mitre, 149
Festival de la Vendimia, 193, 200
Fierro, Martin, 2
Fiesta de Nuestra Senora de Lujan, 129
Figueroa Alcorta Avenue, 125, 126
fin de siecle, Parisians, 54
financial districts, 98
Finca El Rey, 184
Finca El Rey National Park, 183
see national parks
firebush (*Embothrium coccineum*), 244
Fireland, 243
see Tierra del Fuego
first British settlers, 61
first European, 31
first European settlers, 59
first explorers, 31
First Narrows, 247
first settlement, 31
first Spaniards, 24
first Spanish settlement, 228

fishes
corvina, 279
dorado, 163
piranha, 279
shad, 279
fjords, 241
flamingos, 265
see birds
flan, 106
flora, 268, 270
Florentino Ameghino Park, 129
Florida, 111, 112, 113
Florida Avenue, 122
Florida Garden, 112
Florida Street, 50, 98, 102
football clubs,
Boca Juniors, 275
Independiente, 275
River Plate, 275
Rosario Central, 275
football stadiums
Codiviola, 276
Coredo, 276
La Bombanera, 276
Monumental, 276
football tournaments
Libertadores Cup, 276
World Club Cup, 276
Foreign Ministry, 123
formal declaration of independence, 34
Formosa, 37, 176, 177
fossils, 247, 249
Francis Mallman, restaurant, 106
Francisco de Aguirre, 194
Francisco P. Moreno National Park, 269
Franco-Hispanic, 32
Frank Romero Day Amphitheater, 200
Freezer, meat-packing plant, 248
French Embassy, 105 123
Frondizi, Arturo, 46
Fuegian Archipelago, 243
Fuegian Channels, 254
Fuegian fox (Andean wolf), 244
fugazza, 121
Fundacion, 263
Fundacion Vida Silvestre Argentina, 263
Futalaufquen Hotel, 225

G

Gaiman, 227
Gaiman Museum, 228
Galeria del Sol de French, 116
Galeria Pacifica, 112
Galeria Pacifico on Florida Street, 116
Galloping Head, 77, 76
Galtieri, General, 48, 49, 99
gamblers, 135
gambling, 13, 285
Gamboa, Sarmiento de, 210
Gamboler, 135
Gancedo, 177
Garay, Juan, de, 93
Gardel, Carlos, 119
Garden of the Nation, 178
Garganta del Diablo (Devil's throat) 165, 265
gauchesco, 289

gaucho(s), 13, 17, 18, 32, 36, 38, 39, 73, 74, 76, 77, 129, 145, 182, 203, 223, 226, 285, 288
  dress, 36
  life, 285
geese, Ashy-headed, 268
geese, Upland, 268, 269
Geweurtztraminer, 196
  see wines
Giant Horned, 267
Giol, 201
Giol Wine Museum, 199
  see museums
glacial mountains, 20
Glacier National Park, 215
  see national parks
glaciers, 20, 209
Godoy Cruz, 201
golden age, 39
golf, 279
Gonzalez Videla, 196, 201
goose, Kelp, 270
GOU (Grupo Obra de Unification), 42
Government Building, 98, 178
Government House, 103
Government Palace, 130, 199
government tourist bureau, 253
Goya, 162
Graf Spee, 153
graffiti, 102
Grand Prix, 91
grandes dames, 44
Great Depression, 42, 54
Great Dusky Swifts, 265
Greater Rhea, 263
Green Grove, 127
Gregores, 269
Grenadiers Regiment, 103
gringo outlaws, 225
Guachipas Valley, 180
guanacos, 26, 28, 148, 228, 244, 247, 248, 264, 268, 269, 270
Guarani, 290
Guarani natives, 163
guardamontes, 289
Guayaquil, 34
guerrillas, 48
Guifra Alley, 115
Guiraldes, Ricardo, *Don Segundo Sombra*, 289

Hall, Basil, 34
handicraft stall, 112
  see Kelly's
Harberton Bay, 251
Haush, Indian tribe, 245
Head, Francis Bond, 74
Heisdieck, Piper, 196
Hemorrageo Cerebral, 68
Hereford, 149
Hernandez, Jose, 289
Higado (liver), 106
highest peak in the Western Hemisphere, 20
  see Aconcagua
Hipodromo, 128
hippie market, 127
Historical Museum, 116, 162, 198

history, 92, 173
Holando-argentina, 149
Holland, W. J., 78
Holly genus (Ilex), 166
Holmes, Sherlock, 38
Holocene, 26
horse stables,
  Belgrano, 278
  Buenos Aires, 278
horseback trekking, 13
horsemanship, 290
Hoste Islands, 252
Hosteria Kaiken, 251
Hosteria Petrel, 251
hosteria, 181, 184, 247, 251
House of Representatives, 107
Howler Monkeys, 266
Huacalera, 185
Huahum, 218
Hudson, W H, 36, 210, 262
Huechulaufquen, 219
hueco de cabecitos, 123
Huehupen, 251
Huemul,.Andean, 269
Humahuaca, 183, 186
Humahuaca Valley, 267
Humberto 1 Street, 116
hunting, 25
hunting ground, 19
Hunting Tradition, 26, 27
Hurlingham Club, 61
  see clubs
Huzaingo, 199

Ibera Marshes, 266
Iberian Peninsula, 33
Ibises, 270
Ice Age, 24
Idle Days in Patagonia, 210
Ignacio Mini, 164
Iguazú, 159, 161
Iguazú Falls, 19, 165, 261
Iguazú National Park, 164, 264
Iguazú River, 164, 165
Illia, Arturo, 46
Imbert, Colonel, 44
immigrants, 24, 39, 54, 49, 200
Inca empire, 24
Incas, 28, 175
Incipient Agriculture, 27
Independencia Street, 152
Indian dialects, 285
Indian tribes, 288
  Mapuche, 213
  Ona, 248
industrialization, 55
Ingeniero Jacobacci, 225
ingenios, 178
interior, 62
Interlagos, 234
intermarriage, 60
International Hotel, 165
International Monetary Fund, 52, 65
interregnum, 46
Intransigent Youth, 65

Intransigent Party, 55
Iraola Avenue, 127
Irigoyen, 78
Iruya, 186
Isla de los Estados, 254
Isla de los Pajaros, 228
Isla ecapasela, 251
Isla Grande, 243, 246
Isla Grande de Tierra del Fuego, 243
Isles Malvinas/Falkland Islands, 234
Itaipu Dam, 164
Italian lilt, 60
Italian Riesling, 196
Itati, 163
Ituizango Streets, 153

J

J Roca, 150
Jabiru Storks, 266
  see birds
Jacanas, 266
  see birds
jacaranda, 122
jaguar, 265, 268
Jague, 176
Japanese Botanical Garden, 126
Jesuit Church, 153
Jesuit missions, 113
Jesuit Monastry, 153
Jesuit ruins, 159
Jesuit university, 32
Jesuit, Complex, the, 151
Jesus, 212
Jockey Club, 123
  see clubs
Johnson, Hugh, 196
Jones, Carol, 221
Jorge, Trucco, 219
Jose Menendez, 250
Jose Ormachea Petrified Forest, 230
Jose San Martin, 34
Judicialist Party, 55
Jufre, Juan, 194
Jujuy, 20, 27, 32, 149, 175, 179, 184, 267, 175
Jujuy province, 261
Julio Roca, 39
jungle, 13, 24
jungle ruins, 162
Junin, 44
Junin de los Andes, 219
juntas, 33, 36, 47
Justicialist (Peronist) Party, 65

K

Kaiken, 234
Kandahar, 222
Kau Yatun, 234
Kau-tapen ("fishing house" in Ona) Lodge, 249
Kavanagh Building, 122
KDT Sports Complex, 126
  see sports
Kelly's, 112
  see handicraft stores
kerchief, 28

King penguins, 234
King, J Anthony, Colonel, 73, 234, 235
kioscos, 108, 111
Ksar Expeditions, 254

L

La Biela, 123
La Boca, 64, 97, 113, 116, 118, 121, 120
La Boca Museum of Fine Arts, 120
  see museums
La Bodega del 900,199
La Caleta, 227
La Caminita, 117, 120
La Canaba, 108
La Casa Blanca, 115
La Casa de Esteban Lucas, 115
La Casa Rosada, 115
La Cornisa, 184
La Cumbre, 153
La Cumbre Pass, 202
La Estancia, 111
La Falda, 153
La gloriosa jotape (the Peronist Youth song), 102
La Historia Official, 51
La Hoya Ski Center, 226
  see skiing resorts
La Isla, 153
La Lucila del Mar, 138
La Manzana de las Luces, 113
La Merced Basilica, 152
La Pampa, 268
La Pastorella, hotel, 222
La Paz, 109
La Perla del Atlantico, 140
La Plata, 130, 262, 275
La Polvorilla Viaduct, 184
La Poma, 182
la Quebrada de Cafayate, 180
La Quiaca, 186
La Rioja, 28, 32, 175, 176, 196
La Rural, 201
La Toma, 203
La Vuelta de Rocha, 120
labor, 54
Labor Ministry, 55
labor unrest, 54
LADE, 233
  see airlines
Lago Argentino, 64, 269
Lago Belgrano, 269
Lago Fagnano, 246, 251
Lago Kosobo, 251
Lago Pueblo National Park, 217, 222
  see national parks
Lagos Yehuin, 250
Laguna Escondida, 251
Laguna Blanca National Movement, 268
Laguna Blanca National Park, 217
  see national parks
Laguna de los Horcones, 202
Laguna Pozoulos, natural Monument, 186, 267
Lakes, 20, 24
  Lake Alumine, 217, 218
  Lake Amutui Quimei, 217
  Lake Argentino, 233, 234
  Lake District, 177

Lake Futalaufquen, 225
Lake Nahuel Huapi, 212, 220
Lake Llanquihue, 218
Lake Molinos, 153
Lake Paimun, 219
Lake San Roque, 153
Lake viedma, 234
lanchas, 129
Land of Fire, 241
  see Tierra del Fuego
Lanín, 270
Lanín National Park, 217, 218, 219, 268
  see national parks
Lanín Volcano, 218, 219
Lanusse, General, 46
LAPA, 137
  see airlines
Lapataia, 246
Lapataia National Park, 216
  see national parks
Las Chinas, 288
Las Cotorras, 252, 254
Las Cuevas, 202
Las Heras, 127, 199, 201
Las Heras Avenue, 127
Las Leñas, 193, 202, 253
Las Orquideas, 165
Las Pailas, 182
Las Perdices, 262
Las Toninas, 138
Lasifashaj River, 251
  see rivers
lassoes, 285
Last Tango In Paris, 50
Late Ceramic Period, 28
Latin America, 31
Lavalle, 98, 113, 263
Lavalle Plaza, 104
Lavalle Street, 50, 98, 111
Lavalle, General, 263
Lawrence, Clara, 253
Lawrence, John, 253
Le Cheminee, 219
Le Per, 199
Le Village, 219
Leandro Alem, 111, 122
Leleque Ranch, 225
lena dura (*Maytenusmagellanica*), 244
lenga, 250
lenga (*N.punillo*), 244
Lent, 163
Lerma Valley, 183
Letters from Paraguay, 78
  see books
Lezama Park, 92, 116
Lezama, Gregorio, 116
Libertador, 127
Libertador Avenue, 122, 124-125
licuado, 109
lighthouse, 138
Lihue Calel, 268
Lion's Sea, 92
Llama, 25, 27, 28, 20
Llanquihue lakes, 218
  see lakes
Llao Llao hotel, 220
local potentates, 31
locro, 181

longest road, 108
  see Rivadavia
Lopez, Francisco Solano, 37
Los Alceres National Park, 217, 225
  see national parks
Los Andes, 184
Los Canelos, 254
Los Cardones National Park, 183
Los Glaciares, 269
Los Glaciares National Park, 217, 233
  see national parks
Los Gringos, 254
Los Molles, 177
Los Penitentes, 202
Los Redonditos de Ricotta, 68
Los Rienos, 251
Los Sarmientos, 176
Los Toldos, 44
Los Toldos caves, 26
Los Toldos site in Santa Cruz, 26
Los Troncos Inn, 226
lost city of the Caesars, 212
Luján, 66, 108, 129, 201
L'Eau Vive, 130

M

Macuco, 266
Macuco trail, 265
Madariaga, 263, 264
Magdelena, 262, 264
Magellan, 31, 73, 210, 230, 245
Magellanic penguins, 228, 234
  see penguins
Magnone, Guido, 280
Maipu, 34, 123, 201
major port, 18
  see Buenos Aires
Malacara, 227
Malargue, 202
Malbec, 196
  see wines
Mallco River, 218-219
malls, 111
Malvinas (Falklands) Islands, 49, 51, 61, 92, 99, 232, 234
Malvinas/Falklands War, 122
Maned Wolf, 267
Manuel de Coyte, 104
Manzana de las Luces, 113
Mapuche Indians, 213
  see Indians
Mar Chiquita, 139
Mar del Ajo, 138
Mar del Plata, 126, 136, 137, 139, 140, 177
Mar del Sur, 140
Mar Dulce river, 31, 92
  see rivers
Mar y Sierras, 136
Maradona, Diego, 121, 276
maras, 228, 270
Maria, 43
maroma, 286
Marques de Campero, 186
Marsh Deer, 267
marshy Mesopotamia, 17
Martin, Benito Quinquela, 117

Martyrs Valleys, 226
MAS (Movement Towards Socialism), 128
Massero, Admiral, 53
Mataco, 61
mate, 18, 223, 68, 153, 159, 166, 285
Mato Grosso region, 19
May Revolution, 33
Mayas, 175
mazorca, 36
mazzamorra, 181
Mburucuya, 266
meadows, 20
Mendizabal, Rosendo, 118
Mendocinos, 198
Mendoza, 31, 32, 34, 78, 149, 194, 195, 196, 198, 200, 201, 202
Mendoza, Hurtado, de, 194
Mendoza, Pedro, de, 31, 92
Mercado Artesanal, 183
Mercedes Sosa, 68
Merlo, 203
Merlot, 196
mesas, 230
Mesopotamia, 19, 61, 161, 175
Meso-America, 24, 27
mestizo, 20, 93, 285
metalworking, 25
Metán, 179
methods of transportation, 73
metropolitan area, 95
Metropolitan Cathedral, 103, l98
Mi Buenos Aires Querido (My Beloved Buenos Aires), 118
Mi Noche Triste (My Sad Night), 119
Michelangelo, 115, 234
Middle Ceramic Period, 27
military, 46, 50
milongas, 118
Mini-centro, 111
Miramar, 137, 140
miscegenation, 3
Misiones, 19, 37, 163, 164, 166, 261
Mitre, Bartolome, 37
Moat, 251
Mocona Falls, 166
Moet, 196
Molinas Café, 107
Molino, 182
Molinos, 181
Molinos Dam,153
Molinos Lake,153
mollejas, (sweetbread) 106
Monmartre,106
monoliths, 27
Monte, 262
Monte Hermoso, 140
Monte Olivia, 252
Montes Martial, 254
Montevideo, 32, 36, 118
Montoneros, 46
Monument to San Martín, 200
Monument to the Flag, 161
Monumento Natural Bosques Petrificados, 230
morcilla, 106
Moreno Glacier, 233, 269
Moreno Street, 113
Moreno, Mariano, l33
Morrill, G.L., 74

Mostacchio, 254
Mothers of Plaza de Mayo, 48, 99, 104
motifs, 28
Mount Cachi, 182
Mount Chapelco, 219
Mountain Caracaras, 269
mountain climbing, 209, 280
mountainous desert, 17
Mountains
  Aconcagua, 280
  Almacenes, 280
  Capelco, 219
  Cathedral, 280
  Caracars, 269
  Cordon del Plata, 280
  Cupula, 280
  El Plata, 280
  Fitz Roy, 280
  Negro, 280
  Nevado Excelcior, 280
  Otto, 221
  Pan de Azucar, 280
  Pico Bonito, 280
  Rincon, 280
  Tolosa, 280
  Tronador, 221
  Tupungato, 280
  Vallecitos, 2
movie theaters, 111
Mt Otto, 221
Mt Tronador, 221
mudejar, 152
mulattoes, 59
Mundo Animal, 130
Municipal Palace, 130
Municipal Aquarium, 198
Municipal Planetarium, 127
Muscovy Ducks, 266
Museo de Bellas Artas, 129
Museo del Fin del Mundo, 254
Museo Provincial de Bellas Artes, 130
museums, 103
  Giol Wine Museum, 199
  Museum of Fine Arts, 125
  Museum of Natural History, 198
  Museum of Natural Sciences, 130
  Museum Patagonia, 220
  Museum of Transportation, 129
music, 289
Musters, George, 216, 212
Mylodon, 26
Myrtle Forest, 221
myth, 290

N

Nahuel Huapi National Park, 217, 220, 221, 268
Nahuel Huapi, 218
Nahuel Huapi Lake, 220
Napoleon, 93
Nassauvia, 254
national anthems, 118
National Ballet, 110
National Cavalry, 126
National Congress, 104
National Council of Education, 116
National drinking habits, 63

national heroes, 103
National Historic Monument, 166
national identity, 59, 67
national parks
    Chaco, 266
    Iguazú, 164, 264
    Lago Pueblo, 217, 222
    Laguna Blanca, 217
    Lanín, 217
    Lapataia, 217
    Los Alerces, 216
    Los Cardones, 217, 225
    Los Glaciares, 183
    Nahuel Huapi, 220
    Paine, 234
    El Palmar, 262
    Finca El Rey, 183
    Francisco P. Moreno, 269
    Glacier, 215
    Calilegua, 267
    Palmar, 166
    Pueblo, 268
National Parks Commissions, 280
national sport, 64
National Symphony Orchestra, 110
Natural Sciences Museum, 203
Navarino Islands, 252
Necochea, 137, 140
neo-tanguistas, 119
nervosa , 268
Neuquen, 177, 216, 268, 280
New Republic, 53
New World Mexico, 27
New York Times , 112
Nicochea Street, 120, 121
nire (Nothifagus antartica), 244, 251
no nomes (no names), 48
    see desparecidos
NOA, 175, 183
NOA region, 177
NOA (Nor-Oeste Argentino), 175
Nobel Prize, 51
nomadism, 27
Non-Aligned Movement, 65
non-indigenous plants, 18
Northern Hemisphere, 215
Northern Lake District, 213, 216, 217, 225
Northwest Argentina, 175
Norton, 201
Nothofagus, 244, 268
Nuestra Senora de Santa Maria del Buen Aire, 92
Nueve de Julio Park, 178
nunataks, 233

O

Obelisk, 105
Obera, 166
obliqua, 268
oenophiles, 196
official language (Spanish), 60
Ojos del Salado Volcano, 176
Oktoberfest (German festival), 145, 153
ombu, 18
Ona, 61, 253
Ona Indians, 248

    see Indians
Ona (Shelknam), 245
Once, 108, 110
Once line (railway lines), 97
Ongania, Juan Carlos, General, 46
Onohippidon, 26
Orange, 230
original native inhabitants, 59
Orlandi, Augusto, 151
Ortiz, Roberto, 42
Ostende, 139

P

pacas, 265
Pacific, 20, 31
Pacific ocean, 218
Padin, 253
Paella Valenciana, 105
Paili Aike caves, 26
Paimun, 219
Paimun Inn, 219
Paine National Park, 234
    see national parks
painters, 112
Paisaje Dardo rocha, 130
Paisaje de Defensa, 116
paisanos , 232, 233, 290
Palace of Justice, 53
Palacio de San Jose, 166
Palermo, 94, 97, 118, 125, 126
Palermo Chico, 125, 126
Palmar National Park, 166
    see national parks
Palermo barrios, 121
palo borracho trees, 122
Palo Borracho (drunken trees),105
pampa, 93, 145, 286
Pampa de Achala, 268
Pampa Deer, 267
pampa humeda, 18
pampa seca, 18
pampas, 13, 17, 24, 73, 78, 92, 146, 149, 264
Pampas Deer, 263
Pampas Gray, 263
Pan-American Highway, 241, 246
panqueque 91
Paraguay, 18, 176
Paraguay Street, 112
Paraguayan War, 37
parakeets, 268
Paramo, 248
Parana, 18, 25, 37, 161, 162, 164, 176
Parana River, 19, 264
    see rivers
Paranacito, 166
Paris of Latin America, 94, 110, 122
    see Buenos Aires
parks, 91, 125
Parque 3 de Febrero, 126
Parque de los Menhires, 179
parrilla (grilled), 106, 128
parrillada mixta, 106
parrilladas, 95
parrillas (steak house), 106
Paseo de Bosque, 130
Paseo Victorica, 128

Paso Beban, 252
Paso de la Patria, 163
Paso Garibaldi, 251
Patagonia, 13, 20, 24, 26, 28, 39, 44, 61, 73, 209, 210, 213, 214, 216, 228, 230, 232, 243, 249, 290
Patagonian Museum, 220
patero, 176
pathways of death, 32
pato (game), 277
Patquia, 175, 176
patriarchs, 125
Paz, Carlos, 153
Paz, Jose Maria, 35
peccaries, 265, 268
pedemonte, 105
pejerrey, 178
penguins, 270
  colonies, 13
  King penguins, 234
  Magellanic, 234
Peninsula Mitre, 254
Peninsula Paramo, 248
Peninsula Valdés Hotel, 227
pensions, 139
peones, 248, 290
People's Revolutionary Army (ERP), 46
per capita GDP, 54
Pereyra family, 130
Perils, 74
Perito Moreno, 230
Perón, 42
  Peronism, 55, 65, 67, 114, 119
  Peronist, Justicialist Party, 46
  Peronista, Feminist Party, 45
  Peronists, 53
  Perón, Maria Eva Duarte, 44, 65, 99, 102, 124
  Perón, Isabel, 122
  Perón, Juan Domingo, 27, 55, 144, 203
Peru Street, 113
Peruvian Incas, 24
petiseros, 277
phantom paddle-steamer, 161
pialar, 286
piasnos, 290
Piazzola, Astor, 119
pibe de Abasto, 119
piedmonts, 20
Piedra del Aguila, 216
Piedra del Aguila Hotel and Ranch, 216
Pigafetta, 210
pigeons, 107
Pilar Basilica, 123
Pinamar, 137, 139
Pinot Blanc, 196
  see wines
Pinot Noir, 196
  see wines
Piper Hiesdieck, 196
  see wines
Piramides, 270
piropo, 68
Pismanta, 177
pizza, 95, 107
pizza a la piedra, 121
pizzeria, 97
plains, 20
Plains Vizcacha, 262
Plaza Colon, 98

Plaza de los dos Congresos (Plaza of the two Congress), 107
Plaza de la Victoria, 98
Plaza de Mayo, 43, 46, 49, 93, 97, 98, 99, 102, 103, 104, 112, 114, 115
Plaza del Fuerte (fortress), 98
Plaza del Mercado, 98
Plaza Dorego, 116, 114, 115
Plaza Hotel, 122
Plaza Italia, 127, 128
Plaza Lavalle, 110, 118
Plaza Lorca, 107
Plaza San Martín, 150, 151, 122
plebiscite, 51
Pleistocene, 24, 26
Podocarpus, 268
poetry, 289
political parties, 65
politics, 46, 54, 64, 67, 68, 78, 102, 107, 111
polo, 13, 276
Polvani Tours, 221
ponchos, 218
Ponchos de Guëmes, 182
Pope Pius XII, 45
Popper, Julian, 248
Popular Union, 46
population, 32, 38, 54, 55, 60, 61, 64, 95
Port Famine, 212
Port of San Julian, 210
Port Stanley (Falkland Islands), 49
Porta, Hugo, 278
porteño, 91, 106, 135, 13, 39, 53, 62, 92, 93, 97, 102, 108, 121, 123, 126, 136, 285
Portrerillos, 201
Portrerillos Hotel, 201
Portuguese, 31
Porvenir, 247
Posadas, 163
Posonby, Lord, 36
post-independence era, 38
pottery, 25, 27
Pozuelos, 186, 267
prairies, 18
Precordillera, 175
prefecture (coast guard), 246
Prefecture, Almanza, 251
Prefecture, Puerto, 251
Prefecture, Williams, 251
prehistory of Argentina, 28
pre-Colombian societies, 27
Proceso, 67, 68
provinces, 20, 33
Provincial Road 111, 38
Provincial Legislature, 130
psychiatry, 67
psychology, 67
pucaras, 28, 175, 185
puchero (boiled stew), 105, 181
Pueblo National Park, 268
Puente del Inca, 202
Puenzo, Luis, 51
Puerto Bandera, 234, 269
Puerto Blest, 221
Puerto Canoas, 165, 265
Puerto Deseado, 230, 232
Puerto Iguazú, 164
Puerto Madryn, 223, 227, 228
Puerto Montt, 218

Puerto Natales, 232, 234
Puerto Piramides, 228
Puerto San Julian, 230
Puerto Santa Cruz, 230
pulpería, 116, 114, 115, 290
pumas,145, 268, 146, 148, 278
Puna (desert), 20, 185, 267,
Puna Teal, 267
Puna, 175, 186
Punta Arenas, 212, 232, 235, 241, 247,
punta banca (game), 140
Punta de Vacas, 201, 202
Punta del Este, 126, 135
Punta Inino, 264
Punta Medanos, 138
Punta Mogotes, 136, 140
Punta Norte, 228, 270
Punta Rosa, 263
Punta Tombo, 227, 228
Puntra Medanos, 138
Purmamarca, 185, 267
Puyehue pass, 218, 220

Q

quebracho tree, 19
Quebrada, 185
Quebrada de Escoipe, 183
Quebrada de la Flecha, 181
Quebrada del Toro, 184
Quechua, 61
Queen of the Harvest, 200
Queso y Membrillo (or Batata), 106
Quetrihue Peninsula, 221
Quilmes,175, 180
Quilmes Club, 275
Quimei Quipan Inn, 225
quinoa (an Andean cereal), 27
Quinquela, 117
Quintana Avenue, 123
Quorom, 108

R

racetracks, Jockey Club, 278
racetracks, San Isidro, 278
Radical Civic Union, 39, 42, 55
    middle class support, 39
    1916-1930 government, 42
    Argentine major political party, 55
Radical Party, 49, 51
Radicals, 53
Radio Argentina, 44
Radio El Mundo, 44
railway system, 18
rallies, 102
Ramon Carcano Plaza, 123
Ranch Banchero, 121
rancho, 249
rastra, 289
Rawson (provincial capital town), 227, 228
rebenque, 289
recado, 233
Receptivo Puerto Madryn, 227
Recoleta
    new neighborhood, 94

barrios, 97
    Norton Quarter, 121, 123, 125
Recoleta Cemetery, 45, 123, 124
Recoleta Plaza, 121
Recoleta priests, 124
Reconquista, 162
Reconquista Street, 123
Red-tailed Comet, 268
Rega, Jose Lopez, 47
Reiseberg's, "Cape Horn", 245
religion
    characteristics, 67
    Sanavirones and Comechingones, 147
Resistencia, 163, 266
resort beaches, 13
Restorer of the Laws, 36, 37
Retiro, 94, 97, 118, 121, 122, 123, 129
Retiro line, 97
Retiro Train Station, 122
revolutionary junta, 33
rheas, 228, 268
Rhine Riesling, 196
    see wines
Riacho San Jose, 228
Riesling, 196
    see wines
Rinconada, 186
riñones (kidneys), 106
Rio Azopado, 251
Rio Carlo, 250
Rio Colorado, 20
Rio de Janeiro, 247
Rio de la Plata, 31, 32, 54, 92, 95, 97, 118, 124, 194
Rio de la Plata estuary, 18
Rio de la Plata River Basin, 18, 19
Rio Ewan, 251
Rio Gallegos, 216, 230, 232, 233, 234, 247
Rio Gallegos Bank, 225
Rio Grande, 185, 246– 249, 250, 253, 254, 270
Río Hondo, 177
Rio negro, 196, 216, 268, 280
Rio Negro Valley, 213
Rio Olivia, 251, 252
Rio Salado, 137
Rio Turbio, 234
Riobamba Street, 108
Riochuelo, 95, 114, 115, 117
Riochuelo Canal, 117
Risario, 275
Rivadavia (longest road), 35, 105, 107, 108, 111
Rivadavia Avenue, 97
Rivadavia, Bernardino, 33, 35
Rivadivia, 111
rivers
    Anizacade, 153
    Iguazú, 164-165
    Parana, 19, 264
    Uruguay, 19, 166
    Lasifashaj, 251
    Mar Dulce, 31, 92
    Suquia River, 146
    Upper Pinturas River, 28
Road of the Seven Lakes, 220
Road #3, 216, 230
Road #40, 216, 225, 230
Roaring Forties, Furious Fifties, the Screaming Sixties, 243
    gale-force winds

robalo, 254
Robards, Terry, 196
Roca, 216
Roca, J (architect), 39, 151
Rocas, Julio, President, 94, 122
Roca, General, 213
Rodeo, The, 290
Rolero, 122
rookeries, 228, 235
Rosario, 78, 149, 161, 54
Rosario de la Frontera, 177, 179
Rosario de Santa Fe, 153
Rosas Juan Manuel de (tyrant,
  Federalist government), 35, 92, 93
Rose, 196
rotiserías, 254
Rubens,104
rugby, 278
Rural Society, 127, 128
Russian revolution, 233
Ruth Benzacar's Gallery, 112

S

Sabatini, Gabriela, 278
Sabato, Ernesto, 53
saber-toothed tiger, 261
sainetes, 118
Saint Teresa of Jesus, 152
sainthood, 34
salchicha, 106
Salesian Mansion, 248
Salinas, 261
Salinas Grandes salt flats, 176
Salon de Profundis, 152
Salta, 20, 32, 149, 175, 179, 183, 184, 194, 196, 267
salteñas, 173
Salto Grande Dam, 166
San Agustin del Valle Fertil, 175
San Antonio de los Cobres, 183, 184
San Antonio Este, 216
San Bernardo, 138
San Bernardo Convent, 183
San Bernardo Hill, 184
San Carlos de Bariloche, 181, 268, 280
San Carlos Monastery at San Lorenzo, 161
San Clemente, 263
San Clemente del Tuyu, 136, 137, 263
San Felipe, 201
San Fernando del Valle de Catamarca, 176
San Francisco, 162
San Francisco Basilica, 114
San Francisco Church, 183, 199
San Huberto Lodge, 219
San Ignacio, 159, 164
San Ignacio Church, 113
San Isidro, 264
San Javier, 178
San Jose, 249
San Juan, 20, 27, 175, 194, 195, 196, 203, 232,
San Justo, 249
San Lorenzo, 115
San Luis, 18, 20, 194, 195, 202, 203
San Luis del Palmar, 163, 266
San Martín, 35, 161, 165, 166, 195, 215, 219, 220
San Martín de los Andes, 215, 217, 218, 219, 268
San Martín Municipal Theater, 109

San Martín Museum, 198
San Martín Park, 199
San Martín Plaza, 123
San Martín's crossing of the Andes, 31
San Martín, Jose, de, General, 103, 104, 125
San Miguel de Tucuman, 178, 180
San Miguel del Monte, 262
San Pablo, 250
San Pedro Church, 115
San Pedro Gonsalez Church, 116
San Raphael, 202
San Roque Chapel, 114
San Salvador de Jujuy, 177, 185, 186
San Sebastian, 248
San Telmo, 97, 113, 114, 115,
Sanavirones, 146
Santa Ana Chapel, 152, 201
Santa Clara del Mar, 139
Santa Cruz, 28, 230, 232, 268
Santa Cruz Province, 28, 215, 230, 232, 268
Santa Cruz revolt, 233
Santa Fe, 25, 35, 37, 54, 74, 123, 127, 128, 161, 162
Santa Fe Avenue, 123
Santa Maria, 176, 179, 180
Santa Maria de los Buenos Aires, 31
Santa Rosa de Calamuchita, 153
Santa Teresita, 137, 138
santerias,163
Santiago, 194, 202
Santiago de Chile, 149
Santiago de Liniers, 32
Santiago del Estero, 25, 32, 146, 149, 175, 176, 194
Santo Domingo, 176
Sarmiento, 39, 103, 127
Sarmiento Avenue, 126
Sarmiento Domingo Faustino, 37, 203
sashimi, 63
savage Unitarians, 36
Schagrin, Joseph, 196
scrub vegetation, 20
Scuba diving, 228
seaside casino, 13
Seclantas, 182
Second World War, 60
Secretaria de Turismo, 153
Semana Tragica (Tragic Week), 42, 55
semisubterranean, 25
Senate, 107
Seno Almirantaszo, 251
settlements, 25, 93
Shelnam Indians, 61
Sheraton Hotel, 122
Shipton, Eric, *The Land of Tempest*, 269
sí, 68
Sierra de la Ventana, 18
Sierra de la Ventana Tres Picos, 264
Sierra de Tandil, 18
Sierra Subandinas, 20
Sierras Chicas, 147, 268
Sierras de Cordoba, 147
Sierras de Guasapampa, 147
Sierras del Pocho, 147
Sierras Grandes, 147
Siewart C2, 32
silver, 17
ski resorts
  Bariloche, 279
  Las Leñas, 279

La Hoya, 226
  Mendoza, 279
  Rio Negro, 279
ski tournaments, 13
skiing, 209, 279
  see sports
slaves, 38
slums, 53, 60
Small Circuit, 221
smuggling, 32
snacks, 126
Sobremonte Historical Museum, 153
soccer, 97, 120, 275
Social Aid Foundation, 44
social atmosphere, 97
social welfare, 55
Socialist Party, 39
Sociedad Popular Restauradora, 36
Solco, 182
Solis Juan de, 31, 92
solitary beaches, 140
sortija, 286, 289
Sourrouille, Jean, 53
South Atlantic, 243, 248, 251
South Atlantic islands, 17
South Atlantic War, 49
South Georgia island, 235
South Pacific, 243
South Pole, 17
Southern Lake District, 233, 217
Southern Patagonia Icecap, 269
Southern Quarter, 113
Southern Right whales, 228
**southern sector of the Gran
Chaco**, 19
Spaniards, 31
Spanish, 31, 32
Spanish Conquest, 147
Spanish explorers, 17
Spilimbergo, painter, 112
sports
  cricket, 279
  mountain climbing, 209, 280
  skiing, 279, 226, 209, 279
  tennis, 278
  polo, 276
  soccer, 120, 275
  golf, 279
  windsurfing, 275
  equestrian, 277
  rugby, 286
  yachting, 279
  fishing, 279
standard of living, 67
state religion, 66
Statue of Christ the Redeemer, 202
Statute for the National Reorganization Process,
  48
Stephenson, Miriam, 153
steppes, 20
Stirling, W.H. Bishop, 253
stone sculptures, 25
stone watchtower, 202
Strait of Magellan, 241, 246, 247, 212, 20, 24, 216,
  234, 243
Strait of Magellan Embrace, 214
street fair, 127
Strong, Captain, 234

students, 63
St. Andrew's, 61 .
St. George's, 61
Suarez, 121
Suarez Street, 121
subantarctic, 17, 20
Subantarctic Zone, 243
subtropical, 19
suburbs, 53
Sub-Prefecture, 253
Suerte!, 91
Suquia River, 146
  see rivers
swans, Black-necked, 269, 268
Sycamore, 95
Sycamore trees, 120

T

taba, 153
Tafi culture of Tucumán, 27
Tafi del Valle, 179
Tafna, 186
Talampaya, 176
Talampaya Canyon, 175
tambos, (places of rest, supply and storage), 28
Tandil, 264
tango, 13, 62, 118, 119, 121, 136, 153
Tango Argentino, 118
tango orchestra, 119
tanguista, Astor Piazzola, 118
Tante Elvira, 254
tarragon, 106
Tastil, 175, 183
Teatro Argentino, 130
Teatro Martin Fierro, 130
Tehuelche, 61, 76 ·
Tehuelche Hotel, 226
Tehuelche natives, 73
tennis, 278
  see sports
Termas de Reyes, 177, 185
Termas de Río Hondo, 177
terrain, 20
Terray, Lionel, 280
Territorio Nacional de Tierra del Fuego, 246
terrorists, 48
Thomas Turner, 78
Tiahuanaco empire, 24
Tierra del Fuego, 13, 17, 20, 24, 26, 61, 73, 234,
  241, 243–249, 254, 261, 270
Tierra del Fuego zones, 26
Tierra del Fuego (Land of Fire), 243
Tierra Mayor Lodge, 252
Tierra Mayor Valley, 251
Tiger Herons, 266
Tigre, 128, 161
Tigre Hotel, 129
Tilcara, 175, 185
Timbuktu, 209
Tin Tin, 182
Tinogasta, 176
Tipa (*Tipuaria*), 268
Tipuana, 95
tipus, 122
Tira de asado, 106
Tito Testone, 222

Toba, 61
Todos los Santos, 218
Tolhuin, 246, 251
Tolkeyen, 253, 254
Tolombon, 180
Tolosa Hotel, 227
Tomo Uno, 106
topography, 17
Tornquist, Ernesto, 264
Torrontes, 196
Torrontes grape, 180
Tortoni Café, 105
Toso, 201
Toto Toucan, 265
toucans, 265
Tour D'Argent, 226
tour ship, Europa, 247
tour ship, Lina C, 247
tour ship, The Jason, 247
Tourism Office, 199
tourist office, 150
tourist ships, the Jason, 254
tourist ships, World Discovery, 254
towns, 25
Transvaal, 230
Trapiche Peña Flor, 201
Trelew, 223, 216, 227, 228
Tren a las Nubes, 183, 184
Tres Arrollos, 123
Trevelin, 223, 225, 226
tribal ways, 61
tribes, 25
triumvirate, 43, 33
Tromen, 218
truco, 114, 135, 95
Tucumán, 20, 32, 34, 107, 149, 175, 177, 178, 179, 194, 267
Tucumán-Catamarca border, 27
tucu-tucu, 244
Tunel, 245
Tunel site, 26
Turner, Thomas, 73

U

Ubajay, 166
ubre (udder), 106
UCRI(Intransigent Radical Civic Union), 46
ultra-Bohemia, 78
Union of the Democratic Center, 55
Unitarian League, 35
Unitarians, 36, 93, 288
Unitarios (Unitarians), 33
United Provinces of South America, 34
United Provinces of the Rio dela Plata, 35
Unity Horn, 245
Universidad Nacional de Córdoba, 147
university, 67
University of La Plata, 130
Upper Pinturas River, 28
Upsala, 234, 269
Upsala Glacier, 269
URCP (People's Radical Civic Union), 46
Urquiza, Justa Jose, de, 37
Urruchua, painter, 112
Uruguay, 18, 25
Uruguay River, 19, 166

Urquiza, General, 93
US Embassy Lincoln Library, 112
Ushuaia, 13, 215, 216, 235, 241, 246, 247, 248, 251, 252, 254, 270
Ushuaia Bay, 252
Uspallata, 201, 202
Uspallata Pass, 194, 201
usted, 63

V

Vacation Coast, 135
Valdés Peninsula, 64, 227, 228, 261, 270
Valeria del Mar, 139
Valle Carbajal, 252
Valle de la Luna, 175, 176, 203
Valle Hermoso, 202
Valle Tierra Mayor, 252
Vallecitos, 201
valleys, 20
Vaquerias, 153
Varela, Colonel, 233
vegas, 249, 250
vegetation, 18, 265
Venter, Martin, 230
Ventisquero Moreno, 233
Vespucci, Amerigo, 31
Via Peatonal, 153
Viamonte, 112, 251
viceroyalty, 32, 33, 93
Victoria Island, 221
vicuñas, 265
vicuñera, 186
Vidal, EE, 78
Videla, General, 48
Videla, President, 53
Viedma, 53, 216
Viejo Almacen, 115
Viejo Boliche, 222
Vilas, Guillermo, 278
Villa General Belgrano, 153
Villa Gesell, 137, 139
Villa Nougues, 178
Villa Union, 175, 176
Village fests, 153
Villavicencio, 202
Vinchina, 176
Viola, General, 48
violence, 75
Virgin of Itati, 163
Virgin of Lujan, 129
virus, 68
Viscount of Falkland, Lord Anthony Cary, 234
Visitors' Center, 165
Visser, Conrad, 230
viticulture, 20
Vizcacha, 263, 148, 268
volcanoes, 176
voz, 63

W

wanderers, 78
Washington Post, 112
waterfalls, 13, 164
weed, 18

Welsh, 223
Welsh culture, 225
Welsh Eisteddfods, 13
Welsh in Patagonia, 223
Welsh Tea, 223
western Puna, 24
whales, 270
Whistling Herons, 266
widest street, 108
wild Argentina Route 3, 262
wild west atmosphere, 75
wildlife, 209, 262, 265
Wilkens, Kurt233
windsurfing, 275
windy plateaus, 17
wine country, 193
wines
  brands, 196
working class, 102
World Cup (1978), 275
World Cup (1986), 275
World War, 155
World War I (post), 223
World War II, 43, 55, 60

X–Z

xenophobia, 36
Xiu Xiu, 194
Yacaratia Trail, 266
Yacireta, 163
Yachting, 279
Yaganes Turismo of Rio Grande, 251
Yahgan, 251
Yahgan shell, 251
Yahgans, 245, 246
Yamana, 61
Yapeyu, 166
Yatay Palm, 262
Yavi, 186
Yerba mate tree, 166
yerba mate (a form of tea), 19
Young Turks, 42
youth, 68
Yrigoyen, Hipolito, 42, 55
Yukon Valley, 24
Zapala, 217, 268
Zarate, 161, 166
Zarzuela theaters, 104